711 9983

D0909553

THE SIX WIVES
OF KING HENRY VIII

THE SIX WIVES
OF KING HENRY VIII

Paul Rival

Translated from the French by
Una Lady Troubridge

HEINEMANN : LONDON

William Heinemann Ltd
15 Queen Street, Mayfair, London W1X 8BE

LONDON MELBOURNE TORONTO
JOHANNESBURG AUCKLAND

First published 1937
This edition 1971
Reprinted 1971 (twice)

434 63740 8

Printed Offset Litho and bound in Great Britain
by Cox & Wyman Ltd,
London, Fakenham and Reading

CONTENTS

ILLUSTRATIONS

Between pages 168 and 169

I

THE INFANTA CATHERINE OF ARAGON

(1485—1501)

Queen Isabella as Wife and Mother.

ISABELLA, Queen of Castile, and Ferdinand, King of Aragon, who ruled in Spain at the time when Louis XI, King of France, was growing old and when the child Charles VIII was dreaming on the terraces at Amboise, were to all appearances as happy as a King and Queen could be. They were renowned for their power and for their victories. They were handsome in the Spanish style, they even resembled one another slightly, being cousins, with a resemblance just sufficiently pronounced to consolidate their mutual physical attraction. Their faces were long with full cheeks destined to become flabby, they had sallow complexions and dark eyes. Those of Isabella were round and staring; they were wide open and magnificent. Those of Ferdinand, which were perhaps equally luminous, veiled their fire beneath heavy lids. Isabella was the lioness; Ferdinand the fox.

They were strangers to that insipid happiness, that absolute devotion which are ascribed by poets to the lovers of their phantasies. Among beings of flesh and blood such an absence of anxiety would quickly result in boredom. Isabella loved her husband with a violent, exclusive love. Ferdinand, who was slightly her junior and who was attractive to women, did not deny himself distractions. He liked Isabella's dower, her intelligence, her courage, her chastity and all her moral qualities; he did not dislike her face or her body, but he occasionally grew tired of so much majesty. He would escape to less austere and more attractive arms. Journeys, wars and the queen's pregnancies afforded him a thousand opportunities and perfectly valid excuses. Isabella was fully aware of his infidelities. They pained her but not to excess. She was not of those docile women who bribe their husbands with the sacrifice of their worldly goods. She kept a firm grip upon her Kingdom of Castile and clipped Ferdinand's claws by opportune reminders that she was not his subject but an even more powerful sovereign than himself. A hint to this effect would bring him back to the marriage bed, the dispenser of entrancing nights. These storms, which hovered and never broke, and of which they themselves perceived no more than a few distant mutterings, saved them from monotony. As soon as they began the day they were engrossed in such vast interests that night was once more upon them before they remembered the subtleties of the flesh.

God had given them their thrones by miraculous intervention. An elder brother of Ferdinand's had made way for him by a mysterious death, and it was whispered that Providence had been assisted by poison. Isabella had received Castile by a yet more signal grace. Her brother, King Henry IV, who had reigned before her, had been solemnly pronounced by his bishops and nobles to be impotent. Henry had offered proof to the contrary: his wife had conceived and had borne a child. But the

Castilian grandees quietly asserted that the King had sent a substitute to his bed and that the little princess was a bastard. They tracked down the unhappy Henry IV, deposed him and caused him to die of grief. Whereupon the pious Isabella seized the throne, turned out the little princess and drove her to shut herself up in a Portuguese convent. She herself had recently married Ferdinand. They united Aragon and Castile, and in the place of the two smaller Kingdoms became rulers of Spain. But there remained three territories that evaded their grasp: Portugal to the west, Navarre toward the Pyrenees, and in the south the Kingdom of Granada which was still held by the Moors, the tattered remnants of a great empire, misgoverned, rotten, torn by factions and by assassinations, and demoralized by the languid life of the harems, by the charm of the enclosed gardens, the marble courts and fountains. The pious Isabella and the crafty Ferdinand felt their mouths water when they looked toward this luscious fruit.

Every year they made war upon the Moors of Granada. Every year they were the victors, conquered a few fortresses, approached the capital, feverishly visualizing the day when they would behold upon the hilltop among the dark green foliage the red towers of the Alhambra. They had their agents at Granada, Jews or Moors who furnished them with information and fomented dissensions. They saw to it that prophets of misfortune paraded the narrow shadowy streets, replying to the cry of the muezzin by announcements of impending chastisement from heaven. In the course of a skirmish they captured the little Moorish prince, Boabdil. They compelled him to apostatize and then released him, sending him back in the hopes that his weakness and folly would sow disaster. They entered Ronda, Zahara and the most hotly defended citadels. They slaughtered and then, when their troops grew weary of blood, gave quarter. They would pause as they left a town and see the passing, under the high pointed arches of the gates, of terrified throngs of unbelievers; men folded in great ragged burnous, their shaven heads glistening in the sun; women with fleshy faces that had grown pallid in the shadows of the harem, dragging their children by the hand, beating off the grip of drunken soldiers, folding their veils about them. Ferdinand, in full armour, his sharp face seeming more deeply tanned beneath the visor, would watch them with his sinister black eyes. Beside him, upright upon her mule, wrapped in her heavy mantles, her face barely emerging from the linen coif and wimple, Isabella would watch him, telling the beads of her long rosary.

They brought in their train friars in white habits with the great black mantle who preached the Gospel to the Infidels and the New Testament to the Jews. In Seville they installed their confessor, Torquemada. Pyres were lighted under the ramparts of the towns. Thousands of heretics were burned. Everyone trembled before the Inquisitors, even the priests and the bishops. The odour of burning flesh arose like a new incense from the Andalusian plain and from the higher plateaux of the Tagus and the Douro. Isabella's heart bled when she beheld the passing of the holy procession, of the green cross of the days of execution, of the monks chanting from under their cowls, of the condemned whose legs gave way beneath them so that their parti-coloured cardboard mitres swayed in the sunlight. She wept but she conquered her weakness, stifling the voice of Satan. The fire would purify these poor benighted heretics, would cleanse them of their stains and bear them up to heaven. She was giving them to God. Ferdinand collected the spoils of the deceased; he was busy reinforcing his finances.

They had been married for more than fifteen years and already had three daughters and a son when, on the fifteenth of December, 1485, joyful peals were heard ringing from belfry to belfry. Labourers bent over their furrow in the icy wind of Castile, artisans toiling by the fireside raised their heads wondering what new grace had been showered upon their princes: whether the Infidel had suffered defeat or whether the monks were preparing a sacrifice. The conquered Jews and Moors, cowering in their dark quarters, imagined that they distinguished through the clanging of the bells other terrifying sounds: the death-rattle of slaughtered soldiers, the sobs of violated women, the howls of heretics chained to the stake as they felt the first singeing of the flames. But it was only a very faint cry that, from one end of Spain to the other, had set the belfries ringing; the cry of a little girl whom Isabella had brought forth in her gloomy palace of Alcalá; the cry of a red, shapeless, crumpled atom that looked up from its pillow with blue and as yet sightless eyes.

The father and mother were disappointed; girls were of little use in politics; they would have preferred a boy. They resigned themselves to the divine will, however, and asked each other to what great saint they should consecrate their Infanta. Her four elders bore the names of the Blessed Virgin, of her cousin, Saint Elizabeth, of her smaller cousin Saint John. On this occasion they deserted the Holy Family and named their daughter Catherine, in honour of a learned saint who, in very early times and in the land of the Infidel, had allowed herself to be beheaded for her faith, who is the protectress of virgins and of students, and whose name signifies: "without a stain."

It was this same Infanta Catherine who, twenty-four years later, after other and too brief espousals which were abruptly severed by death, became, to her deep misfortune, the first of the six wives of King Henry VIII of England.

Childhood.

Catherine grew up among her sisters, surrounded by monks. She heard several masses every day and recited the various offices like a nun. Isabella macerated herself, making strange vows to God and wearing underneath her royal robes hair shirts that scraped her flesh. She took her five children with her when she travelled, lodging them and herself in monasteries. Catherine saw the Castilian countryside, green in March, golden in June and grey with the coming of July and the harvest. She grew to know the sudden squalls of the Sierra and the tepid Andalusian breezes. She wore great black capes that protected her alike from the cold and the sun. Priests expounded to her the sacred sciences. She learned Latin in order to be able to please God by addressing Him in that language. She also learned dancing, solemn and measured steps that gave her suppleness and grace since the most saintly of Infantas must some day prove attractive to the princes of this world. Her women would sit upon the ground striking their tambourines and guitars. Her sisters and her brother would mark the rhythm by clapping their hands while they laughed at her gravity.

She had not yet attained her seventh year when Isabella and Ferdinand set out for the siege of Granada. She was urged to redouble her prayers; new vows were invented for her use. She implored the angels and her holy patroness to entice the Moors to disaster, and on the very day of Saint Catherine's feast her prayers were answered. The infidel king, Boabdil, yielded up Granada. God had listened to Catherine's infant petitions and six weeks later, on the feast of Epiphany, she took part in the triumph. She entered Granada behind Isabella and Ferdinand. She visited the newly purified and reconsecrated mosque. She passed through the narrow white-walled streets to the sound of clattering hoofs, of the clashing of cuirasses, of psalms and acclamations, under the floating folds of gaudy banners. She knelt upon the stone floor and sang the *Te Deum*. That night, in the Alhambra, she saw the great courts with their delicate traceries shining in the flare of torches and she fell asleep to the sound of feasting, behind windows from which she had glimpsed the Albaycin with its shifting lights and the dark outlines of trees under the relentless January moon.

Heaven rained favours upon Isabella. One year after the taking of Granada, it bestowed upon her a limitless continent beyond the ocean, discovered by Christopher Columbus with the aid of three small vessels. Isabella had provided the ships; she was therefore entitled to the new world. Columbus presented her with some red men of whom the scriptures themselves had made no mention. She learned that in islands deluged with sunshine under trees with crimson foliage lived an entire race of simple pagans whose souls she was called upon to save. She was responsible for them before Heaven; she was their god-mother. Columbus also brought with him gold which Ferdinand demanded but which Isabella refused to relinquish.

Catherine was delighted with the red skins of the foreign slaves, with their stiff shining hair and their long, gentle faces. She taught them the catechism. She also played with wonderful birds as frail as butterflies which quickly perished in the bitter winds of Castile. Visits were made to Granada, to listen to the Arab songs, to gather roses from thorny stems that clung to the boles of the cypress trees. Catherine would dabble her fingers in the little fountains of the Generalife. She would gaze at the frozen summits of the Sierra, gloriously outlined against the sky.

She knew that a day would come when she must leave this land; she would be married to a foreign prince and speak a stranger tongue; she would no longer see her people, Isabella, her sisters, their priests. She believed that this would entail suffering, but she wel-comed the thought. She was eager to bear her cross. Her eldest sister had long since departed to be Queen of Portugal. From the Alcazar at Toledo, Catherine, looking down upon the yellow Tagus flowing grimly at her feet, imagined Lisbon and its estuary.

Ferdinand was much too wise a king to marry his daughters carelessly. He sought for glorious and useful alliances. Above all things he wished to consolidate the union of Spain, to seize the corner which still evaded his grip, the narrow kingdom of Navarre, Pampeluna, the Eastern Pyrenees, the pass of Roncevaux. As it happened, Navarre belonged to a French family who were protected by King Charles VIII. In order to get Navarre it was therefore necessary to muzzle this Charles VIII. Ferdinand decided to bestow his daughters only upon the enemies of France.

There was in Brussels a young man equally qualified to be a good husband and a no less excellent ally. He possessed the two kingdoms of Belgium and Holland and also several rich French territories: Dunkirk, Lille, Arras. His sway extended almost to the Somme; he was in a position to threaten Paris. Moreover, he also held the Jura country: Vesoul, Besançon, Dôle, Pontarlier. On his mother's side he was a grandson of that Charles the Bold who had been such a thorn in the side of Louis XI. His name was Philip, in commemoration of the most glorious dukes of Burgundy. His ambition was eventually to retake Dijon and break the power of France. This ambition caused Ferdinand to smile happily. "We shall each of us have our share. The lad will seize Burgundy. I shall annex Navarre and in addition some of the richest provinces of Italy."

Philip had vast resources. He not only ruled Belgium and the Jura. Germany was at his disposal, since he was the only son of the Emperor Maximilian. He was eventually to receive as his patrimony Austria, the Tyrol and all the Habsburg dominions. It was probable that the German Electors would be unable to resist the lure of such riches and that he would be named Emperor.

Meanwhile he had his father, Maximilian, to assist him. Nor could anyone believe that the mercenaries of Germany would fail to respond when summoned to march on France, pillage Champagne and occupy Paris.

Ferdinand therefore offered Philip the second of his daughters. The Fleming accepted the offer. He was a magnificent athlete. His female subjects were crazy about him and called him: the Handsome. The Infanta Joan could scarcely lay claim to good looks. She was swarthy and lean and she rolled great hungry eyes. She was even more peculiar than plain. She painfully alarmed Isabella and shocked Catherine; the priests affirmed her to be possessed. She blasphemed and did not believe in God. She had to be dragged to Mass and beaten into silence. Ferdinand was particularly glad to dispatch this encumbrance to Belgium. Peace resumed its sway in the royal palaces. The little Catherine breathed a sigh of relief; the priests gave thanks to the Lord. Isabella wiped away a few tears, and very soon afterwards there were great rejoicings in Spain at the marriage of her crown prince. His bride was one of Philip's sisters, Marguerite, a lively, shrewd girl who had in her childhood been insulted by the French and who nourished against them a stubborn hatred. The alliance was gaining strength. France, surrounded from the North and from the South, was threatened on all her frontiers: the Somme, the Meuse, the Jura and the Pyrenees would inevitably brew disturbance and rise against her.

Nevertheless Ferdinand harboured a misgiving. He knew France and her intractability. He required additional allies and remembered the English, the perennial enemies of France, from whom she had so often suffered defeat, dismemberment and exploitation. In London there was a marriageable Prince of Wales. Why not offer him an Infanta?

England was marking time. Of all her French conquests nothing remained to her but Calais. During twenty years she had been torn by internecine feuds. Eighty Plantagenet princes had perished. A taciturn adventurer had finally issued forth out of the shadows, had conquered by treachery, had slipped craftily onto the throne and had for thirteen years silently kept his seat. He killed few people, but he brought legal actions and confiscated. He was seldom seen and was surrounded by guards; he was puny; he coughed, and he governed by gloom, by a paralysing fear. Ferdinand, judging him to be firmly established, offered him Catherine for his heir. Henry VII enquired the amount of her dowry. Ferdinand promised two hundred thousand gold crowns. The bargain was struck and the two children were betrothed. The entire west was thus united against France.

The Betrothal

The Prince of Wales was ten years old, Catherine was eleven years of age. She knelt before the priests, received the ring and plighted her troth to the little unknown boy. But she remained at Isabella's side. Nobody thought it necessary to teach her English. She wrote impressive letters to her future husband in the Latin tongue and the prince replied to her in choice periods culled from Cicero. This was a happy scholastic arrangement: their earliest love-letters furthered their education.

Life was becoming very gloomy in the royal palaces of Spain. Heaven, which had appeared so propitious to Isabella, seemed now determined to smite her. John, her heir, prematurely married to the too ardent Marguerite, died suddenly. The Queen of Portugal, her eldest daughter, was ill. She had however succeeded in banishing the Jews and the Moors from Lisbon, had wrested their children from them to be christianized and had burnt many unbelievers. Unnatural Jewish mothers had been known to cut the throats of their offspring rather than yield them to Christ. In spite of so many holy deeds, the Queen of Portugal died, and Isabella sent the widower her third Infanta in compensation.

She adopted as her minister and confessor a begging friar who had lived for three years in a hut made of branches. She made him primate of Castile and Archbishop of Toledo, against the wishes of the court and of Ferdinand and to the great annoyance of the Pope, Alexander Borgia, who had no liking for anchorites. She reformed the monasteries, compelled the monks to do penance, threw such as were licentious into dark dungeons and burnt any who rebelled. But Heaven was not appeased. The Infanta Joan was unhappy in Brussels. Philip was unfaithful to her; she adored him, made him scenes and threatened to kill her rivals. It was said that her mind was affected. In view of the fact that the decease of her brother John and of her sister of Portugal had left her sole heir to her parents, Isabella was infuriated at the thought that this Philip who so misused her daughter must one day rule in Spain.

She was ageing and felt ill. She was heavy with dropsy. Ferdinand neglected her, seeking more youthful flesh. She spent her days in penances; all that remained to her was Catherine. The child knelt beside her in her private oratories at the feet of the great tortured crucifixes. She was wise and serious, having all her mother's qualities and also some of her defects, such as her pride and her violence. She lacked Isabella's political genius, her ability to bow before the inevitable, her arrogant grace and her beauty. Isabella would sadly contemplate the stumpy figure, the short neck and the long, unattractive countenance of the typical blond Castilian; her pale dull eyes. What would the dreary sky of England offer to an unfortunate child whose only charms were of the soul? The people of the North were frequently crude drunkards. She mused on the perfidy of men and on the subterfuges of her Ferdinand. She stroked Catherine's hair, interrupted her prayers and sought to develop her. She made her rehearse her dances, dwelt upon her own memories. Catherine stared at her from under her pale lashes, and Isabella would fall silent. Catherine would take advantage of her silence to examine the portrait of her little prince. He had comely features, the face of a girl and his name was Arthur, like a king of romance.

Ferdinand, wishing to ensure the stability of his daughter's throne, begged Henry VII to dispatch the two pretenders who were languishing in the Tower of London. The English King thought the request reasonable and promptly beheaded the captives. Ferdinand, touched by this consideration, commanded his daughter to prepare herself for departure, while he packed up the two hundred thousand crowns of her dower in iron chests. Henry VII asked that a few comely ladies might accompany his son's bride; at the age of forty-five, after thirty years of use, English women had ceased to attract him.

Isabella packed the trunks. She supplied her daughter with a confessor, a diplomat and an archbishop, waiting women, cooks, scullions and other menials. An escort of gentlemen and those comely ladies so insistently demanded by the father-in-law. The day of departure dawned. There were tears, blessings and prayers and Catherine, mounted upon a mule, took the road to Galicia. Ferdinand returned to his schemes and his pleasures.

II

A PUNY PRINCE AND A KING WITH A COUGH

(1501—1509)

The Journey to England

CATHERINE and her escort made their way across the parched fields of July. They would set forth at sundown and travel all through the night, refreshing the hoofs of their mounts in grasses wet with the morning dew, and halting as soon as that dew had evaporated, they would sleep all day in closely shuttered rooms. They were astonished at the coolness of Galicia, at its clouds, at its trees, at the mists that veiled its horizons. At length Catherine beheld the ocean and a little flotilla with furled sails but streaming pennons. She went on board, crossing a gangway covered with a Moorish carpet. She heard the grinding of the anchors as they were weighed, the cries of the sailors, the first spreading of the sails; she felt the motion of the sea.

Her pleasure was of short duration. A tempest arose, and beat the vessels toward the South, pushing them in the direction of Africa and fresh storms. Through the narrow slits of the port-holes she caught a glimpse of a long flat coast, then of islands—the Canaries, Madeira or the Azores—then of vast and terrific seas. They tossed about for two months and finally sighted the grey rocks of Cornwall. On a day in October they glided into Plymouth Sound. They disembarked, rejoicing at the sensation of the solid earth beneath their feet. The Archbishop, the diplomat and the confessor examined their Infanta, judged that her beauty had suffered severely, that the comely ladies-in-waiting themselves were distinctly the worse for wear and prescribed a brief repose. The future bride being barely fifteen years old, there was no need for undue haste.

They waited for several days. Catherine began to use her eyes and was astonished at what she saw in her new kingdom. Great clouds, hustled by the west wind, billowed above the rocks. She went to church. Folk ran alongside to acclaim her. They were sturdy, dark-haired and bandy-legged. They had fine light eyes and broad, ruddy cheeks tanned and pickled by the salt air. They smelt of strong liquors. She folded herself in her mantles to keep out the cold and in order that none should see her face.

At length her three companions decided to leave Plymouth. They travelled by easy stages. They passed through heather, through meadows where the long grass caught at the horses' feet, through woods where the thinning foliage dripped large drops. The roads were heavy with mud and the days short. At nightfall they were joined by the baggage waggons bringing their beds, their gold and silver plate, the crowns of the dowry and the blue and green tapestries for the bedroom walls. Then the country altered. The wind became less violent and the clouds heavier. They encountered thick fogs which muffled the sound of the church bells. The people were no longer dark as in Plymouth. They were blond

and fair-skinned, they had fine muscular bodies and quiet
eyes and they did not loaf along the roads. They could
be glimpsed for a moment in passing, snug in their
cottages beside great wood fires. Catherine missed the
blue sky; she felt further from paradise and these English
appeared to give very little thought to eternal life. They
seemed to be devoid of all cravings, either for heaven or
for women; they lived a life bereft alike of grave sins
and of fierce passions. They devoured meat that dripped
blood, drank cider and about them lingered the smell of
their orchards. Catherine, shivering with malaria under
her drenched mantles, was nauseated by their placidity.
She was homesick for her arid Spain, for the tough
strong-tasting flesh of the Spanish sheep. She would rise
very early and pray with her priests until the coming of
daylight.

She had been travelling for twenty days when she was
informed that she was about to meet her father-in-law
and Prince Arthur, her betrothed. She promptly shut
herself into her house. Nobody must see her before the
wedding. Meanwhile the Archbishop and the diplomat
endeavoured to keep back the King. But Henry VII thrust
them aside. "I will see her," he exclaimed, "even if she
is abed," and he marched into her room, followed by the
little Prince Arthur. She knelt before them.

She examined them closely from head to foot. They in
no way resembled their athletic subjects. They were
pale and weedy and appeared to be soaked in fog. The
father, at forty-five, was bent like an old man: it was
amazing that this long, hollow stalk had been capable of
making war, had worn harness and conquered a kingdom.
His face was narrow and bony and his mouth like a gash.

[17]

His eyes blinked, his nose was pendulous, melancholy and flabby. The son, even thinner than his parent, had anxious eyes, stiff curls and an uncertain, childish mouth. He eyed Catherine shyly and murmured a few sentences which his tutor translated into Latin. The Spaniards found it hard to understand Latin spoken with the Oxford accent: they stammered. Henry seized the diplomat by the arm and in French, a precise language well adapted to financial matters, began to speak of the dowry.

They all set out together for London. As he rode, the King coughed. Arthur also coughed, which perturbed the diplomat and the Archbishop. At every paroxysm they started and exchanged anxious glances. Would this sickly husband live? Could he survive the ordeal of marriage or would he expire in the nuptial bed? What would Ferdinand say if after a few days of matrimony his daughter was sent back to him, a widow? There is nothing more difficult to dispose of than a damaged Infanta who has not had the time to be fruitful. They asked to be allowed to examine Prince Arthur. They stripped him and inspected him minutely and were compelled to admit that he was normally developed. Only his excessive emaciation shocked them. His skin was flaccid and lifeless and his ribs stuck out like those of a famished dog; they were able to count them one by one. But at fifteen leanness is not unusual. They hoped that Prince Arthur would put on flesh and dared not further oppose the marriage.

Catherine's First Espousals.

In London all the family was waiting. Catherine threw herself at the feet of her mother-in-law Queen Elizabeth, who raised her and took her in her arms. The Queen's face was charming but worn; from under her coif strayed heavy locks of gold. She was pregnant and seemed borne down by the weight of the new life within her, and also by that of her own past sorrows. Even the love she felt for her children brought her little happiness or hope. She was a descendant of a sinister race. Her father, King Edward IV, the son of a sire who had lost his head, had strangled his own brother, and had himself later died mysteriously under her eyes, probably of poison. Another of her uncles and her half-brother had been executed. Her own brothers, the celebrated Princes in the Tower, had been suffocated in their prison and their murderer, her atrocious uncle Richard III, crooked and hunch-backed, had seized her and sought to marry her. She had withstood him, had remained in prison and later had fallen into the arms of his conqueror, the consumptive, coughing Henry VII, a murderer like all the rest of them, but a sly, shamefaced assassin who assumed the airs of virtue. Even her mother had betrayed her and had tried to oust her from the throne. She had been compelled to countenance her imprisonment and the confiscation of her goods. She watched Arthur anxiously. She knew him to be ill and was not allowed to nurse him. For political reasons he had been removed from her care. Being Prince of Wales he must live in a distant castle, alone with strangers. She shuddered to see him so pale.

[19]

Beside Elizabeth Catherine saw an old lady who looked more cheerful, her energetic countenance closely swathed in a linen wimple. This was Henry VII's mother, Margaret. She dressed as a nun but had always known how to combine worldly affairs with those of heaven. Isabella would have approved of her. She understood politics and it was to her wisdom that Henry VII owed his throne. She had dragged him forth from obscurity and invested him with her own rights. In order to gain him partisans she had remarried twice, selecting in one instance a minister of the enemy and persuading him to break faith upon the battlefield. The victory once assured, she had decided that she was weary of the married state, had shown her ex-minister the door and had given herself entirely to God. The unfortunate husband had realized that his only safety lay in submission. His family were threatened. Henry beheaded one of his brothers. The aged Margaret adored theology. She acquired a learned confessor whom she commandeered from Cambridge University. She studied; she lived among holy things and was engaged in translating the *Imitation*.

Then came the children. Queen Elizabeth pushed them toward Catherine, whose face brightened. Two smiling little girls, one already tall, Margaret, fat, inclined to heaviness but amiable; the other, Mary, a tiny blonde of five years old with delicate features and the fairness of angels or of the children of England. A nurse bore a baby in her arms, and then, thrusting aside his sisters and the nurse, the King's second son, Henry, Duke of York ran toward Catherine.

He was fat, lively and muscular and at ten years old

might have passed for twelve or thirteen. His hair was tawny and he had the resplendent complexion that goes with red hair. His eyes were narrow but sparkling. His strength was that of the young male and his chubby cheeks those of a baby. One felt him to be fed on red meat, upon fat roast mutton luscious to the palate, upon prime beef dripping red gravy before the great fires. He exhaled the open air, the meadows, the forests, mushrooms and cold mists. Added to which he could be serious when occasion required it; he was learned and delighted his grandam Margaret by his application to his Latin studies, pleased the lords and the soldiery by his taste for hunting and sport, and appealed to the Queen's women by his love of music and his skill in playing the lute, the organ and the flute, over which latter instrument he gently swelled his childish cheeks.

There was little conversation, to the great relief of the interpreters, who sweated at their own inadequacy. Catherine gave the order for the unpacking of her dresses and her household effects and proceeded to show off her Spanish dances. Young Henry was astonished at the sound of the guitars and of their harsh music, at the leisured undulations of the dancer.

On the wedding day Catherine appeared dressed in white with her fair hair flowing onto her shoulders as is seemly for a virgin. She was carried in a litter to Saint Paul's Cathedral, where the priests awaited her. The pieces of money, of which the King allowed a sparse provision to be thrown to the populace, fell into thick mud. Arthur, even paler than usual, appeared half frozen in garments that were too heavy and too ornate. In the evening there was a banquet and a ball. Catherine danced again, but alone; Arthur danced with his aunt. The festivities were showing signs of wilting when Henry, seizing his sister Margaret, started a lively measure. He adored jigs, which showed his powerful legs to advantage. He threw off his doublet and bumpers of wine began to go round. Well fed and filled with good liquor the lords and ladies became more cheerful. Presently Catherine and Arthur were escorted to their chamber. A bishop blessed the huge tester bed. The Spaniards disrobed Catherine, while the English removed Arthur's shirt and they were slipped into bed, naked. The curtains were then drawn to conceal them and those intimately concerned settled down in the room for the night, watching for any suggestive movement of the curtains. Distant sounds of the ball could still be heard. In the morning Arthur thrust his thin face from between the curtains and remarked: "I am thirsty." A gold cup, brimming with wine, was brought to him, it being fitting that a young warrior's first drink should be manly. He drank it eagerly, observing with an air of triumph: "Marriage is a thirsty business!" In the course of the day his pages crowded round him, begging for confidences and he answered them confidentially: "I spent the night in Spain." Tournaments followed. The lords donned their plumed helmets and gravely broke lances; but as such entertainments were costly, Henry VII very soon put an end to them and decided that Arthur had better return to his Welsh castle.

It was debated whether or no Catherine should accompany him. The Spaniards remembered their little prince who had been consumed by a few months of marriage. But Henry VII was concentrating upon the hundred thousand crowns of the dowry and desired a marriage that should be undeniably consummated and indissoluble. He had an interview with Catherine's confessor and reminded him that God expects husband and wife to share the same bed. The confessor persuaded his penitent and the two children therefore set out together for Wales, that country swept by winds and drenched in fogs, alike perilous to delicate lungs. They were to remain there for the winter. The Queen, who had a partiality for relics, delighted Catherine by presenting her with a costly shrine containing a miraculous girdle of the blessed Virgin, said to be invaluable to pregnant women.

The Little Duke, Henry of York

Henry watched his brother's departure enviously. He had escorted him to the nuptial couch and had listened to the gossip of the pages. Two or three well-grown lads who had been assigned to him as companions, who instructed him in sports, in war and in many other things, considered Catherine plain. He dared not contradict these connoisseurs, but he secretly thought them hard to please. This infanta from an heroic land, this grave mysterious young girl whose shape was already mature and who danced such alluring dances, attracted him. The strains of the guitars, the vibrant strokes of the tambourines had seemed to arouse his sympathies for this soul which appeared to be unawakened, but which he felt might be capable of strong emotions. He fingered his lute, trying to recapture the notes of a jota or a seguidilla.

But the lute and the flute are idyllic instruments, quite unsuited to the raucous Spanish music.

His melancholy was of short duration; it was but a musical pause and Henry was too vigorous to dwell upon it. He returned to his religious books. Fisher, his grandmother's chaplain, attended to his Latin studies and taught him theology, urging him to discourse upon the mysteries of the Trinity and the Eucharist. He was thoughtfully pious and diligently attended lengthy offices, but he was not moved by any ecstasies or troubled by any reflections on the infinite. He had no dreams of paradise and was immune from the impulses of the Spaniards, from their penances, their sufferings, their mystical unions with Christ, their stigmata and their tears. God, holy subjects, and the sacraments were for him matters upon which to compose learned exercises, to construct and demolish theses, to realize and develop his intelligence.

He desired to excel in all things, to be an infant prodigy. He believed himself to be predestinate. He loved riding, the feel of a horse between his knees; he loved yet more to dominate his companions, to vanquish them with the spear, the sword or his bare fists. His favourite exercise was wrestling. Naked to the waist he would seize hold of his father's pages, crush them to him until their bones cracked, roll upon the ground with them, stifling them beneath his weight and compelling them to beg for mercy. He was always victorious, being extremely muscular and a king's son.

The intimate friends whom the King had appointed as his mentors organized sporting events, acted as referees and were prodigal of applause. Henry, more powerful than perceptive, believed in their admiration and swelled with vanity. The intimate friends winked at one another and devised further flatteries. They were impecunious scions of the nobility and had their fortunes to make. They talked to him of women, allowing him to suspect their intrigues and filling him with envious admiration. A gipsy poet who had contrived to secure his favour in early childhood entertained him with tales of gallantry. His friends took him hunting. They hunted the deer in the great royal forests round Eltham, Richmond and Windsor; they became intoxicated with the healthy and virile joy of killing, with the stimulating echoes of hunting horns under frosty December skies. Young Henry revelled in the sensual enjoyment of these manly pleasures.

But a shadow marred his happiness; he was not the first-born: "The crown will never be mine; I shall always be compelled to obey, to receive orders from my brother, from that dreary, sickly Arthur." The intimate friends had hopes that poor Arthur might be removed. Henry was too good a Christian to indulge such thoughts. And in any case, ailing persons and even consumptives had been known to survive. Henry VII was tubercular and had reigned for twenty years.

With the coming of spring the shadow vanished. It was learned that Arthur had expired in his Welsh castle and in Catherine's arms. Henry wept bitterly. Then he enquired whether he was to become Prince of Wales and heir to the crown. He was told that he must be patient. The little Infanta might yet conceal a crown prince within her womb. Henry's admiration for Catherine suffered a sudden eclipse.

There was a pause of some weeks until fate pronounced itself and Catherine finally confessed that she had no hopes of pregnancy. She was bitterly disappointed and so were her dear Spaniards. Were they expected to return to Castile? Henry VII would gladly have sent her home, but in that case it would have been necessary to relinquish the dowry. He temporized. He kept Catherine at his side and she followed the royal family from castle to castle on its perpetual peregrinations. The Virgin's girdle had proved ineffectual.

Queen Elizabeth protected her, but Henry VII found her keep expensive. Soon the good Queen fell ill; Arthur's death had shattered her and she failed to survive another confinement. She died in London, at her apartments in the Tower.

The King's Matrimonial Projects.

As soon as the King had decently mourned the Queen, he began to consider what advantages could be reaped from his bereavement. He might, for instance, marry Catherine and thus ensure the retention not only of the hundred thousand crowns already received but also of the second hundred still owing, while obtaining for his elderly and consumptive embraces a body which might lack perfection but which was none the less youthful and warm. Catherine recoiled and Isabella and Ferdinand refused categorically. They desired for their daughter a lusty young husband who might be expected to have a lasting reign. They therefore demanded Henry.

Catherine was undeniably six years his senior, but a ripe

woman is the more likely to be faithful, to give sound advice and bear healthy children. In order to retain the dowry, Henry VII consented. In the month of June, on Henry's twelfth birthday, he was solemnly betrothed to Catherine. The stout child assumed an air of dignity as he placed the ring upon the finger of a girl of eighteen who was already fully initiated in all the mysteries of sex. He felt the occasion to be his promotion to manhood.

It was a year of weddings. Henry VII celebrated the marriage of his daughter, the gentle and attractive Margaret. In this case the marriage was a serious one, an adult affair of the flesh devoid of empty symbolism. The bridegroom was over thirty years of age and was King of Scotland. Henry VII marked the event by brilliant festivities and tournaments. He sighed heavily over the bills and attempted to levy a special tax, but the Commons would have none of it.

He looked around for other resources and resumed his hunting for eligible princesses. He made an offer for a Neapolitan, then for two French cousins of King Louis XII, the mother or the daughter, impartially. He had no success. He was getting tired of keeping Catherine and fed her sparsely on bread and vegetables. No meat; a princess must remain slim. Isabella was dead and Ferdinand also was contemplating a useful remarriage. Catherine no longer possessed a wearable woollen gown. She was compelled to make daily use of her sumptuous state dresses. Henry VII was thinking of sending her home. On his son's fourteenth birthday he had him taken before a bishop in whose presence he was required to protest against his betrothal and repudiate all engagement.

The young prince acquiesced with a light heart. He had lost interest in Catherine; possibly the intimate friends had enabled him to sample other fruits. Catherine suffered in silence. The old king insulted her and ended by accusing her of improper conduct with one of her monks.

Any pretext was good enough to fill Henry VII's coffers; he ardently despoiled his subjects. His great predecessors had cut off the heads of their nobles; he cut the strings of their purses. He was a pirate and grabbed everything that fell within his reach. Philip of Habsburg and his Queen, the crazy Joan having been shipwrecked on the English coast, were not permitted to depart without paying ransom. They were not mulcted of a bag of crowns but of a fat commercial treaty. Catherine poured out her troubles to her sister Joan, but the lunatic would not listen to her. For her the world held only Philip, Philip's body and his embraces. She had escaped from Spain to join him in Flanders; she overwhelmed him with her jealousy, her furies and her tears. One day she sprang at the throat of one of his blond mistresses, who had to be rescued from her clutches. Catherine, feeling more than ever deserted, saw her depart with her handsome husband.

Not long afterwards news came that Philip was dead. Henry VII was delighted and determined to marry Joan. He wrote at once to Ferdinand and made Catherine write also, restoring her to favour. He cared little, he was at pains to explain, that Joan should be crazy; she was none the less capable of bearing a child. She was also capable of bringing him Castile as her dowry. Unfortunately Ferdinand was himself determined to retain Castile and was preparing to perform his paternal duty by putting the mad queen under restraint. For the moment she was wandering about Spain accompanied by the embalmed remains of Philip enclosed in a glass coffin. Henry VII did not dare invite her to London with her strange baggage, but he did not lose hope and Catherine helped him to the best of her ability.

The Earliest Escapades of a Prince of Wales.

Henry was sixteen years old. He enjoyed his youth to the full. Each day brought him unsuspected powers, more intense pleasures, new victories. He now disdained the pages, wrestling with his adult friends. He loved to throw Compton, Brandon, handsome soldiers of twenty-five years of age, mature and skilful. In his calmer hours he adventured into theology, wrote dissertations by which the worthy Fisher pretended to be impressed, and which enchanted his grandmother. Seated at the organ, he submerged himself in pious music, discovered new harmonies. He would wander by himself in the park, listening to the silence, to the multitudinous resonances of earth and sky, to the sounds of growing vegetation. Everything that was young, everything that had life followed him. Henry VII was little more than a ghost, an indefinite shade hidden behind the casements. He was wasting from day to day and his eyes were growing dim. His death was eagerly awaited and the lords whom he had despoiled were preparing to hang his ministers. Henry shot with the bow, vaulted, galloped in the forests, foundering the strongest horses, hardening himself in the saddle. He breathed in the healthy cold air of the English countryside, delighted in the baying of his hounds, sought to disentangle in the undergrowth the rank scents of deer and boar. He would also ride across the heather, hunting the fox and enjoying its ruses. He grew to distinguish the savour of the seasons; the heavy atmosphere of winter days when the branches are soaked by the rain and the unwary passer is drenched with a cold shower. The taste of the foggy days when progress is slow and the neighbourhood of a village is apprehended by the lowering smoke screen and the smell of baking bread. The green taste of spring with all the may-trees in bloom, of that first night in May which all folk spend out of doors in the meadows, in the forests, rich and poor alike, and from which the lads come home with great armfuls of foliage, with the may-tree to be planted at the threshold, and from which young maids return with too tender memories and not infrequently a child in the womb. But Henry feared the flesh. It terrified him like a deadly sin. Fisher and his grandam Margaret had brought him up like an acolyte; he had retained the modesty of a great child and blushed easily. But his friends Compton and Brandon were less pure than Fisher. Compton was ready to find him mistresses: Brandon hinted at improper adventures. No lie was too dastardly for Brandon if he wanted a woman. He secretly married two of his cousins, deserted them in turn and caused the marriages to be annulled. There remained a daughter whom he put out to nurse. Henry beheld hell yawn at such disclosures; nevertheless, he listened and dreamed of them over his organ and his theological tomes. Brandon was so comely and so confident that it was impossible to despise him.

Day by day these two friends gently urged their prince towards sin. Is a man worthy of the name while he remains virgin? One may be a monk or a saint and go to heaven, but earth has its pleasures which outshine those of paradise. And then, at sixteen years of age, is it courage that counsels chastity, or fear? Henry, by nature a braggart, was forced to recognize that his chastity was scarcely courageous. And after all, argued the tempters, is the sin so great? Is one bound to listen to these old priests who are so often hypocrites steeped in vice, liars and whitened sepulchres; who would be the worse? Nobody was suggesting that he should violate women or even lie to them. There are so many who are willing, so many who are eager. Would it not be happiness enough for any little peasant girl to be of service to her prince? Especially when that prince was the handsomest of young men. The scent of woods, of the chase, of horses; the sensation of the sweating labouring beast between one's knees, engender wild emotions of the flesh. Henry yielded to the advice of his guides, ventured and found the game agreeable. Peasants are a prince's best initiation. They do not make him shy and, simple animals though they may be, their flesh may have its subtleties.

But rustic fruit quickly becomes monotonous. The thought arises of more complex flavours, of variety, of less instinctive responses. The pleasant word mistress is well chosen. There are things to be learned other than hunting, music and theology. Friends, even those most experienced, can only teach theory. The time came to return to the court and seek a cultured partner, a godmother.

[31]

He chose her—or she was chosen for him—from the noblest family in England—the Howards, who were of the blood royal. The lady had married slightly beneath her. The Howards, having produced too many daughters, had been compelled to provide for them as best they could. This one was the wife of a younger son, rich but scarcely noble, a scion of great city merchants. Thomas Boleyn, while still in his first youth, had seen war service in Cornwall. He was a good fighter and a better schemer. He knew how to line his pockets. Elizabeth Howard had borne him two daughters and a son, but she was still comely. Henry could hardly have made a better selection. For so handsome a prince, so muscular but so innocently ingenuous, Elizabeth was filled with tender consideration. The milk that had nourished her latest-born, Anne, still swelled her breasts. By the side of this experienced body, responsive to the lightest caress, Henry enjoyed an amiable affection, an almost maternal devotion, pleasures enduring, deep and varied. The village girls had given him only passing gratifications, as crude as ale and as depleting in their effect. Elizabeth taught him that there existed harmonies more moving and more refined than in music itself and that even the strains of the organ are not comparable to those drawn from the flesh when it is shattered by delight. He would leave her bed contented, serene and full of a happiness as exalted and as rarely lovely as moonlight. Meanwhile Thomas Boleyn perceived nothing, or deliberately feigned blindness.

In this manner Henry attained his eighteenth birthday. His father still clung to life, and with his lungs in tatters somehow contrived to breathe. He even aspired to remarry and demanded the hand of the ardent Margaret of Habsburg, who, at twenty-four years of age, had already proved fatal to two lusty husbands. He weathered autumns and winters, but April was his undoing. The sharp airs and the spring sunshine consumed the remnants of his vitality. So soon as he knew himself to be dying he wished to found a hospital, to give some money to the poor. But it was then too late and it was loaded with ill-gotten goods that he winged his way to the Judgment Seat.

III

THE CROWN, THE FLUTE AND THE CONJUGAL BED

(1509—1512)

A Joyful Event

THE people do not love wisdom. Henry VII had given his subjects peace. It was rare to see drunkenness. Business prospered and France paid tribute. The taxes were heavy, but the money thus extorted remained in the State Treasury, ready to meet necessary expenses. England should have considered herself fortunate. But peace engenders thoughts of death and England was bored.

The demise of this admirable king was hailed with acclamations. Strapping messengers left Richmond at a hard gallop and, waving their cloaks, flung the news abroad at the street corners of Westminster and the City of London. The lords issued forth in cavalcades followed by their fully armed retainers. Merchants and artisans paraded the streets and buzzed in the pleasant April sunshine. They shouted: "Long live Henry VIII" until they were hoarse and then looked around for fresh amusement.

They seized the late king's tax-collectors and their myrmidons in their lairs, thrust them into the pillories at the street corners, pelted them with rotten vegetables, organizing competitions in accuracy of aim. When they considered them to be sufficiently battered, they released them, perched them back to front astride ancient nags and paraded them from street to street. Everyone shared in the enjoyment; even the housewives, who, from the upper windows, were able to souse the unhappy riders with noxious odours. When night fell, torches were lighted. It was not until a very late hour, when London was replete with shouting, with vengeance and with wine, that the wretched victims were flung into the prisons and left to repose in solitude and filth.

Then it was time to think of the obsequies. The king's body was embalmed. A wax mould was taken of his face for the purpose of making the effigy that would rest upon the catafalque. The crypt at Westminster was being prepared. Apprentices and gossips issued forth from the City and clustered round the Abbey. It had been an excellent idea to die in April and be buried in May.

The new king wept for his father. He conformed to custom, but we may be permitted to doubt whether he would have recalled the old man to life had he been able to do so. A crown is not relinquished once it has been attained. But God did not put him to the test; the kings of England were empowered to heal the scrofulous by touching their throats, but not to resuscitate the dead. One must not be too ambitious.

It is very agreeable to be king when one is eighteen years old, in good health and addicted to all pleasures. Henry VII had not been a bad father, but he had kept a tight hand on his gold. Young Henry demanded the keys of the strong rooms. He was going to be able to delve in the coffers, to devise tournaments, to show the populace his prowess as an athlete, to eat and drink rare and delicious things, to satiate the court. He would also have to rule, which was a more delicate matter.

Two crews were available for the ship of state: the soldiers and the priests, the army or the church. The men of war were Henry's playmates, the lords, the generals so long without employment. The churchmen had the support of Henry's grandmother, Margaret, and of his tutor, Fisher. The men of war were good company but smacked somewhat of original sin. The churchmen gave forth an odour of righteousness and were profoundly boring. Henry hesitated between these two crews. But he did not hesitate when it came to consigning to the dungeons his father's two financial advisers who were universally detested. The financial slogan of the new reign was clearly to be: Less income and more expenditure. Such a slogan never fails to be popular, but unfortunately it cannot long be maintained.

Henry formed a piebald government of priests and soldiers. These came to an agreement on one point: that of sharing the spoils of the two disgraced financiers. Each man carried off his share, particularly the scholars and the priests. A pious and youthful lawyer, Thomas More, protected by the priesthood, was made sheriff, and a dawning personality, the brilliant chaplain, Wolsey, who had already been climbing for several years, received a magnificent country mansion which had belonged to one of the fallen.

Compton and Brandon, the useful friends, obtained lucrative sinecures. The generals clamoured for war; they were weary of a peace that precluded pillage. Their leader was old Howard, the father of Elizabeth Boleyn. He had several sons who were fretting at inactivity and thirsting for carnage.

The Howards, father and sons, were counting on their Elizabeth. She proved of little use to them, for Henry was cooling off. Having become king he felt it incumbent on him to cleanse his life and turn to thoughts of serious import. Compelled by his mourning to forgo his customary diversions, secluded, living in close proximity to the shrivelling remains of his father which nobody had decided to remove, emotionally stirred by Requiems and De Profundis', he had meditated upon virtue and the duties of a sovereign. He had told himself that a frivolous king is a bad example and that he would acquire merit in dismissing Elizabeth. The most ingenious of women ends by repeating herself and Henry was attracted by a new mistress: virtue.

Countries overseas are always useful to princes as a destination for obtrusive persons whom they desire to honour. England had lost every foreign possession save Calais. Boleyn received an important appointment in that town and his wife was asked to vacate the king's heart.

But a young man who has ceased to be pure cannot regain his innocence. God does not require that he should do so but only that he should legitimize his indulgences. For this end marriage was invented. Henry therefore resolved to marry and was unanimously applauded, since the throne must have an heir.

Betrothal.

There was nothing to compel Henry to marry Catherine. His betrothal to her at twelve years of age had been no more than an empty ceremony and two years later he had repudiated it. Catherine could perfectly well be sent back to Ferdinand. It was only necessary to return her dowry. But where was another bride to be found? Only French women were available and nobody wanted a French woman. Pious folk considered them too frivolous, while those of an adventurous temperament wished to remain allied to Ferdinand and make war on France. The lords therefore favoured Catherine and the bishops were impressed by her piety. Henry's saintly grandmother, Margaret, saw in Catherine a granddaughter after her own heart and, most vital of all factors, Henry himself found her attractive.

She drew him because he reverenced virtue and because, since his childhood, she had for him represented Purity, the spotless spouse. At his earliest meeting with her, when he was ten years of age, he had felt the first promptings of his virility and had thenceforth refrained from bullying his sisters. He had intuitively divined the mystery of her womanhood and had thrilled with admiration for the stranger. He had detested his brother for taking her from him. Even the lewd jests with which the pages had soiled her name during the days which followed her marriage had, while stirring his senses, only increased his feelings of tenderness. Later, while despising her a little for her shabbiness, her widowhood and even for her holiness, he had not ceased to respect her. It had been her image that had risen before his eyes as he lingered over his musical compositions. Others undoubtedly excelled her in beauty. Elizabeth was livelier, but Catherine, by her very silence, moved him. His seclusion after his father's decease, his meditations upon death, the chanting of the priests and the strains of the organ, thoughts of eternal life, tears, all these things led him back to the neglected Infanta. He desired to worship her and perhaps to do her violence; to kneel at her feet and also to destroy her. She was twenty-four and he was eighteen; he felt like a small boy before her and wished to demonstrate to her that he was a man. He loved her.

The old king was buried on the ninth of May. He was borne from Richmond to Westminster through town and country accompanied by a resplendent procession. The crowd was stirred by the torches flaming in the sunshine, by the songs of birds which vied with the intoning of psalms, by the mingling of death and springtime. Henry created a sensation. He was very tall, very ruddy and tawny-haired: a slightly substantial deity to rejoice the eyes of women. Old crones declared that he resembled his grandsire Edward IV, whom no Englishwoman had ever been known to withstand. Romantic dreams hovered that night over more than one London pillow, and more than one husband in his cotton nightcap was surprised at the ardour which greeted him under cover of the darkness.

Catherine was profoundly happy. God had answered her prayers. For six years she had waited, a prey to desires and trances. Virgin or wife—and she swore that she was virgin—Arthur's caresses had served to arouse her. A girl of sixteen years is not far removed from womanhood after five months of sharing her bed, and no marriage, however childish, can be pure. Catherine came of passionate stock. Her brother John had died of sexual excess and unbridled desires had rendered her sister Joan insane. Her mother Isabella had loved Ferdinand to the last day of her life, and he in his turn was now spending himself in the arms of a youthful French-woman. Catherine resembled them in the fullest degree. She had grown up at Toledo, at Seville and in the Alhambra, to the rhythms of Moorish music. For her emblem she had chosen a pomegranate, the symbol of life, the bitter-sweet, bleeding fruit. In her love for Henry, desire was mingled with anguish and with a kind of despairing maternity. It was as a little boy of twelve years old that he had placed the betrothal ring on her finger and had melted her heart which had already cherished hopes of motherhood. She had been touched by his innocence and had longed to shape his character, but he had been removed from her influence and com-pelled to repudiate his betrothal. She beheld him lured into sin by the impious courtiers, by people whom she would gladly have seen burnt at the stake, in accordance with the custom of her country. She knew all there was to know, about the peasant girls, the Boleyn; a court has a thousand ears. She feared that Henry would be thrust down into hell and prayed for his salvation all the more ardently because of her belief that she alone had power to save his soul. And suddenly, just as she was about to give way to despair, he had returned to her. Clad in his mourning and in the full splendour of his royalty he had come to her in the beautiful

English springtime and had humbly begged her to be his wife.

Henry's First Marriage.

Henry married Catherine in June. She appeared once again dressed in white and she unbound her hair as when she had married Arthur, so that all might know that she was still a virgin. That night Henry came to her bed and she, whose memories were only of the futile and ghostly Arthur, welcomed a youthful Hercules who was still as comely as Apollo. In the nuptial bed, consecrated to the Lord, he revealed to her entrancing devices, of which she had dreamed when Satan tempted her, the very thought of which she had sought to banish by prayer and exorcism. She realized with rapturous shame that he had acquired his experience from his peasant girls and from Elizabeth Boleyn, but the following morning she heard three masses with edification and found it easy to visualize heaven.

It was a glorious June with occasional showers that served to refresh English lawns and hearts. The King and Queen were crowned at Westminster. The music, selected by Henry, was exquisite; standing upon the resting-places of the quiet dead they inhaled the incense of the angels.

All that summer they were happy. Henry's grandmother, Margaret, died and they buried her reverently but without tears. She had been saintly, but her death caused them little emotion: their bodies were teeming with the powerful essences of life. Very soon Catherine knew that she was pregnant and that their love had

received the divine approval. They were face to face
with that strange hour when, seeing the woman about to
become a mother, the man is filled with an increased
respect and becomes almost as a child himself before
her. They were busy preparing the cradle and were
hearing in anticipation the cries of the infant when
Catherine miscarried. They looked at one another in
astonishment. Why should God punish them?

But their sorrow was short-lived. A month later they
were again permitted to hope. They decided to travel
and to see their kingdom, and set out towards the north.
They were pleased at being received with acclamation
and wished their people to behold their happiness. In
the autumn they returned to their palace by the Thames.
Catherine travelled in a litter for fear of jeoparpizing
their hopes. But the idyll was too perfect and they were
asked to shed blood. Henry VII's two financial advisers
had been tried and for several months had been awaiting
death. The military party demanded their heads and
had the full approval of the bishops. Catherine would
have liked to spare them, but Henry dared not resist.
So the two heads fell.

They tried to forget this bloodshed and the year drew
to its end in the happiest of expectations. Catherine
could already feel the movements of her child and her
body was fruitfully swelling. The baby was born on the
first of January and proved to be a boy. Henry presented
him to the assembled lords; God had established His
seed upon the throne of England.

They enjoyed another two months of peaceful happiness. They smiled over their baby son, supervised
his wet-nurses and his cradle-rockers, listened to the

lullabies with which he was soothed to sleep. On a day in February the child died. Catherine was filled with terror and Henry began to ask himself in what manner he could have offended God and wherein could lie the sinfulness of this union which he had believed to be so holy. His old companions drew nearer: did he intend to spend his entire existence in the bed of one woman? Was he not twenty years of age with all his life before him? Was it his ambition to be an uxorious and monogamous king, remaining with folded arms while all Europe was at war? This was not only excess of conjugal virtue, but torpor. A king is only great with sword in hand. God had given him the strength of Samson and the subtlety of David; it was high time to display them on the field of battle.

Wolsey.

When one is desirous to fight it is always well to choose a holy cause. Most opportunely the French were just then engaged in attacking the Pope; they had penetrated into Italy and it was obviously the moment to fall upon them from the rear, pillage their fields and snatch from them some of their provinces. More urgently than ever, the military party clamoured for war. Old Howard was polishing his armour while Catherine, prompted by Ferdinand, was offering up petitions to the god of battles. The bishops were wailing over the perils of the poor Pope and demanding that the French, an unbelieving and corrupt people, should be severely chastised. From behind the skirts of the clergy there began to emerge the king's Chaplain, Thomas Wolsey, who also desired war.

This Wolsey was of fairly humble origin. He was the son of a wealthy Ipswich cattle-merchant and he had entered the Church in the belief that it would help him to rise. His ability astonished the University of Oxford; then he slipped somehow into royal employment, climbing with agility, noiselessly and unobtrusively. After a successful stroke of business, Henry VIII appointed him his Chaplain. He approached the great, advised them and acquired experience. The Church was behind him. He stood out among the bishops who were frizzled, worn and tremulous, by reason of his tall stature, his handsome, fleshy face, his resounding voice and his piercing eyes. He adored festivities, banquets, balls, masques, gold, women and life. He resembled Henry VIII, but with more depth, more poise, fewer tortuous scruples and also greater maturity—he was forty years of age—and greater magnificence. Or, rather, Henry might more accurately have been said to resemble him, but only as a copper coin may reproduce a gold piece, bearing the same effigy. Henry VIII, by the side of Wolsey, always appeared as a coarser replica, the squire beside the Knight, the deacon beside the priest. As it happened, the accident of birth had given a throne to the inferior while placing the superior in the rank and file. Wolsey set to work to remedy that accident. He wormed his way into Henry's intimacy, studied his character and understood it without difficulty, since it was but a reflection of his own. He gently suggested to him those ideas that he thought desirable and, pretending admiration, imposed his own views. He had as yet no official title, but he was gliding into power, stroking and caressing an unsuspecting England.

Insignificant ministers may hold office in times of peace, but genius reveals itself in war-time. Wolsey felt himself to be the possessor of genius and he decided that England should go to war.

Projects of War.

At the mere idea of attacking France England went mad with delight. France was the land of past victories, of pillage. She had been harried during more than a hundred years. Merchants began to dream of contraband, peasants of the joys of leaving their furrows, of fighting, of sending their arrows into living flesh, of raping Norman virgins and of roasting the feet of the Norman farmers in order to extort from them their woollen stockings. People about the court were yet more excited; they were already counting upon lands and castles. Old Howard, now too decrepit to ride, was having a litter constructed for his use. The Howard sons were commissioning their ships, Thomas Boleyn was appointed to an embassy, while Brandon and Compton received commands. Wolsey contented himself with the commissariat, a responsible but lucrative charge. The English were perfectly confident of victory. They had the whole of Europe on their side: to the north, the States of the archduke Philip, Belgium, Holland, French Flanders, Artois and the Franche-Comté; to the east, Germany, led by the Emperor Maximilian; to the south-west, nearly all Italy, the Pope Julius II, the Venetian Republic, and

Sicily; to the south, Spain, under the command of Ferdinand. France was to be crushed and Catherine wrote joyful letters to her father in the brief intervals between telling her rosary.

Henry was much less delighted. He was by no means convinced that he would like war. He preferred innocuous sports: wrestling, or fencing with blunted weapons. War was full of unexpected mishaps and misdirected blows and was not controlled by any laws of fair play. What may not happen to the most doughty of champions if he is attacked from the rear or compelled to fight at odds of ten to one? What can he be expected to do against cannon or against those venomously whistling arrows which insinuate themselves between the joints of any armour or pierce an eye or the throat? Was not Goliath also a doughty champion, and yet three pebbles thrown by the young David had put an end to him? Moreover, on reflection Henry began to wonder whether he himself was indeed so invincible a champion or whether Brandon and Compton had not used discretion and sometimes allowed themselves to be vanquished out of tact.

And in any case, what did he stand to gain by the war? A certain number of provinces overseas? Henry particularly disliked travelling and was perfectly content with England. She was wealthy, fruitful and green and obedient. Her castles were overflowing with produce, her coffers were bursting with gold. Why, then, go in search of hazards, risking his crown and even, possibly, his life? His father had been nothing but a usurper, and might he not himself be overthrown? he was not without enemies. There still remained certain turbulent

pretenders whose claims were undeniably better than
his own. He had two of them safely under lock and key
in the Tower, but others were at large on the Continent,
serving the King of France. He scented traitors in his
own court, people who flattered him while waiting to cut
his throat. What might not these people do if the king
left England, if he crossed the Channel and was beaten
in war? All these considerations gave him food for
thought.

The End of a Honeymoon.

Henry was asking Heaven for advice and was hearing
three masses daily with ever-increasing piety, but God,
by some incomprehensible caprice, was withholding His
approval. He was refusing issue to the most chaste of
kings, the most faithful of husbands. All Henry's hopes
evaporated in miscarriages, still-born infants or others
that were short-lived. This appeared to be doubly unjust,
since in any case Henry had ceased to find much enjoyment in Catherine's bed. Gradually, as he attained
mature manhood, she was losing her prestige of seniority,
of an elder adored since childhood and so long inaccessible. Above all, she was losing, by reason of her sterility
and of God's manifest displeasure, that celestial aureole,
that perfume of serenity, of religion, of incense, which
had at first proved so irresistible to the pious young man.
He was no longer convinced that he pleased Heaven by
cohabiting with her; he doubted whether she were indeed
a saint and was sadly becoming aware that she was a very
unsatisfactory sinner. Satan had endowed her as meanly

as the Almighty; she was not good-looking and she lacked sexual ingenuity. Henry was astonished that he had been so long in perceiving it, that he had not sooner believed what his friends averred. He gloomily contemplated her short neck, her dull eyes, and reflected that she was perpetually pregnant to no purpose, feverish, ailing; in short, a woman seldom in a condition to be touched at all. Added to which she was obsessed by a ridiculous prudishness and by a devastating self-respect, submitting all her qualms to her confessor, an insufferable monk whom she had brought with her from Spain. To sum up: a wife to be revered but a most unfulfilling bedfellow; she was doubtless a great queen, but she was by no means a titbit for a king's palate.

Moreover, she was the reverse of docile, and she made him scenes, believing that in virtue of her six years' seniority she could treat Henry as a child and deny him even the most trifling of escapades. She ended by boring him and he began to look about for an adventure. He might have recalled Elizabeth Boleyn, but Catherine would have known of it and he feared her scenes, and in any case he had no particular inclination towards Elizabeth—he knew all about her and she thus lacked mystery. Since he was now determined to sin, he intended to get some profit from doing so. He confided in Compton and asked him to arrange something. Compton was full of resource: he approached a very great lady, a Buckingham, Henry's own cousin and married to boot. The lady did not refuse and promised discretion. Compton pretended to be desperately in love with her himself; possibly he received his share of her favours in order to prepare her, to instruct her in her duties. In any case he was the protective screen, the go-between.

Henry felt a renewal of vitality. He was still sufficiently ingenuous, sufficiently Christian and there still, despite his great muscles and his crown, lingered about him enough of the acolyte, to experience an entrancing thrill at the very fact of sinning. To the pleasure that he received from the amiable embraces of his new mistress was added that of telling himself that many years of purgatory would be added to him as payment for these forbidden relaxations. He also took a secret delight in deceiving Catherine, but her ignorance was of short duration.

She watched; the entire Court spied and gossiped. A sister of Lady Buckingham, one of Catherine's maids of honour, learnt of the intrigue with indignation, and revealed it. A brother, head of the Buckingham family, protested furiously that his honour was assailed. Catherine went in tears to her confessor, who, in the face of such blatant adultery, invoked the wrath of Heaven. Together they raised an abominable uproar. The lady's husband was compelled, in his turn, to open his eyes and join the hue and cry. He carried off his wife to the country and Henry, ashamed of having been discovered, remained with empty arms, bereft of his beloved, chaste of necessity and reduced to the con-jugal couch. After a few days of embarrassment he remembered that he was king, announced that he would no longer be interfered with and had no intention of remaining in leading strings. He banished the Bucking-ham tribe from Court, including the spying sister and the too scrupulous brother, and dismissed the Spanish monk who confessed and abetted the Queen. Catherine wept, and he left her to her tears.

He was becoming accustomed to the idea of sin and was even clearing his Court of the canting old bishops. Wolsey was his chaplain and advised him to live cheerfully. Wolsey himself ate and drank freely, organized masked balls and hunting expeditions, fenced with Henry and enjoyed all the fruits of the earth. Wolsey continually had women in his bed and disdained to repudiate his bastards. Henry found him an agreeable companion. It was quite possible that he robbed the treasury and sold his support to the highest bidder; but he spent inordinately, his house was the most beautiful in London and Henry would escape at night to sup with him. Catherine, alone, would vainly await his return.

IV

THE PLEASURES OF WAR

(1512—1515)

Resistances.

BETWEEN the sampling of two dishes, in the interval between two masquerades, Wolsey advised war. The Howards, old and young, Brandon, all the military party demanded it. Compton thought it would compensate him for his disastrous Buckingham venture and reimburse him for his expenses as go-between; while the bishops and Catherine wailed over the martyr Pope. Henry only yielded partially: he formed an alliance with the Pope, with Venice and with the mountaineers of the Swiss cantons. Ferdinand also joined the alliance, but without sending a single soldier.

Henry had a great respect for the Pope, the respect of a theological student for the examiner, the bestower of diplomas. Pope Julius II, however, cared little for theology: "If you want honours send me soldiers and money." Henry pretended not to understand and let a year go by. As certain lords pestered him he sent the most obstreperous to Ferdinand to fight against the Moors, but immediately on their arrival they quarrelled with the Spaniards and returned home in a rage.

The following winter there was nothing for it but to mark time. The French were carrying everything before them in Italy and Julius II was in difficulties. They had a young general who at twenty years of age was sweeping the country. They took and sacked Brescia and smashed the resistance of the Pope's troops and the Spaniards at Ravenna. But their prodigy general was killed in a skirmish and the French, disheartened, evacuated Italy. Hearing of their misfortune the English again began to urge Henry. Such an opportunity could not be neglected. But Henry moved slowly. He sent a messenger to Louis XII to demand of him fully a quarter of his kingdom. Louis shrugged his shoulders and got ready to meet the English army, but the English army did not make its appearance.

Ferdinand made an offer to his son-in-law to conquer Guyenne for him if he would send him some troops and Henry despatched a brilliant force, thanks to which Ferdinand was able to occupy the Kingdom of Navarre. Of Guyenne there was then no further mention. Spain was an uncomfortable country and, moreover, the English army was attacked by dysentery, grumbled and mutinied. Henry, informed of the fact by his father-in-law, advised him to massacre the mutineers, but these had already taken ship for England: Christmas was drawing near and they had yielded to the double lure of homesickness and plum pudding.

Nor was the fleet more fortunate. One of the younger Howards was killed at sea by the French and the following year another of them, who had sworn never to return to the Court until he had avenged his brother, was also killed. The French began to pillage the coasts of England.

A third Howard, the most distinguished of them all and now the heir to the estates, bore down upon them with a new fleet. They evaded him and took refuge in Brest.

The Battle of the Spurs.

At length the English army embarked for Calais and the first detachments landed in May commanded by the flower of the military party. Wolsey was in charge of the commissariat. Henry still hung back awaiting a perfectly calm sea; the fine athlete was a bad sailor. At length, on May 30th, he crossed, but so great an effort necessitated several weeks of recuperation. Banquets, balls and tournaments were organized at Calais for his benefit; he was provided with a few comely Frenchwomen and he was able to compensate himself for Catherine's conjugal claims.

The unhappy Louis XII, less handsome, older and much less vigorous, had no time to think of amusement. His forces were now being beaten in Italy. To the east an army of Swiss and Germans had invaded him and setting fire to Burgundy as they went were making for Dijon. And now, as formerly in the days of Crécy and Agincourt, a hungry English horde was coming across the sea. He appealed to his ancient ally, the King of Scotland, that James IV who had married Henry's elder sister, but who hated England. Anne, Queen of Brittany, incurably romantic, sent a ring to James IV, electing him her champion. She was lame and had never at any time been handsome, and now she was elderly, prudish and cantankerous; but James IV, seeing only the ring, was able to dream of a fairy princess.

Henry continued to enjoy himself. He had ordered Catherine to rule England during his absence and to dispatch the claimant to the crown whom he held captive in the Tower. He could easily have had him secretly poisoned or suffocated or impaled on a red-hot spit. Such had been England's methods for over two hundred years when dealing with princes who proved obstructive. But Henry revolted against such hypocrisies and preferred the procedure of a public execution. Since, however, he also preferred not to soil his hands with blood, he handed the affair over to Catherine, who accepted it as a matter of course. She had inherited great energy from Ferdinand and Isabella, and lost no time in depriving the captive of his head, and as James IV of Scotland, with Anne of Brittany's ring on his finger, was threatening England from the north, she also commanded old Howard to raise an army.

Henry at last made up his mind to move. The daughter of the old Emperor Max, Margaret of Habsburg, who was governing the Low Countries, was begging him to come into the Artois. She hoped to persuade him to thrust back the French and thus to utilize him in order to appropriate a large section of Picardy and extend her Low Countries as far as the Somme. He had a reputation for being easily gulled, a simpleton who could be used to pull the chestnuts out of the fire.

The Emperor Maximilian was arriving with four thousand Germans to the assistance of his daughter Margaret, but he assured Henry that he asked nothing better than to serve under his command. Henry was

much flattered at the prospect of having an Emperor
as a subordinate, and since it is incumbent upon a
commander to pay his troops he bestowed on Maximilian
a large salary. The unhappy Henry's gold was melting
hourly.

On a fine day in August the French made their appearance; a heavily armed force that shone and glittered as it
moved like a dragon covered with scales. The troops
bristled with lances and displayed floating many-coloured
standards in the sunshine, through the clouds of dust.
The plumes upon the helmets and on the horses' heads
could be discerned. They bivouacked casually, not
expecting to meet the enemy; they had in any case been
ordered to avoid action.

To Henry his own army appeared very inadequate,
but old Maximilian quelled his fears. They were only a
few miles from the famous field of Agincourt upon which,
a century earlier, an eminent force of French cavalry in
heavy armour had found itself sinking in the mud, its
horses bogged to the girths, trapped and immovable.
England still rang with the legend of that magnificent
slaughter. Her archers had merely fired into the masses
and her pikemen had fallen upon that paralysed army
with nothing to do but to seek the joints in their
enemy's armour in order to thrust and kill. Louis XII's
forces, on reaching the locality, were also, for their part,
reminded of Agincourt.

Max set his four thousand Germans on horseback and
made each man take an English archer before him. The
French were astonished to behold this cloud of horsemen.
They were unable to charge these hovering hordes; the
arrows whistled and harassed them, the horses kicked

and reared. They forgot that they were led by princes of the blood royal, by the Chevalier Bayard and the heroes of the Italian wars. In their imaginations they saw a second Agincourt; their horses hoofs would sink in the mud and they themselves would be slaughtered like cattle. Amazed at not finding themselves rooted to the ground by some strange enchantment, they deserted Bayard, Bussy-d'Amboise, La Fayette and Dunois' grandsons and fled, believing themselves to be pursued by an army of sorcerers. Driving their spurs into their horses' flanks they urged them onward until they fell dead beneath them. Max and Henry had only to collect the remnants of the French army, including Longueville and Bayard, level-headed soldiers who had scorned to make their escape. Henry decided that this war was amusing; he believed himself to be a hero and that he had regained God's favour. Moreover, Catherine was once more pregnant.

She also, for her part, was winning victories. Her general, the aged Howard, carried in a litter, had beaten the Scots. His eldest son, the pride of the family, had left the fleet and had led the forces. The King of Scotland, James IV, had been killed and the Highlanders compelled to take refuge in their mountains.

They had left behind them the remains of their King. Howard annexed them and informed the Queen. She wrote to Henry that she was in possession of his dear brother-in-law's body and would have liked to send it to him—presumably pickled—but that she feared such a proceeding might shock the English. She deplored a prejudice which prevented her from despatching so touching a gift to her husband. Her Spanish family had a positive passion for treasuring corpses, both of enemies and friends. The crazy Joan was still clinging to that of her husband. James IV's embalmed mummy would have made an elegant pair with that of Philip. But Catherine was compelled to renounce the idea. Brother-in-law James's coffin was thrust into a storeroom and promptly forgotten by everybody, including his widow.

In Flanders Henry proceeded with his victories. Margaret and Max persuaded him to take two French frontier towns whose independence made them uneasy: Thérouanne and Tournai. He had promised the citizens of Thérouanne protection for their houses, but who can be expected to keep promises made to foreign civilians? As soon as it was taken, Thérouanne was set on fire. Then, with the coming of the October rains the flat fields of Flanders became unpleasantly muddy and Margaret and Max carried off Henry to entertain and restore him. They put themselves to both trouble and expense in order to do honour to so great a prince; they arranged tournaments at which he could display his prowess and they showed him Charles their nephew and grandson and the hope of their family. Son of the crazy Joan and of the deceased archduke Philip, he was Henry's nephew by his marriage with Catherine. Margaret was rearing him and ruled on his behalf. He was fourteen years of age, sickly, sad and cynical. Small of stature, he was plain in appearance, with thin hair and staring blue eyes. He was solemn but unimpressive, with a projecting underjaw and a mouth like an ill-tempered dog, but he flattered his English uncle, figured at the tournaments in order to please him, which he considered necessary though he thought him a frivolous fool.

Henry remained the official master of Thérouanne and Tournai, but Margaret sent her own troops to occupy those towns. The troops obeyed Margaret, but were paid by Henry. Max talked of marrying his grandson Charles to Henry's sister Mary. It was true that she was three years older than Charles, but she was as flighty as he was serious, which might be expected to establish the balance. Margaret meanwhile delighted everyone. She coquetted with the King's friends while Henry himself sampled the Flemish women.

The Hunt for a Dowry.

Henry missed the English forests and the wide, open hearths where the hunter can dry his clothes after the chase and imbibe great bowls of steaming hot punch. Viewed in the perspective of five months' absence, even Catherine was recovering some of her past charms. The child that she carried in her womb appeared to be intending to come to full term. Toward the end of October, Henry returned to England. There were two weeks of embracing, of caresses and of connubial chastity, and before he had exhausted the happiness of finding himself safely at home after the hazards of so turbulent a campaign, the child was born. It was a boy and obviously came straight from a benevolent and forgiving Heaven.

But the rift in the clouds was not destined to endure. Almost before Henry had had time to show his son to the Court, to revel in his first wails, the child, like all his predecessors, died. Catherine, her heart frozen, sat beside an empty cradle: "You must indeed love me, Lord, to confer upon me the privilege of so much sorrow!"

The King's friends assumed an air of affliction and demanded lands and titles as consolation. The tribe of Elizabeth reaped a rich harvest. Old Howard became Duke of Norfolk, young Howard—Thomas—Earl of Surrey, and Boleyn the son-in-law, also by name Thomas, did not allow himself to be forgotten. Compton received favours and Brandon outdid them all. He obtained the spoils of the pretender whom Catherine had beheaded and was made Duke of Suffolk. He was not, however, content with a dukedom but was determined in addition to marry a princess. He was nearly thirty-five years old, and was just ripe for an advantageous marriage. A younger man may be fancied by the daughters but the fathers will think him of little account. Older and with acquired honours, the fathers will be amenable, but there is a risk that the daughters will be reluctant. At thirty-five a man is to be reckoned with and has not yet lost his charm.

On the journey to Flanders Brandon thought he had succeeded. He spent his time flattering and caressing Margaret. She encouraged him in order that he might help her to manage Henry, but once the treaty was signed she dismissed him. He was not, however, the man to lose courage and he transferred his attentions to a more youthful object and made love to Mary, Henry's little sister. So long as Catherine failed to rear a child, Mary remained the heir to the throne. Should Henry break his neck out hunting, die of a surfeit, of a fever or of a chill, she would be queen and her husband king, or at the very least, he would be prince consort.

She was pretty with very smooth fair hair, a high fore-head, delicate features, light eyes and a small nose and mouth. Her shape was slim, her skin like satin; she was lively, sensual and in love with love. Brandon paid her attentions. He was old enough to be her father and for that very reason captured her fancy. She forgot her pages and Charles of Flanders, who was only a child, whom she had never seen and whose portraits were unprepossessing. Brandon was at her side, Brandon shone in tournaments, Brandon who fascinated all the Court ladies, Brandon who knew all the secrets of life, especially those tender ones that aroused her curiosity. Brandon was romance, the forbidden fruit; in daring to love her he risked his head. Could she, in the circumstances, be expected to withstand him?

But politics interfered to shatter this idyll. A French prince, cousin to Louis XII and now a prisoner at the English Court, persuaded Henry to throw over Max and Ferdinand and enter into an alliance with France. Louis XII had for some months past been a widower and the Frenchman suggested that he should marry Mary. Louis XII, on being approached, asked for the little princess's hand, offering in exchange a substantial sum. Henry's friends, particularly Wolsey, were largely bribed with French gold and Henry was persuaded to agree to the bargain. Brandon's ambitious dream was shattered.

The Romance of Mary of England.

Mary shed a few tears when she learnt that she must leave Brandon. But she was also told that she would be

Queen of France, and that the French were a very dissolute people. Mary had no prejudices in favour of austerity. She had never seen Louis XII and was therefore able to picture him as handsome, or at any rate as reasonably presentable. At the age of fifty-three many princes are still attractive. She did her best to console Brandon and persuaded Henry to allow him to accompany her to France in the character of *cavaliere servente*. This arrangement would at any rate ensure a honeymoon prior to her marriage, which was fixed to take place in the month of August.

However, she did not cross the sea until October, and the autumnal tints added their charms to the melancholy of her parting from the comely Brandon. At Abbeville the French dismissed all her English ladies, a proceeding which struck her as lacking in gallantry. But when she at length saw Louis XII she was appalled. He proved to be a weedy little old man with shaky knees, a bulbous, peasant nose, arms as long as an ape's, tired eyes and decayed teeth. Having been sickly ever since his earliest youth, he led a semi-invalid existence, dined at six and went to bed at seven; but the worst of all was that immediately on beholding Mary, this pitiable wreck fell violently in love.

Mary was inconsolable and found no comfort even in her pompous coronation at Saint-Denis. She thought only of Brandon and could think of but one means of seeing him again: she must become a widow, and at the same time, if possible, the mother of an heir who would secure for her the regency. She was not lacking in courage and she remembered many things that she had learned from her handsome lover. She gave her old husband not a moment's rest, affording him the most devastating delights and astonishing revelations regarding the temperament of Englishwomen. The aged Lothario fulfilled her expectations; in eighty nights—or, to be exact, in eighty-two—he collapsed, dying blissfully of excess on the first day of January, 1515.

No heir had appeared and Mary saw herself compelled to leave France, but she hesitated and could not make up her mind. She was still entitled to some days of respite, since a child is not always punctual in arrival. There may be delay, or indeed, if God so decrees, the parturition may be premature. She looked around for a partner, and, there being no time to send for Brandon, cast her eyes upon Francis, the handsome nephew and son-in-law of her late husband—Francis, who was only observing the legal delay before proclaiming himself king under the title of Francis I.

Francis was fond of women. He was comely, lusty, and admirably adapted to produce an heir without loss of time. He was flattered, reciprocated Mary's advances, called upon her and was just about to fall into her net when his mother stepped in and interfered. If he gave a child to Mary he would give her the throne. He himself would merely remain Duke of Angoulême; he would, in other words, be nobody. He would probably not even be retained as Mary's lover but would speedily be replaced by the comely Brandon. Nor would he find much con-solation in the knowledge that he was secretly the father of the little king. Francis, for all his ardour, paused to reflect. He allowed Mary to sigh, was exceedingly respectful, and was careful not even to touch her white robes. The necessary period of delay being passed, Francis duly became King of France.

For Mary nothing remained but to pack her baggage. In February Henry sent Brandon to her; ambition having failed her, she was at liberty to return to her romantic love affair. This might be a poor consolation, but it was the only one available and she urged Brandon to marry her. But when it came to the point, Brandon had misgivings; he feared for his head and tried to evade her. Mary was appalled; everything was failing her, even the remnants of her shoddy romance. She appealed to Francis, who, having achieved security, no longer had any reason for avoiding her and had again become sensible of her charms. Francis explained to Brandon that it was his duty to marry her, promising at the same time to afford him protection. Mary for her part made him ashamed of his cowardice.

The King of France was powerful and Mary might prove vindictive; Henry, in any case, was across the seas. Placed between two risks, Brandon chose the more distant and married. Barely two months had elapsed since the burial of Louis XII and nobody had ever seen so rapid a remarriage. They spent the spring in France and Francis won over Wolsey. Henry sent them his forgiveness and in May they crossed the Channel. Brandon had recovered his cheerfulness and Mary tried to imitate him, but Brandon's defection had disappointed her, and in any case he lacked novelty. She had left England to be a queen and she returned a mere duchess, the wife, moreover, of a parvenu. She regretted France and her handsome twenty-year-old King with his long nose, his broad shoulders, his bright, subtle eyes, who had come so near to forgetting his greatness for her sake, and sacrificing his throne for a night in her arms. It seemed to her that princesses can be very unfortunate.

Henry's Court impressed her as dreary. Brandon, the married man, was a bore. Wolsey, now a bishop, paraded his purple robes. Catherine grew plainer with each successive pregnancy, while Henry seemed weary of experienced mistresses. He told himself that flowers must primarily be fresh, he eyed the Queen's maids of honour, and aspired in his turn to be the teacher.

V

A TOO IMPRESSIVE NEIGHBOUR

(1515—1520)

Legs Slim and Legs Muscular

HENRY was not yet twenty-four years of age, but he felt that the first flower of his youth had faded. Among the Kings of Europe he was no longer the prince of adolescents, the cynosure of all eyes. Francis I was three years his junior, an insufferable neighbour who also loved sports and a gay life. Moreover, he had many qualities that Henry lacked: self-possession and charm and those peculiarly French characteristics which are so displeasing to God; he liked women unashamedly and dared to pursue and possess them openly. He ate sparingly and kept his muscular form free from redundant flesh. He had been brought up by two very exceptional women: his young mother who adored him and called him Cæsar and his elder sister, the poetess, whose devotion to him was such that she never experienced any other love. He dressed well and had an understanding of the arts; he bought pictures and statues and entertained Italian painters. He also possessed that mental equilibrium that enables a man to lead the most licentious, the most natural and pagan of existences without ever falling to a purely animal level. Henry felt himself put to shame. His chastity and his theology gave him the air of a sacristan, his heavy sports savoured of the peasant and the indulgence of his appetites suggested the drunkard. In order to please him somebody declared that Francis was his inferior in the shape of his legs, which lacked muscle and erred on the side of slimness. Henry displayed his full calves and plump thighs. He would even descend to questioning the ambassadors. "Is he really as tall as I am and have you remarked his legs? Look at mine!" And the ambassadors would duly bend down and admire these marvels in their closely fitting hose. He would walk with his feet apart so that all might observe the play of his muscles. He believed that it gave him a nonchalant aspect, but it merely caused him to waddle like a duck.

There was one thing that aroused him to extreme annoyance. King Francis had a pronounced liking for war and appeared to be quite indifferent to its risks. The lunatic actually dared to cross the Alps and succeeded in reconquering northern Italy. He also vanquished the Swiss at Marignano. This was sacrilege, since the Swiss were a serious, moral people, who observed order even when they pillaged. It was unseemly that they should be routed by the dissolute French. Moreover, on the battlefield, Francis I committed the gravest follies. He only conquered by reason of his temerity, of his absurd disregard of rules and of danger. Henry, in his wisdom, felt himself to be quite incapable of such heedlessness. But a man is not always proud of being wise. Francis was entirely devoid of modesty and had had himself knighted by the Chevalier Bayard. Henry was pained at this touch of melodrama.

But how could this scatter-brain be put in his proper place? How was he to be checked without personal risk? It was necessary to revive ancient alliances, to conduct skilful intrigues, but who was to direct them? A council, a commission are never effective. A single individual must hold the reins; Henry being incapable, the lot fell to Wolsey.

Wolsey Prime Minister.

Wolsey kept a sharp eye on his own interests while easily manipulating those of others. He understood sovereigns: Ferdinand of Spain, Max and Margaret of Austria and their young Charles of Flanders. In all Europe only the Vatican held any mystery for him. Priest though he was, he had remained too crude, too forthright to plumb the motives of the red-robed foxes who were plotting in Rome. England's gloomy skies had made him too brutal, he had been reared upon too heavy a diet in the cattle merchant's house in Ipswich. The Pope, however, had made him a cardinal; Henry gave him a knighthood and the kingdom.

He grasped at his honours greedily and proceeded to build a palace. He maintained an army of retainers, a vast concourse of servants. The greatest nobles came to kiss his hand and to offer him their sons as pages. When his cardinal's hat arrived from Rome he had it placed upon a table and all the English dukes assembled to do homage to it. Nobody had ever beheld the worship of a hat since bygone ages in Switzerland, in the days of Gessler and William Tell, but the flower of English nobility duly made obeisance. Not one of them refused to salute the hat or thought of drawing a bow upon Wolsey.

Henry still believed himself to be the master. Wolsey was very tactful in imposing his decisions. Wolsey invited him to intimate suppers, hunted with him, evoked memories of Oxford in order to allow him to discourse upon theology; promised him paradise and meanwhile set his feet upon a flowery path leading to beatitude. He comforted Henry in his mundane difficulties and when in January, 1516, Catherine was again delivered of a child, a daughter undeniably sickly and plain, Wolsey hastened to remind the King that in England females could inherit the throne and that in any case a man who had fathered a daughter had good grounds for hoping that a son would follow. Henry was so deeply moved by his sympathy that he invited Wolsey to be godfather to the princess.

Francis I was still in Lombardy diverting himself with the lively Italian women. With the coming of spring in 1516 Henry and Wolsey hoped that the old Emperor Max would attack him. Max collected an army and descended from his Tyrol. But on reaching Lombardy and beholding the French outposts his enthusiasm flagged. He had a vision from heaven of two aged saints who strongly advised him to return home. Since it is unseemly to argue with the saints, he obeyed, but sent a proposal to Henry, offering to appoint him heir to the Empire if he would send troops to attack France. Henry thought the suggestion fantastic; he had other matters to occupy him at home.

A Riot of the Unemployed.

The workers in London were unemployed; they lost patience and demanded the expulsion of foreigners. "England for the English!" In May, stimulated by the heat of the sun, they revolted, seized the foreigners, thrashed them and held them to ransom, routed the police and even attacked persons connected with the Court. Henry thought them insolent. He suddenly decided that the air of London was unhealthy in springtime and retired to his fortified palace at Richmond, to make a cure in safety behind its ramparts.

Wolsey, the indispensable, made all necessary arrangements. He quietly allowed the unemployed to exhaust themselves with shouting, then he let loose the police upon them and captured several hundred simpletons who were so imprudent as to parade the streets. Of these he selected forty who were handed over to the executioners, hanged, drawn and quartered and their remains set up above the city gates. After which he wrote to Henry, telling him that all was quiet and that his presence was urgently required in London to witness a new masque.

Henry thereupon returned majestically accompanied by his wife and sisters and repaired to Westminster Abbey. Wolsey had lined all the streets with soldiers. He then brought into the King's presence four hundred strikers whom he still retained in his prisons. They were thrust into the great hall, clad only in their shirts, which inadequately concealed their gaunt, famished forms. Henry sat upon a dais hung with the royal arms and narrowed his little eyes as he stared imperturbably at the wretched rabble. Wolsey, in his scarlet robes, approached the throne and, in his capacity as a servant of Christ, asked that the unhappy rebels should be pardoned. Henry refused. Catherine and her two sisters-in-law fell upon their knees; Henry again refused. Then Wolsey resumed his jeremiads, actually contriving to squeeze a few tears from his shameless eyes, and so great was this prodigy that Henry's heart was touched to forgiveness. The four hundred scarecrows tore from their necks the nooses of hempen rope that had been draped around them, flinging them in the air with wild cheers and capers of joy.

But none of this put an end to the strikes. With the coming of winter the starving populace made another attempt. Wolsey raised a bourgeois army to subdue them; more gallows were erected and silence supervened.

But kings cannot hope for a quiet life. The next occurrence was an epidemic which provided an unexpected remedy for the strikes. People died in masses and Henry beheld the fell disease wreak havoc in his own palace. Cooks died, then pages and even the nobles themselves. Henry remembered that he was a good horseman, leaped into the saddle and left the town. Wolsey lost no time in following his example and neither of them returned until the dead had been buried, the air purified by braziers and, in fact, until everyone had ceased talking of the fever.

Bessie Blount.

The fear of death awakens desire. Catherine had a number of comely attendants and Henry selected one of them as a mistress. In all the kingdoms of the earth the Queen's ladies have supplied a harem for the King.

His eye had lighted for a moment upon a niece of Elizabeth Boleyn. But preferring fresh fields he chose another Elizabeth, a girl of twenty-three or twenty-four years of age and of very generous proportions. She was not rich and had been reared in the country in a distant castle not far from Wales. But she had already lived for some time at Court, her parents having procured her employment with the Queen in order that they might be relieved of her expenses, and with a view to her acquiring social polish and a husband. The husband did not make his appearance and she was beginning to be anxious when she caught the King's eye. There was never any question of love at first sight, Henry had been seeing her for more than ten years, but she was willing and she had a backing of tactful friends. Henry gave her a trial and found her charming, decided that there was something to be said for being the first in the field, but blushed at the mere thought that such conduct might be suspected. Sin, so far as he was concerned, was only palatable when concealed. His intimates, those who had acted as panders, must also provide him with retreats. He would set out, on the pretext of hunting, and visit his Bessie in secret pavilions. The scent of her sound and wholesome flesh mingled with that of forest foliage. She was as refreshing as a summer shower.

She also proved fruitful and Henry was both ashamed and proud: proud of his virile prowess, ashamed that his sin should be rendered obvious, should sully the purity of his castles. The young Bessie was promptly removed from court: Catherine was given to understand that she

was ill and in need of country air. Wolsey, now master
of all English convents, by joint command of the King
and the Pope, had no difficulty in providing a secure
shelter. In Essex, only a few miles from London, was a
small convent of Augustinian canonesses, and thither
Bessie Blount retired. There she spent the winter and
the spring, for her pregnancy dated from the autumn
season of hunting. Henry would ride to visit her through
the young green of the grass, the blossom on the hedges,
and in June her child was born. It was a son and Henry
marvelled at the miracle by which God, the God of
virtue, should thus reward sinners. Henry felt himself
to be absolved and kissed Bessie and the child. He had it
baptized Henry and also, following the example of his
early Norman predecessors, Fitzroy, being the ancient
French for "son of a king."

The child was Bessie's glory and also her undoing, for
Henry took her son from her and forbade her return to
court. His virtue would not permit of his risking a
scandal, and in any case, Bessie, for reasons unknown, had
ceased to attract him. Wolsey undertook to relieve him
of her and as Bessie did not seem unduly attached to the
King, Wolsey found her a husband young, well born
and well connected, the possessor also of an ancient
French name: Taillebois. This estimable youth had been
brought up in Wolsey's household and had been most
carefully trained to docility. He felt it an honour to
enter so glorious a bed and to find it yet warm from his
sovereign's occupation. Wolsey, moreover, had paid his
debts. Bessie, for her part, was delighted with a husband
over whom she could domineer, whose time was at her
disposal, who could furnish her with regular pleasures

devoid of anxiety and console her for the loss of her son by supplying her with a litter of other children.

Henry, happy to have sired a son, returned to the embraces of his holy Catherine; he resigned himself with a good grace to the performance of his conjugal duty, but his efforts in that direction failed to meet with success.

An Emperor of Nineteen Years of Age.

Important changes were taking place in Europe. Ferdinand had died and had bequeathed Spain to his grandson, Charles of Flanders, who thus enclosed France on the north and the south, by Belgium and the Pyrenees. There followed the death of Charles's other grandfather, the Emperor Max. Max was by no means old, but he had grown morose, and for fully four years before his death he had dragged about with him, wherever he went, the coffin and the winding sheet destined for his obsequies. As soon as he felt the approach of death he insisted upon making the responses to the prayers for the dying. He commanded that prior to his burial his hair should be cut off, all his teeth extracted, and that his body should then be placed in quicklime.

With his death arose the question of replacing him. The balance of power demanded that the Empire should be offered to a German prince. But the Germans were poor and the Kings of Europe were rich. Francis of France wished to become Emperor, a desire which was shared by Henry of England and yet more passionately by Charles of Spain, who claimed the succession as Max's grandson, as the sole heir to Austria and the Tyrol and of all the Habsburg inheritance. The German Elector princes met and Henry and Wolsey were compelled to realize that they were unable to buy them. Charles promised Wolsey to obtain the papacy for him at the next conclave and Henry renounced the Empire, and in order to frustrate the ambitions of the too fortunate and too ingratiating Francis, exerted himself in favour of Charles. Marguerite, Charles's aunt, borrowed from the German bankers, giving them as security the town of Antwerp and Belgium bribed the electors liberally. Charles was elected and became the Emperor Charles V. With the exception of France, England, a few Swiss cantons and a few scraps of Italy, Charles became the possessor of the whole of Europe.

Henry should have been alarmed, should have formed an alliance with Francis I, but Charles, with his puny physique, his long mournful countenance, did not humiliate him. Charles despised tournaments and cared little for women. Charles was Catherine's nephew and had promised Wolsey the papacy. Finally, Charles was a menace to France and every Englishman detested the French.

Francis wrote to Henry that he wished passionately to meet him. He calculated that he could win him over by display, but in this he was much mistaken. Henry replied that he would come to France, but seemed in no hurry to redeem his promise. Francis insisted. Henry replied that he would not trim his beard until they had met. Francis retaliated by growing a beard himself. This he could very well afford to do, since beards were then beginning to be fashionable. But Henry's beard was red and of unbecoming growth; it outlined the jowls that it should have concealed. Catherine, who knew that the appearance of this beard signified the imminence of a French alliance, acted the coy and capricious spouse, complaining that the bristles offended her delicate skin when Henry favoured her with his caresses. Whereupon Henry shaved his beard while Francis cried shame on him and kept his own, and Henry began to entertain the idea that people might believe that he feared to encounter the handsome Francis.

"I shall soon be looked upon as a mule, an overrated warrior, a miser or a beggar." He consented therefore to cross the Channel and ordered his nobility to deck themselves in resplendent garments. Each one of them dived into the family coffers, the poorer among them mortgaged their lands. The Frenchmen also sold farms and mills. Between Guînes and Ardres, upon the frontier of the English fief of Calais, two camps were erected, two cities draped in cloth of gold.

The Field of the Cloth of Gold.

It was June. Henry was on his way to Dover when Charles suddenly landed at that port and proceeded to Canterbury. He wished to embrace his uncle Henry and his kindly aunt Catherine and also to resume discussion of the papacy with Wolsey. He appeared shy, devoid of ambition, and might almost have been the English King's vassal. Henry was moved at finding himself so magnificent in comparison with this sombre shadow. He promised to avoid any treaty with Francis and to visit Charles immediately after the interview.

When he finally entered his loyal city of Calais he settled down to rest for several days, being determined to appear to the fullest advantage before Francis and the hypercritical ladies of the French Court. He had also decided not to venture far from his own territory and the frontiers of the small English stronghold.

Wolsey had provided him with a vast palace in the fields; it was built of wood, but the timbers were concealed beneath satin, brocades and tapestry hangings. Around this palace the nobles erected their fantastic tents.

He issued forth from Calais in great pomp to the blare of trumpets. He advanced in the sunshine accompanied by his courtiers on prancing horses. He was also surrounded by an efficient guard. After him rode Catherine and her ladies, with their hair unbound and eight hundred soldiers with waving plumes. These were succeeded by a number of priests in splendid vestments, by the yet more magnificent military nobles, by fifty ushers, and finally by Wolsey, his cardinal's robes tucked up revealing the scarlet calves that firmly gripped his horse's belly, while his ornate cardinal's hat hung on the nape of his neck.

Equally resplendent, the Frenchmen also made their appearance in the brilliant June sunshine. Francis galloped to meet Henry; they dismounted and embraced. Francis was insolently graceful but Henry's eyes were glued to his legs. They were undeniably slender, but legs are by no means everything. The tall lad was vibrant with a fiery ardour that dazzled the eyes of women. Catherine's own ladies were entranced and Henry felt himself blushing at the thought of his own timidity, of his elementary adventures.

The Englishmen out-topped the Frenchmen by inches, but they felt stiff and awkward beside these damnable little swarthy men who danced attendance upon their women, smiling at them and making themselves understood by signs, admiring their fairness for all that they thought them dowdy. Henry's friends grumbled and counselled caution. The French were apt to be treacherous. They might spread a snare for Henry, trap him and bear him off a prisoner. To such suggestions Henry was easily susceptible. He paid only ceremonial visits to Francis, accompanied by an adequate guard. On the way back he would conceal himself, change garments with one of his attendants, and be uneasy and alarmed at the slightest sound.

Francis displayed less reserve. One fine morning he appeared alone in the English camp, invaded Henry's bedroom and found him in bed. He kissed him, crying: "I am yours. I am your prisoner!"

Henry, unable to believe his senses, lay rubbing his little eyes, still puffy with sleep. Francis insisted upon being his valet, hauled him out of bed and put on his shirt. Henry made an effort to impress him by placing on his shoulders a magnificent jewelled collar; but Francis had provided for all emergencies. He drew from his pocket a man's bracelet of equal value and clasped it on to Henry's podgy wrist. At length he departed, saturated with sentiment, brotherly love and romanticism. Henry felt ridiculous. This great lad with his spindle shanks had given him a lesson in courage. He found the pill very bitter.

Each day was marked by knightly exercises. There were tournaments and lances were broken. Crowded upon the gradients of specially erected stands the women laughed and applauded. The victors bragged and swaggered in the shade of their plumed helms. The conquered chewed the cud of their shame and dreamed of a war that would permit of their slaying their conquerors. At every meeting Henry and Francis ran five courses, and as regularly, five times in succession they overthrew their adversaries. They took good care not to tilt against one another. The evenings were devoted to an exchange of banquets. In the matter of cooks the two kings were equal, but Francis's great banqueting hall put Henry's in the shade. The English hall was hung with satin only, the French one with cloth of gold. This cloth of gold was an affront to England; the wives of the Englishmen felt themselves to be eclipsed. Queen Catherine was undeniably plain, and for that matter so was Queen Claude of France. The latter, moreover, had one leg shorter than the other, but she was nevertheless younger than Catherine and had contrived to bear sons. Francis paraded his mistresses, including the resplendent Château-briant. He showed off his sister, the chaste and sprightly Marguerite of Angoulême, and his mother, Louise of Savoy, less gentle and less chaste, if rumour was to be credited, but still comely at forty. The elderly Englishmen lowered their eyes, deploring the scandal, while the young ones demanded leave of Henry, in order to visit France and spend some months in Paris.

Henry sought rancorously for a means of humiliating Francis and remembered his own prowess in wrestling. One day, in his salon, in the presence of the Queens, he grasped Francis by the neck, exclaiming: "Brother, let us wrestle!" He had calculated that the long-legged man must give way to his great weight, and Francis, taken unawares, was indeed staggering when he was seized with disgust and sudden fury. Slim legs are agile, and Francis, hooking one of his spindle shanks round one of King Henry's renowned calves, gave a lift and sent the heavy body hurtling into space. King Henry landed upside down among the voluminous skirts of the two Queens. The carpets were soft and so were the portly King's buttocks, but Henry arose gasping with discomfiture and bellowing with fury. The bystanders intervened, Catherine remarked that dinner was served and led the way to the dining hall. That day Henry had little appetite; the next day he was a mass of bruises and at the earliest opportunity he gave the order to strike the tents and departed in a rage.

He proceeded to Belgium, saw his nephew Charles and assured him that he had no use for Francis. Charles was, as usual, exceedingly humble. He accompanied his uncle Henry as far as Calais and there embraced his aunt Catherine. Peaceful family life took the place of tumultuous pomp and feasting. The English were delighted with an Emperor so mild and so gentle and they embarked for home with restored composure. The London merchants greeted Henry with rapture; Charles's dominions remained open to them and they would be able to sell their cloth and their sheep in Flanders. Wolsey, the Howards, Brandon and Compton added up the sums received from the King of France. They rejoiced that the treaty had not been concluded, and hoped to be able to squeeze gold out of Charles also, by playing off one party against the other.

VI

TWO FLOWERS ON ONE STEM

(1520—1523)

Mary Boleyn.

THE beauty of the English summer consoled Henry for his humiliations in France. He resumed his enjoyable rural life, moving from castle to castle, from Windsor to Richmond or to Greenwich. After the dreary grey plains of Calais, shorn so bare before July was ended, his own parks and meadows refreshed his eyes. He had discarded his brocades and wore light doublets of silk and roomy hose. He revelled in the open air and flourished exceedingly.

He rose very early, as do the pure of heart, and after amply fortifying himself with meat and wine he would hear three masses before mounting and riding forth into the country. He chose comfortable horses with broad backs and easy paces and favoured a moderate speed lest he should become overheated and sweat. He went hawking, attended by his fowlers, bearing the hooded falcons on their wrists. When a heron or wild duck was sighted, they would halt, unhood and release the falcon, which would soar into the heavens, to the sound of the bells on its spurs. Henry would lean back in the saddle, following its course with his eyes and watching the clouds as they floated by.

The fields were parti-coloured, patched with red and white, with poppies and with wild carrots. The Thames flowed at the foot of the hills and on the horizon hovered a blue grey cloud of fog, the smoke of London's early morning fires. The hollows held churches with low, sturdy belfries. Butterflies still heavy with dew tried their wings but quickly alighted on the hedges.

They would turn towards home by nine or ten o'clock and from the meadows would come the sounds of scythe and sickle. Green fields were mown and later fields of gold. The cows lay down in the shade and there was no more bird-song save the sudden shrilling of a rising lark. Henry would dismount and enter his palace, grateful for the soothing shadow of its halls. His friends and servants would undress him, wash him and dry him and clothe him again in fine linen. He would eat a second breakfast and then turn his mind toward spiritual thoughts.

Cool and comfortably ensconced in those wide arm-chairs that to him seemed restful after hours in the saddle, Henry would send for his books of theology, the Fathers of the Church, Saint Augustine or Saint Thomas. He studied the arguments of these great saints, seeking out errors and remoulding dogma to his own taste. Doctors of divinity would wait upon him, his tutor, the aged Fisher, his grandmother Margaret's one remaining friend; the delightful Thomas More who at scarcely forty years of age had already been the pride of Oxford and who combined a rich and genial imagination with a fund of honest simplicity and sound judgment. Both of them adored their king. They kept his footsteps in the narrow way of pure orthodoxy.

Then would come the statesmen: Wolsey, the Howards, father and son, and Henry would lend them an inattentive ear. Politics, the art of ruling men meant little to him in comparison with the art of discovering God. Politics are fraught with awkward realities, but theology offers an open field. At noon Henry would eat again, a meal followed by an interval for digestion, and repose during the heat of the day. Then he would repair to the gardens and indulge in sports for his figure's sake. From every game he emerged victorious. His companions missed the ball, aimed awry at the quintain and were overthrown at every wrestling bout. Not one among them would have dared to retaliate; only the insolent French king had been so presumptuous.

Sometimes Henry would go on the river, in his enormous, ornate barge propelled by oars, past the drooping willows. At Greenwich he would take pleasure in the tidal traffic. He would watch the great sailing ships, loaded to the water's edge and exhaling exotic odours, making their leisurely way towards the port of London. From a barge that followed his own, the strains of viols, flutes and lutes added enchantment to the evening air.

At dinner the musicians were again to the fore; playing upon a raised stage in the centre of the hall. Young girls would sing or children with shriller voices. Henry found a voluptuous gratification in mingling the grosser pleasures of the table with the more elusive enjoyments of music. And thus the day would draw to its close, and with night came the shameful and delicious hours, the hours of temptation, the hours of sin.

Henry had lately taken a new mistress, and she would be awaiting him in secret chambers, in houses concealed in the depths of his parks, far from Catherine and far from the conjugal bed. He had discovered her in France at the court of Francis. She was an adept at those Paris refinements which, while they scandalize, are irresistible to the most virtuous of men. She was, however, an Englishwoman and came of a blood that had already appealed to Henry. Her name was Mary Boleyn and she was the daughter of that Elizabeth Howard whom Henry had loved when he was seventeen. And now it was Mary who was seventeen years old.

Henry had noticed her first because of her gaiety, because she was in love with love and because of other more intangible things that lent an elusive savour to sentiment. She was Elizabeth over again, but Elizabeth with a difference: younger, less arrogant and more docile. In her he recovered his adolescence, and at the same time realized in her company, more than in that of any other, the lapse of those thirteen years which were now but a memory. He enjoyed the melancholy of a vanishing youth allied with the satisfaction of being thirty years of age, and in his desire and in its realization he discerned a tinge of incest, of something so fleeting and so evanescent that he hardly knew whether it were dream or fact. Mary was by nature simple, yet life had made its mark on her; she was youthful, yet at the same time over-mature. Neglected from her infancy by her parents, abandoned to the vicissitudes of foreign courts, she had not been able to protect herself from men. At Fontainebleau, at Amboise she had refused no one. Her heart was generous and her body responsive. Francis himself had known her favours. Within the flesh of this gentle creature slept all the alluring sins of France. Henry, in the security of his rustic retreats, in the pauses between the songs of the nightingale, made it his pleasant business to awaken them.

He was exceedingly happy. At thirty years of age, happiness is seldom unattainable to the male. To matters of government he gave little thought. Wolsey had allied himself with Boleyn and with Howard in order to make him a present of Mary; on her loving bosom he pillowed his head, and there the trio left him to his slumbers.

Buckingham.

Wolsey, the successful climber, took pleasure in baiting the nobles. There was a touch of the schoolmaster in this priest from Cambridge and he aspired to the control of other people's private lives, of their expenditure. He imprisoned his Grace the Duke of Northumberland because he threw money out of the windows, built castles of unseemly splendour and maintained an unnecessarily numerous retinue. At the expiration of his sentence, Northumberland attempted no revenge, but made a humble reappearance at the Court, apologised and swore to serve his gracious master, Wolsey, to whom he offered his son as a page. And the boy, young Percy, before whose ancestors kings had trembled, bore the scarlet train of a cattle-dealer's son.

Thus encouraged, Wolsey struck at bigger game and proceeded to attack the blood royal. The proudest of all the nobles was that Buckingham who had formerly refused to give his sister to Henry. Living in disgrace upon one of his estates, he had still remained very powerful and had married his daughter to Thomas Howard, the brother of Elizabeth Boleyn. Wolsey accused him to Henry of conspiring, of intentions upon the king's throne and life. He mentioned the revolts of Buckingham's forebears; the Duke's own father had perished on the scaffold. His was a dangerous family indeed, a dynasty of assassins. Henry clung tenaciously to life; he was in excellent health and Mary Boleyn was kind. He was terrified.

Wolsey secretly arrested several of Buckingham's servants and had them tortured. They said everything that he desired. They revealed that Buckingham was surrounded by magicians, that he sought the advice of the devil. Satan had promised him that his son should be king, that Henry and all his line should perish. Henry shuddered. Such people were capable of casting a spell upon him, of bewitching him, of afflicting his body with mysterious maladies, of shrivelling his flesh and drying up the marrow in his bones. He began to believe that he was indeed victimised; he actually felt himself to be growing thinner and anxiously prodded his thighs.

Buckingham, however, was one of his vassals and Wolsey could not seize him without risking a rebellion. He begged him therefore to wait upon the King. Buckingham obeyed and appeared at Greenwich, where he was promptly arrested by guards, hurried into a barge and taken to the Tower. It was April and Wolsey was loath to trouble Henry in so pleasant a season, so, for the moment, he took no further action. The May-tide celebrations were at hand. Henry and Mary, clad all in green, spent the entire night in the woods. In the morning they and their friends came home, singing and bearing branches of young foliage. Moreover, Henry was in training for the impending tournament. Meanwhile, in the dungeons, Wolsey's judges and his torturers were at work. Buckingham's servants, broken and dismembered, continued to supply the required information. They declared that their master wished to murder Henry, to seize the crown and—unpardonable outrage— behead Wolsey.

Wolsey appointed a tribunal of nobles and ordered them to deliver over to the executioner this Buckingham who was their natural leader, and whose only crime had been to put into words or at least to imply that with which every one of them inwardly agreed. He appointed the aged Howard as president, thus compelling him to condemn his daughter-in-law's father. He met with no opposition, they wallowed in their shame, they condemned Buckingham, and Howard read aloud the sentence. He wept as he read, doubtless at his own cowardice. Buckingham forgave his judges, refused to sue for pardon and on the 17th of May was beheaded on Tower Hill.

Henry had been ill for the space of three days. He had no thoughts of Mary, of hunting or of other pleasures. His body lay helpless; he tossed upon his bed, sweating with anguish. Wolsey, always cheery, his cheeks glowing pleasantly in the reflection cast by his scarlet robes, sat by his bedside, encouraging him and reminding him of Buckingham's alleged sorceries. Caught between two terrors, Henry stood firm to the end and allowed the axe to fall. When all was over, when he saw that the heavens had not opened to punish his crime, he felt his life-force resume its normal rhythm; he breathed again, and put a tentative foot to the ground. He worshipped Wolsey for having taught him how a king should act and for having played his part in the murder. Had he been unsupported the blood would have choked him. But Wolsey seemed so placid that all thoughts of remorse faded. May offered him its gentle rains and its flowers and Mary's willing lips were sweet.

Reply to Luther.

Chance or Providence favoured Henry. On the Continent, Charles, his ugly little nephew, was attacking Francis and pressing him hard. The Pope himself was at war with France and Catherine was murmuring rosaries. Henry sat at home listening to the exquisite litanies intoned by his musicians. He did not dispatch a single soldier. From the summit of their white cliffs, without exposing themselves to the chances of battle, the English sat in judgment. Then came less favourable news and it was known that Charles was retreating before Francis. Wolsey and Henry offered to arbitrate. They temporized, keeping Francis entertained, and affording their friend Charles an interval for recuperation, after which they gave their decision against Francis, pronouncing him to have been the aggressor. Wolsey collected tips from both litigants, while Henry beheld himself as God's elect, ordained to control the quarrelǝ of princes.

He even came to the conclusion that Heaven had chosen him to defend religion and confound heretics. If he was not a priest, he was at any rate a doctor of divinity, he was learned in theology and the Lord had enlightened him. He was unable to endure the thought that an ordinary German monk, the Augustinian friar, Martin Luther, should presume to attempt to reform the Church and claim to enunciate a new truth. This Luther put forward the most curious views, alleging that it was not possible, by gifts of money, to shorten the sufferings of the dead, the duration of their sojourn in purgatory. Yet who could deny the magnitude of the sacrifice which a man made in parting with a portion of his worldly substance for the salvation of souls? Luther also cried out against the sins of the clergy and against the fact of their maintaining mistresses; and yet he himself contemplated marriage as a palliative for the desires of the flesh. Here were indeed strange views. Nor did he hesitate to attack the sacraments, wishing to transform, to suppress them, defying the Pope. He had publicly burned the Papal bulls, declaring himself to be inspired by God. Henry was outraged: he who aims at the Pope touches the King, since all authority is interdependent. Wolsey, with his own eyes fixed upon the papacy and with promises of support from Charles at the next election, was filled with respect for the Holy See.

Both Henry and Wolsey desired that Luther should be burned and they wrote to the Duke of Bavaria advising him to slay the heretic. But Luther had vanished, and since he had promised the joys of paradise to those German princes who would pillage the possessions of the Church, none of these princes was able to find him.

It was, however, possible to discredit this abominable monk, to vanquish him by argument. Henry felt that it was time for him to display his talents, to show forth that light with which God had endowed him, and he made up his mind to write a book. He commandeered the assistance of Wolsey, and that of his aged army of learned bishops. All his grandmother Margaret's friends issued forth from their lairs, pored over textbooks and prepared notes. Henry, between two hunts, two excursions on horseback or on the river, between two assignations with Mary, would listen to their views, promote discussions between them, and together with them would labour for the great cause. He tabulated arguments, rounded sonorous Latin periods, and in pompous phrases thundered at Luther, the accursed *fraterculus*, the satanic wolf, maintaining that the sacraments were inviolable and upholding the Pope's absolute infallibility. A sumptuous copy of the book was dispatched to Leo X, a young Medici Pope delicately addicted to pleasure. Leo X expressed himself as deeply moved, his elegant fingers caressed the handsome binding, but he was careful to leave the volume unopened. He despised pedants, even when they were kings; moreover, he found it incomprehensible that human intellects should waste their time arguing about another existence. He himself infinitely preferred this one, with its sunshine, its scents, its women and the frescoes of Raphael. There might perhaps be some excuse for Luther, for a compulsorily chaste monk afflicted by boredom and unruly desires, but a royal theologian was nothing less than an unnatural monster. Given a taste for literature, could he not read Plato, Virgil and Petrarch? He was, however, careful not to discourage such zeal, sent his thanks to his dear son Henry and conferred upon him the title of

Defender of the Faith, after which he summoned his
poets, his engravers and his jesters.

Henry was enchanted with his new title; he was still
sufficiently ingenuous to appreciate diplomas. Wolsey
made enquiries regarding the Pope's health and was
informed that it was fairly satisfactory.

An Amiable Mother-in-Law.

Henry had already loved Mary for a year; in her arms
he savoured a very peaceful happiness. His vigorous but
placid organism was not enamoured of variety. Wolsey
attended to business and Mary provided pleasure; Henry
had only to let himself drift. In order to silence scandal
Wolsey found a husband for the girl: an insignificant
but suitable young man of an accommodating and amiable
disposition, a husband for daytime requirements. At
night he was careful to keep his eyes closed.

The Boleyn parents added to their King's contentment
and provided him, as it were, with a family. Boleyn was a
loyal servant, while Elizabeth was unfailingly obliging.
There are few mothers-in-law so agreeable as a former
mistress if she has the wisdom to abjure jealousy. Such are
experienced in the mysteries of the flesh and are the most
admirable of *confidantes*. The son-in-law has but to hint
his desires, and these are delicately conveyed to the
daughter. They harbour a memory of former happiness,
and a touch of melancholy colours reciprocal affection, an
affection of a slightly indefinite nature which allows of
fleeting returns to passion. This is one of the most
enjoyable forms of the eternal triangle.

Elizabeth and her husband did not always live at Court. They found its etiquette fatiguing and retired to their country estate, Hever, in Kent. In spite of their former amorous adventures they loved one another: after twenty years of common life there must be mutual love or hatred. At any rate, they loved one another in their children: in Mary who obtained for them so many favours, in George who was now eighteen years of age and must be brought to the King's notice, and finally in their little Anne whom they had left at the French Court, there to be instructed in life, in behaviour and in every art that can lead to success. For what was the use of attempting to deny that there was no place like Paris for moulding a young girl? Had not even their ingenuous Mary acquired a measure of worldly wisdom in Paris? On his estate of Hever, Thomas Boleyn lived as a country squire. He supervised accounts, directed labour, interviewed his farmers. He hunted and revelled in the pleasure of being at home, of giving orders. The most servile of spines must at times weary of bending. Elizabeth sat at her tapestry, watching the stagnant waters of the moat and pondering the recollections of her youth. They received their neighbours, their friends and their Wyatt cousins who owned an estate a few miles away. Sometimes Henry would arrive at Hever on an impromptu visit, bringing Mary with him. These were pleasant occasions; he would tell them of his anxieties, of politics, and would disclose the wiles of diplomacy. Charles and Francis were still at war, and Henry's wish was that neither should conquer. Francis caused him increasing irritation while his nephew Charles was revealing himself to be a fox. He had recently prevented Wolsey from securing the papacy, having obtained it for a creature of his own, his former tutor, a sanctimonious thieving Fleming whom the Romans insulted in the open streets. This Charles, with his greedy underhung jaw, appeared disposed to swallow the world.

The two Boleyns supported each other in frequent allusions to the future of their children. Henry bestowed lands and appointments and when European affairs became further involved, he entrusted a new embassy to Thomas, dispatching him forthwith to Spain.

George Boleyn.

George Boleyn, Thomas's only son and heir, lived in closest attendance on Henry, in his bedchamber. Henry had taken the boy as his page, together with five or six others, friends or relations of the Boleyns and the Howards, and young Thomas Wyatt, who was a poet, wrote sonnets and dreamed of Italy. Henry had shaped these youngsters according to his fancy, had instructed them in all those things that he himself loved and in which he found his enjoyment: physical exercises and music. They played upon the flute and the lute, looked after his clothing and his horses and provided him with pleasant companionship. Henry found in them a relaxation from his theological labours, from Wolsey's fierce ambition and even from the society of his former friends, the Comptons and Brandons who had always sought to dominate him, who had not improved with increase of years, who had remained mere soldiers of fortune and were becoming surly into the bargain. In contact with their greying beards Henry felt himself to be a mere boy, whereas among his company of pages and esquires he ruled as absolute master. George Boleyn and Thomas Wyatt obeyed him as docile pupils.

At thirty he savoured for the first time the pleasure of surrounding himself with youth. The laughter of his esquires was a complement to Mary's embraces. They ran his errands, arranged his assignations and Henry found amusement in their escapades and their follies. To them he took the place of a youthful uncle, who must be obeyed but who is consistently indulgent and generous, providing all that is necessary for a pleasant existence and always willing to organize diversions. Like all those who give freely, he thought himself beloved and among them all he himself loved George Boleyn, with whom he was so closely linked, who brought to his mind not only Mary's caresses, but also the pleasures of his adolescence. The lads would cluster round him, would tilt with one another, would go hunting with him; jumping hedges and frequently being unseated, they would scramble up laughing, none the worse for their falls. They danced, drank and surrounded him with gaiety, talking to him only of cheerful subjects. If in their hearts they jeered at his theology, if they thought his paunch absurd and his views old-fashioned, they were very careful to conceal their opinions. They laughed, but they trembled, being well aware that their security was entirely dependent on his favour, and in their light-heartedness dwelt a tinge of fear, a shade of melancholy which gratified their master. Their presence enhanced Mary's charms as a shower of sparks will adorn a star. Henry found in their society something fugitive and ardent; they gave an unexpected savour to the passing hour.

They clamoured for war for the love of adventure, and Wolsey was engaged in its preparation. The new Pope was wilting in Rome and Charles had again promised Wolsey the succession. Wolsey persuaded Henry that it was time to break with France, and promptly had the ambassador arrested. George and his friends were ordering armour. Henry offered no objection and smiled. He had no intention of allowing them to run into danger or of being deprived of his lively escort.

He recalled those English who were living in France and who might be of use to the enemy as hostages. Anne Boleyn was compelled to leave Queen Claude. She returned to join her parents in England, and shortly afterwards there appeared at Windsor and at Greenwich a little girl of fifteen with over-bright eyes and a too flexible neck weighed down by an enormous mass of black hair. She sang and danced but seemed to harbour a smouldering fire. She had held her own against Francis and his Court; she had a nervous laugh and was somehow intriguing. She astonished Henry, who found himself suddenly dissatisfied with the simple pleasures of a tender attachment. Mary's charms paled, despite the returning spring and the nightingales; Anne had the hard glitter of jewels.

She was a problem to her mother and to all the tribe of Boleyns and Howards. To them she remained a mystery. They looked for a husband for her and selected a seasoned soldier, with whom they intended to dispatch her to Ireland. She flatly refused to accept him and they were unable to make her yield. Thereupon they removed her from Court, sending her, with her mother, Elizabeth, to Hever. She remained there without protest and when Henry appeared she would sit in silence sewing or embroidering, but she never took her magical eyes from his face.

Early Thoughts of Divorce.

There is an inexhaustible enchantment to be found in loving at the same time and in one person several women of the same blood. Mary, in the amorous arms of Henry, was now no longer only Mary. Her body was endowed with subtle emanations from those of Elizabeth and of Anne, alien and yet familiar. She glowed with fires which Henry had not yet encountered; in her he sought the secret of her race. He found her complex, evocative of memories, devastating as desire itself. In her he lost his present identity, recovering in her embraces the sharp stinging savour of his earliest fulfilments, the scent of primroses and the autumnal perfume of dying leaves. She had the submissiveness of a wounded creature, of one who had learnt passion and a certain servility from the caresses of the French nobles, of one whose flesh had known the kisses of too many lips. Those of Francis I had left upon her mouth an indelible imprint of lusty desire. Moreover, in her too sapient body he now also found Anne, the immature girl with the relentless eyes, the slender shape, a garden enclosed, untouched by kisses, untouched by so much as the light of day, the body of a dancer, alert, with vibrant nerves, secretly vital beneath its heavy robes. Henry sought in Mary's unbound hair the perfume of Anne's imagined tresses, the spirit of that abundant glory that, springing from her virginal and childish brow, must clothe her entire form in waves of splendour. Henry, lying with Mary in his secret pavilions, found the nights fevered, mysterious and exquisite.

He still kept Mary concealed, which enhanced the romance. His nephew Charles V came to spend the summer in England, in dutiful attendance upon his aunt Catherine. Henry felt it incumbent on him to assume the pose of a faithful husband. Catherine was now thirty-eight years of age and her days were spent in prayer. It was four years since she had conceived and the only fruit of her innumerable pregnancies had been one little girl Mary, now six years old, who was Wolsey's god-daughter. A sickly, intelligent child, already revealing signs of stubbornness, she had a grey skin and red hair. Henry dreamed of a son. He consulted his confessor, reminding him of a verse in the Bible which lays down that a man may not marry his brother's wife.

But so far it was only a question of a secret misgiving, a possibility that was whispered kneeling before a crucifix in an oratory, a scruple, an idea, a dawning hope. Henry would dally with the pleasant hypothesis of how he would shape his life if Catherine died. There could be nothing sinful in suppositions: "Catherine certainly seems ill; she might easily die, and she would undoubtedly go straight to heaven. God might possibly grant me this favour, or alternatively Catherine might agree to a divorce, might even be the one to ask for it. She is so much addicted to prayer, to religious ecstasy. Many other women have adopted that course, among them the most exalted princesses. There was my own grandmother, Margaret, for instance, who in middle age so casually dismissed her husband. I might possibly agree to being dismissed. Marriage, after all, when it can no longer be fruitful, degenerates into a kind of concubinage. I hesitate to impose it upon so holy a woman. I must summon my theologians, seek for passages in the writings of the Fathers of the Church; Wolsey, who is always so ingenious, so learned, will surely find a way of coming to my rescue."

To such suggestions his confessor made indefinite replies. He did not venture to contradict a penitent who was capable of sending him back in disgrace to his monastery or of consigning him to a dungeon for life.

Charles V.

Meanwhile Charles V and Francis I were still at war. Charles, already the master of almost the whole of Europe, intended to swallow France, and Francis defied him. Henry also should have been fighting Charles, who might easily succeed in uniting the West. Francis fought to preserve the individual life of nations, that is to say, the salt, the savour of the world, war also and discord, which are the very breath of life to the English. But their hearts were full of hatred for the French; Henry was violently jealous of Francis and the memory of the unfortunate wrestling bout rankled.

It was not that Henry found Charles attractive; he thought him dull and dreary, a pedantic scribbler and, moreover, a very inferior horseman. Nor was his dislike of him decreased by the fact that he suspected that in this mole of a man there lurked a hidden greatness. Charles, in his person, resembled Catherine. He had her mournful eyes, her short body and her high shoulders; his face was equally disheartening and evoked unwelcome nocturnal recollections.

To Henry Charles remained a stranger, so distant, so cloudy that he did not even awaken curiosity. Henry was quite willing that Charles should be happy; he could not be jealous of a happiness that was outside his imaginings, that must ever to him be incomprehensible. Envy necessitates a measure of understanding, and Henry was well able to understand Francis, a brother whose splendour overshadowed his own. He could not endure the thought of Francis victorious.

Finally, Charles had influenced Henry by promising to obtain the papacy for Wolsey. Henry was now more than thirty years of age. He was beginning to find Wolsey irksome, and would have been happy to see him depart. Not that he had any great expectations that Wolsey as Pope would do much for England; the clergy were notoriously forgetful of favours. But Wolsey's presence at Court disturbed him; he felt himself to be despised by this man, baffled sometimes and duped, yet unable to retaliate. He dared not attack him, or strike at him directly: he felt that Wolsey was protected by genius, or yet more disconcertingly perhaps by an evil star.

Wolsey, for his part, wanted the tiara. He had exhausted all the gratifications obtainable from England. He was sick of his successes, of humbling the nobles, of feeling their abject kisses upon his plebeian hands. He was weary of scheming and of subtle contriving in order to handle the overgrown, cunning lout whom fortune had bestowed upon him as a master. His dreams turned towards escape. "In Rome I shall be free, I shall be omnipotent; I shall be able to further my own advantage. I shall dwell in peace in palaces adorned with statues, with frescoed walls of the purest beauty amid gardens of perpetual greenness. I should like to see the sunshine of the South and Rome will be an all-sufficient paradise for my declining years, a delicate enchantment for my tired senses."

Henry and he were therefore agreed upon the advisability of assisting Charles. Their fleet was dispatched to threaten the French coast and Howard, head of his family since his father's decease, enjoyed the supreme gratification of sacking Morlaix.

Henry's Secret Hatred.

These little maritime excursions by no means satisfied the Emperor Charles. He wanted an army, well equipped, well fed and well paid, which would land at Calais, march on Amiens and on Paris and threaten the King of France. He made it clear to Wolsey that such was the price of the papacy.

The Cardinal found himself in a quandary. An army is expensive, especially when it is English. Wolsey had not sufficient money in his coffers to raise one and was faced with the necessity of imposing a special tax. This, however, could only be accomplished by summoning the Lords and the Commons. Without Parliament, no money, no army and no tiara.

Wolsey detested Parliament. He was well aware that its members had little liking for governments that govern. Since his accession to power he had let them sleep, contenting himself with the ordinary resources rather than risk summoning these cavillers. But the time had come when Parliament must meet; he knew very well the danger he must face, that the session was likely to curtail his powers, but consoled himself with the thought: "Once I am Pope, I shall sink into voluptuous oblivion of all these annoyances."

There were rumours throughout the length and breadth of England. The giant Wolsey was an oppressive burden and it was believed by many that his fall was approaching. Everyone was against him: the schemers because he stood in their way, humiliated them, spread himself unduly and prevented them from pilfering at their ease; honest folk because he reduced them to silence, because he violated the rights of citizenship, governed without asking their advice and because, instead of talking he acted. Henry himself was among his enemies. He feared Wolsey too much to attack him directly, he had so long regarded him as superior and invincibly fortunate; now the desire arose to try his strength, to discover whether the minister's good luck was vulnerable.

It was a curious struggle, for it was in Henry's name that Wolsey was asking Parliament for money, while Henry was stiffening the Commons against him. He gave them as leader his friend Thomas More, a virtuous man of simple and openly liberal outlook, a fine writer and a learned philosopher who believed in promises and accepted them as actions. The members debated, they cut down credits. As for the war which almost everyone desired even more earnestly than Wolsey—the Cardinal considered only his personal interests, while they were influenced by their fanatical hatred of France—they themselves wrecked it with their endless squabbles. It collapsed. An army, commanded by Brandon, was finally dispatched, too late, to France. It came to grief at Amiens, at Laon and then at St. Omer. It was drenched to the marrow by the October rains and thus frozen to the bones it settled down to warm itself by the fireside.

Wolsey's foundations were shaken. The fissures were slight, but Henry proceeded slyly to enlarge them. Well-informed persons began to realize that the powerful minister's prestige was diminishing. A few months later came Charles's public defection. At the elections consequent on the death of Pope Adrian VI, so far from suggesting Wolsey as candidate he either permitted or supported the election of a Medici, a Florentine Cardinal. Wolsey, seeing his dream vanish into space and compelled to swallow this heavy affront before the eyes of all Europe, figured in the matter as a foolish dupe. His enemies raised their heads and nudged one another. Henry, still timid but opening a watchful eye, meditated the traps that might presently be set. Wolsey, still magnificent in his scarlet robes, felt the solid earth giving beneath his feet.

VII

FEMININE CUNNING *VERSUS* PRIESTLY WILES

(1523—1528)

The Charm of Anne Boleyn.

THE heart of Henry was uneasy. Two years had elapsed since Anne Boleyn's return from France; she was growing up, she was seen at Court. She had been appointed a maid of honour to Catherine. She still retained the grace of a timid woodland creature but with the addition of something new, a dreaminess, a languor shattered by sudden peals of laughter. She had nothing of the quiet flower that opens in due season. She grew by fits and starts, expanding and then folding her petals. She used her eyes like a woman and then shrank in dismay.

Henry would seek her in Mary's apartments. There she served her sister, sitting upon the floor, seemingly modest and innocent. She feigned obtuseness, reducing Henry to confusion. She would dance for him, but with the simplicity of a child, much as she might have played with a skipping rope. Henry, while pretending barely to look at her, would extend his puffy hand and finger a lock of her black tresses. These tresses appeared more living than her flesh, they seemed to sway in rhythm with the music, they had the vivacity and beauty

of a lovely and captive animal. Anne would sing him the
airs of France, the verses of Marot and of Marguerite,
and Henry would ask himself whether he was lured by
the novelty of the songs or by Anne's clear voice in which
there were modulations so true that they seemed almost
hard and rang on the ear like a struck goblet of glass.
She would fling back her small head upon her long sinuous
neck and the sound would rise up and issue forth from
her virginal body as pure cold water from a shadowy
spring.

She would accompany herself upon the lute, or upon
the tremulous treble virginals, seeking to re-evoke
around the melodies the delicate harmonies dreamed of
by their creators. Sometimes she would sing all the
four parts in turn, while Henry listened enthralled. From
song to song, from voice to voice, Anne would transform
herself, changing like a Proteus or like a siren, becoming
as it were four women, four spirits. The musical Henry
would listen and dare to hope. At such times she would
become for him purely a delight of the ear, but a delight
so deep, so complex, so fourfold and intense that he
would retain its savour in his memory until, from the
recollections hovering in the silence he himself could
reconstruct a harmony.

For sounds he possessed the sensibility of a wild
beast. He was Pan enslaved by Echo and enchanted by
his pipes. If his overfed, athletic body remained gross,
if love itself had so far brought him but rude fulfilments,
his ear was capable of exquisite thrills, and it was to his
ear that Anne appealed. Thanks to her French songs,
so varied, so elusive, he was able to imagine for himself
a paradise, a tenuous world devoid of matter, of colour

or of shape, in which the lightest physical contact would be profanation. An immobile world in which sounds would be transformed become melodies and finally resolve themselves in fulfilment. She herself would only dance and stir the air the better to evoke in him by movement and furtive gestures the desire for their resolution in silence and repose. She would glide across the floor like a Salome, with an innocent face and parted lips.

Then he would watch her as she departed, gathering about her her marvellous hair. Mary would lay her arms round his neck drawing him gently towards the bed. There she would serve the needs of his body, but later, in the quiet watches of the night, to the rhythmic accompaniment of Mary's light breathing, Henry would lie, seeking elusive harmonies.

Anne would occasionally leave the Court; Elizabeth would take her daughter to Hever. There she would hunt the fox and the deer and learn the manifold cares of housekeeping. Henry would arrive, watch her shyly and depart; he was not as yet quite certain that he loved her. He was filled with astonishment at discovering that he missed her. Was not Mary still at his side? He would ride far into the forests and visit his son, the bastard offspring of Bessie Blount. He made a handsome allowance to the mother and was filled with amazement to think that he had loved her. Now his sympathies were all with her husband, the lusty Taillebois who gave her a child every year. Henry yawned, danced, played tennis, wrestled, tilted with George Boleyn, Norris and Mary's other friends. He talked business with Wolsey and laid sly snares for him. Then Anne would return.

He seldom saw her during the day-time. She would spend those hours sporting with her young friends. Through windows and walls he would listen for her voice, would recognize her sudden laughter that moved him so deeply. But other voices would mingle with hers, the voices of women, irritatingly commonplace, the full sonorous voices of young men, voices of those he had thought he loved and whom he now detested. Then he would be astonished at his own distress. How could he conceive that she might be attracted by beings so soulless and crude? Could anything on earth be as empty and as foolish as these adolescent lads. They might be bright of eye and limber of body, but Anne was elusive as a breath; she was like the summer breeze in the woods.

Percy.

There came a day when he found her changed. She avoided him and refused to dance. She seemed to have acquired a hatred of music. When he ordered her to sing her passionate notes amazed him. Her songs in which he had so revelled filled him with unease and he divined that she had fallen in love. She lowered her eyes and sat in silence, appeared shy yet inundated by a gentle radiance, bathed in dew.

She was betrothed, and to the dreariest of all young men; awkward, melancholy, a beaten cur. Only twenty years of age, however, and of a well-nigh royal lineage: Percy Northumberland, the possessor of a vast fortune, and said to be madly enamoured of Anne. A perfect marriage for a girl with a will of her own. "He will release her from her family," thought Henry, "deliver her from her oppressive clan, and she will twist him round her little finger. She will take lovers, if she so desires; such as attract her, possibly myself. But perhaps she is really in love with Percy; who knows the recesses of these virginal hearts? What do I know of her? Or of Percy? She will go with him to some distant castle and be hidden from all eyes: I shall see her no more.

"Or perhaps she will remain here, among us, shamelessly, brazenly flaunting her happiness. She will dance and sing, still warm from his embraces. She may also yield herself to me, and that will be yet more painful; all my life I shall be seeking the traces of the ineffaceable stain."

Already his eyes were seeking that stain. He longed to clasp Anne's frail body in his arms, to close her heavy lids with his kisses so that she might no longer see Percy, to crush her mouth beneath his lips so that she could no longer breathe the same air.

And still Anne gave no sign of comprehension. Henry began to lose patience; he found it impossible to credit her innocence. Everything about her was false and deceptive, even perhaps her love for Percy. Everything about her caused him suffering: her long silences broken by her sudden laughter, her eyes into which would come a gleam, a glitter that would scorch him like flame. Had she not, perhaps, engineered the whole affair as a means of compelling him to declare himself? Did she perhaps despise him for his diffidence, for not daring to take her, he, the colossus with his balanced nerves, he the sapient, the all-powerful? Nevertheless, he dared not risk it: he was afraid. In her presence he lowered his eyes; he said not a word to Elizabeth or to Mary; instead he sent for Wolsey and ordered him to remove Percy.

Nothing could be easier: Percy was terrified of Wolsey, who had had him in his household as a page since childhood and who had seen to it that he was well disciplined. He sent for him and told him he must give up Anne. Percy was very deeply in love, but he did not attempt defiance. He babbled, wept, threw himself upon his knees and made less than no impression on Wolsey. Then he gave way and promised obedience, then sought to retract his promise. Wolsey summoned Percy's father to the rescue; together they mustered a council of friends, dragged Percy before them, bullied and insulted him. The friends joined in the hue and cry and the unhappy Percy collapsed. They dispatched him forthwith to a distant garrison, reminded him that he had been betrothed at fourteen and married him off, leaving him to spend the nights mourning Anne in the arms of his astonished little bride.

But Anne did not weep. She left the Court and went into retirement at Hever. She detested men: Percy for having been so poor a creature, Wolsey for having insulted her by daring to suggest that she was not a match for a Northumberland, she in whose veins ran the blood of kings. She also hated her Uncle Howard and her father, Boleyn, for having failed to defend her. All men trembled before the fat King. Not that women were any better; her mother and her sister had sold themselves and were ready and willing to sell themselves again. She determined to pursue her revenge alone and unaided.

Henry, ruefully, watched her depart and fell back upon Mary's insipid bosom. Like Percy, he was troubled with insomnia, but he did not weep and a great hope sustained him.

Pavia.

Charles and Francis were still at war. The Empire was shattering itself against France. All England hoped that Charles would be victorious, with the exception of Wolsey, who thirsted for vengeance, and of Henry, who wavered and wished only to be on the winning side. The problem lay in deciding which was the stronger. Wolsey was secretly receiving French envoys and Henry, who knew of it, did not interfere.

During the autumn of 1525 it seemed for a while as though Francis would triumph when Charles's army, which had vainly invaded Provence, was compelled to retreat across the mountains. Francis pursued it and recaptured Milan. But the handsome conqueror had a frivolous mind; courage, charm and imagination do not suffice in war; serious mental concentration is essential. In February, 1526, Francis met with unnecessary defeat at Pavia. He was captured and left to languish in an Italian prison until the spring, when Charles commanded that he be brought to Madrid, where he was closely guarded in a narrow tower.

England rejoiced and Henry, delivered from his doubts, felt extremely happy. Bonfires were lighted at all the London cross-roads, and fountains ran with wine. The populace gorged and swilled and gave free course to its rejoicing in the streets, in the drifting fog of a March night to the last flare of the dying bonfires. Wolsey publicly gave thanks to God.

Deprived of her leader and of her armies, France appeared defenceless and Henry decided that it would be glorious to invade her. He had hopes of capturing half the kingdom, of occupying Normandy and Guyenne, the Plantagenet provinces and even perhaps of having himself crowned King in Notre-Dame. But this grandiose project was of short duration; there was not enough money in the treasury and Henry dared not summon Parliament, he was too much afraid of their stubborn independence. He therefore told Wolsey to levy a tax without their intervention, by direct decree. The peasants revolted, threatening to march on London. This foretaste of battle made Henry reflect and he decided to renounce his campaign.

When one is afraid of being attacked it is opportune to invoke Christian brotherliness and the pious precepts of peace. Henry, prompted by Wolsey, changed his course. He perceived that Charles was becoming too powerful and began to nourish a tender affection for the captive and impotent Francis. His conqueror at the wrestling match no longer humbled him; he was caged, he was losing flesh, he was unhappy. Henry, with Wolsey to lead him by the hand, bestowed his compassion upon the poor unfortunate, and out of the greatness of his soul intimated to Charles that he must not be unchivalrous.

What would become of England, cut off by the seas, almost floating, as it were; how could she expect to seize her share of Europe if Europe should be united under a single prince? For his own sake, Henry must clip Charles's claws. His amiable nephew, usually so humble, was losing his head as the result of victory and was beginning to fancy himself the master of the world. He was talking of marrying the small Mary, Henry and Catherine's only daughter, who was not yet ten years of age: he had dreams of eventually ruling over England. An arrogance so immense and so suddenly unleashed, such dreams of inheritance, alarmed Henry. Catherine, between orisons, was assuming airs of conquest which did not by any means enhance her charms. Wolsey whispered to Henry that divorce was possible. It was not against the will of God and Francis desired it. The Medici Pope, Clement VII, disturbed by Charles's increasing ambitions, would soon allow himself to be won over. Henry listened, pricking his ears: "Wolsey will rid my bed of this dull-eyed bigot; he will prepare for me a new bridal couch, and I shall bring to it youth and joy."

Wolsey intended, when Henry should be free, to marry him off again to a Frenchwoman. Two were available; one rather mature, but undeniably charming, Francis's sister, Marguerite. She had a large nose and attractive eyes; was said to be frigid but brilliant. The other, Renée, a daughter of Louis XII, was not good-looking but was virginal, barely fifteen years old and already learned with a marked taste for theology. Henry allowed Wolsey to go his way; he himself cherished other dreams.

He loaded the Boleyns and the Howards with favours. Thomas Boleyn was made a viscount. It almost appeared as though, intending to be rid of Catherine, Henry was forming for himself a new family.

He even seemed to repudiate his daughter. He sent for the little Henry Fitzroy, recognized him as the heir of his personal estate and gave him the title that his own father, Henry VII, had borne before seizing the throne: Earl of Richmond. Catherine, deserted, menaced, clasped her small Mary to her breast, showing her the flourishing bastard and exhorting her to pray.

Mary Boleyn was still the official mistress and Anne remained in retirement at Hever. Elizabeth appeared to favour this retirement, but she only partially understood her daughter. Henry she knew well, having lovingly helped to form him; she knew less of Anne, who had grown up far from her, who as a woman necessarily remained more impenetrable, and who was careful to guard her secrets. Henry did not dare to question Elizabeth, fearing what he might discover.

Time passed. Wolsey was preparing the divorce, cajoling the French, meditating a new betrothal. He was helping Francis, still a captive, and seeking to intimidate Charles. After a year's imprisonment Francis at length left Spain; he had made magnificent promises to Charles and had casually delivered over to him his two sons. Once back in France and with no thought of the two children, he promptly broke all his promises: Charles protested indignantly, imprisoned the two hostages, and the war began again. The Pope and the Italian princes came to France's assistance, but Henry refused to fight. The French offered him gold and he assured them of his sympathy. Less than ever was he inclined to think of war, for Anne, the fugitive, the reserved, the unresponsive, had lately acquired a new friend.

Thomas Wyatt.

It was at Hever that she met him and he was of Howard blood, being the son of one of Elizabeth's sisters. His name was Wyatt, he was twenty-three and possessed of many attractions. He had known Anne all her life and was an intimate friend of her brother George. Wyatt and Anne had played together as children; he knew all her past, her childish secrets; he had seen her at the time when she had been devoid of all artifice and her innermost heart was known to him. The thought of these facts caused Henry the deepest suffering; he was jealous of all those who had shared her earlier life, even of the girl's own brother George.

Wyatt was married, but it was a loveless marriage. He had been given a wife at the age of seventeen, the daughter of a noble, and comely enough, but he had been careful to refrain from loving her. He was a romantic and dreamed of travel and of sunny climes; he read Petrarch and was himself a poet. The magic that Henry found in music, Wyatt sought in the beauty of words, in their substance. All that appealed to Henry appealed to Wyatt: forests, love and the silver light of the moon. He felt things less deeply, perhaps, being younger and more careless, but for that reason, perhaps, was better able to express them.

More than any other he was to move Anne's heart. He was of her race, his taste was impeccable, his courage dauntless, his emotions incoherent and tumultuous. He loved her much less deeply than Percy, but loving does not necessarily beget love. He made her the theme of his poems. He inveighed against her in the over-elaborate verses of a savage dazzled by the dawn; he worshipped her, comparing her to the fauns in the forest. Better than any other he realized Anne's wild untamed charm, and in praising it, in describing it to her he intensified it. He remoulded Anne in accordance with his desires.

He handled a lance with the prowess of a Saint George and at the Christmas tournaments he had dazzled the Court. Being married, and therefore available only as a lover, he acquired for Anne the lure of forbidden fruit. He visited her at night, climbing to her balcony, or alternatively Anne descended to him and went to seek him in the garden. Seated side by side they would breathe the scent of flowers, the odours of the sleeping forests.

Henry understood. Anne was now bolder, moved by joy and sorrow to flashes of radiance. She was alight with the flame of Wyatt's love and Wyatt glowed in that of her response. She avoided Henry, sought Wyatt and seemed indifferent to consequences. Henry would tear himself from her in despair.

He would gladly have stabbed Wyatt and would have experienced exquisite gratification at the sight of his eyes glazing in death, but he shrank at the thought of murder. Nor did he dare accuse Wyatt of treason and put him upon his trial: he feared to betray his own sufferings. Wolsey murmured an offer of assistance, sent for Wyatt and made him understand that he was risking his future, possibly his head. Wyatt was no fool; perhaps his love for Anne had been little more than a literary adventure, a dangerous amusement devised with her consent, a snare set to entangle Henry. He felt the chill of the axe on his neck, and Wolsey advised a visit to

Italy. Wyatt departed to look for the footprints of Petrarch; the shade of Laura made him forget Anne.

Anne Demands the Crown.

The Boleyns, the Howards began to wake up and to take a hand in the game. They must influence Anne and offer her to Henry or they themselves would be lost. But they trembled lest she should betray them. They sensed within her childish body a spirit so bitter and hard that it alarmed them. They knew that she was aiming at a secret objective; was it her desire to escape from Henry or did she intend to capture him? Why should she withhold her confidence from them to whom the King's heart was so familiar? Uncle and father were affectionately attentive, Elizabeth dwelt on her memories while George, her brother, reminded his sister that he seldom left Henry's private apartments. Mary herself offered to abdicate in favour of Anne, hoping thereby to remain near the King and to obtain favours for her husband William Carey, whom she doubtless found more attractive than Henry and who, after being so long a husband only in name, was now to acquire his conjugal rights. Anne pretended to understand nothing; she held her tongue and smiled at their perturbation.

She pursued Henry, demanding that he define her future. He had betrayed himself by banishing Percy and Wyatt and could no longer hope to shelter behind silence. She had had enough of music, of songs to the flute, of elegies and of childishly abortive desires. Did he contemplate retaining her purely as an idol who would fulfil

his imagination and be subjected to no physical contact?
She mistrusted such dreams, she was not of those who
accept them; she had already hovered near too many
fires. There was in her nothing of the saint nor of the
angel. Her body was intact, but her wings had been
singed; she was nearly nineteen and it was time for her
to live.

Henry hardly listened to her words. She evoked
pictures in his mind and he dwelt on those pictures:
"Nothing of the Saint, it is true," thought he, "but
something of the angels yet remains, something of their
ethereal and intangible grace. The wings have doubtless
touched the flames, but one feels their presence none the
less, throbbing and beating in the air that surrounds her.
Is she perhaps a fallen angel, rebellious, accursed, of a
perverted purity, born of her resistance to the natural
impulse of her senses? The glitter of her eyes is like a
memory of stars, a lingering reflection of the Star of the
Morning, the Satanic lustre of Lucifer himself. I dare not
extend my hand to touch her; her fascination is woven
of magic, she has the lure of whispering elves."

She withheld herself; he had had her sister and her
mother, he should be content with two Boleyns. "He
shall not enjoy the savour of my body; he has treated
me too long with contempt." The vileness of the Boleyns
nauseated Anne, and, moreover, she owed them nothing.
At twelve they had got rid of her by sending her to France
and once there she had been left to her fate. She had
seen her sister prostituted and men snigger when she
passed by, had seen them stop her and whisper obscenities
in her ear, she could feel their breath upon her own neck.
Mary, the fool, had responded to their laughter, had

allowed Francis to have his will of her. In his eyes she had been no more than an animal, an animal that gave him pleasure and that could be lent to his friends. He had spoken of her as "My hack, my mule."

On her return to England Anne had thought herself rescued, but things had only gone from bad to worse. She beheld the shameless shame of the Boleyns and learned the secret of her mother's past. Everyone offended her; primarily her own clan, who after attempting to dispatch her to Ireland only desisted because of their vile calculations; Wolsey, who insulted her in order to rob her of Percy, by saying openly that she was not well enough born; Percy, who had deserted her out of weakness; Wyatt, who had left her out of cowardice or self-interest, and finally the King, who had whipped on the whole pack and who for a few nights of pleasure was prepared to ruin her: "But nothing on earth shall make me weaken. I shall never be a party to furtive assignations, to shame. Perhaps he does attract me, but I shall not be defeated. I shall retain control of my senses, of my heart, and if need be, I can die."

He felt her to be capable of heroic daring, of desperate ventures; he realized that her desire was for him only, that she had always waited for him, whether out of love or because of her ambition. And why, after all, should she be unable to love him? He was handsome, glorious and the master of an entire people. He held the power of life or death. She knew all the simplicity of his heart, his childish tenderness, his love of dreams and caresses. He was the husband of another woman, the man who may not be touched without sin. Moreover, there was another and deeper reason that must remain unspoken:

he had already conquered others of her blood and was bound by association to all those impurities for which she suffered shame, which appalled her and which for years past had haunted her dreams.

She might have yielded and held him by her weakness, but she withstood him. Possibly she feared the flesh and therefore prolonged the prelude. His red hair and his bulky shoulders filled her with repugnance and made her recoil. She would imagine the hour when his lustful crimson mouth would touch her, when she would feel the fevered heat of his breath, when she would be helpless and undone in his arms, and she took her revenge of him beforehand. She wished to see him cringe and beseech, to conquer him before she herself should be conquered. She refused everything: dresses, jewels, castles, honours: "I am no harlot." "Then what can I give you?" "Your hand?" "My hand?" "Yes; marry me and make me Queen."

This was presumption and he recoiled. "I shall only belong to my husband." "But I am already married." "You can get a divorce." Henry reddened with indignation. She was daring to put herself upon the same level as himself and the Queen, she was forgetting the majesty of her Sovereigns. Anne remained silent, she had played her last card; he might shut her up in prison for life or have her beheaded for high treason; he might accuse her of witchcraft and set his bishops to examine her, condemn her to the stake and thus be free of her by fire. Less than a hundred years had passed since London had seen a princess walk its streets barefoot, carrying a candle, asking pardon of God for having bewitched her husband, Humphrey, Duke of Gloucester, the brother

[117]

and uncle of kings and Lord Protector of the Kingdom. All her accomplices had been burned.

Henry's Indecision.

She had hit the mark. Henry was goaded beyond endurance; such natures as his require the goad. He did not understand his own suffering. What was this mere child that she should treat him as a stout middle-aged man who must keep his distance and who must be amenable to her whims? All the other women, including Catherine herself, had worshipped him on their knees. This one disdained his kisses, made conditions and exacted payment. Henry's body did not suffice her, that royal body that aroused perpetual admiration; those columnar legs, that circular red beard, those broad jowls and those handsome eyes. Then, in God's name, what kind of man did she want? She appeared unmoved by his musical appreciation, by his political shrewdness, by his theological learning, by his divine inspirations or his communications with Heaven. She was not impressed by his combat against the infamous arch-heretic, Luther, by his being the officially appointed Defender of the Faith. She despised the lover and aimed at the crown.

For the first time in his life, at thirty-five, he experienced a spontaneous desire which had sprung from the deepest roots of his being. Up to that time he had known only imaginary emotions such as may come to children in their dreams; he had only pursued shadows. He had neither reigned nor loved. His royal gestures had come to him from Wolsey, his amatory gestures from Elizabeth

and from all those others whom he had not himself
chosen, but who had been brought to his bed by the
Boleyns and the Howards, by Compton, Brandon and
above all by Wolsey. Not one virtuous girl, not a virgin
among them; they had all been experienced, ripe and
moulded by others. He had remained a pupil, learning
not love but amorous exercises and had been spurred
merely by imagination and a puerile desire to imitate,
never by the real, deep original impulse of his nature.
And how monotonous, how shallow, how primitive
had been his pleasures, in their almost animal simplicity.
He had been completely ignorant of that searing anguish,
of the suspicions, of the jealousies, of all that men must
suffer when they set out on adventures of the heart. He
had known less than nothing of all those emotions which
enrich, refine and subtilize desire. Had he ever known
so much as the rut of the lesser creatures, of those who
fight and kill and thus ennoble their savage instincts?
He had only been supplied with peaceful pleasures, with
the gross satiation of the stud or of the kennel.

He saw Anne again and allowed her to explain her
reasons for desiring to be Queen. She was not ambitious;
she only thought of him and wished that their love should
be clad in beauty, should walk openly in the light of day;
that it should be sung by poets, that nothing should soil
it; neither concealment nor ignoble adultery. A great
King must be above deception. Already his furtive
caprices had lowered him. Why must he be compelled
to blush for his love? His only shame lay in his union
with Catherine, a deadly sin thrust upon him by self-
constituted advisers, a sacrilege. He had never loved that
plain and ageing woman; his very nature had rebelled at

such a union, his consciousness of the divine laws. Anne became almost pedantic in her quotations from Leviticus: "Thou shalt not marry thy brother's wife." For nearly twenty years he had endured this sinful connection, sacrificing his first ardours, the flower of his youth. He had thought to serve God and had been enslaved to Satan. Had not all his sons died in the cradle? He must therefore free himself, cut these pernicious bonds. The Lord's command was to increase and multiply. Catherine was no longer able to conceive, while Henry was in the prime of his virile strength. Was he prepared to allow his race to perish? Was not it a law that love should beget life? Why else should he now experience this new desire, this ardour, this mysterious and devouring impulse to give himself and to possess? A child must be born, a future king, and this Messiah, this prince should be the fruit of Anne's womb. The powers of Heaven were drawing them together, they were in themselves but humble instruments, their duty was to submit, to worship and to obey.

To Henry she appeared so entirely ethereal that almost he was persuaded to believe her and to stifle his recollection of her earlier sorceries. The hard glitter of her eyes might be that of the stars. Lucifer was resuming his wings and arising again to become the incorruptible, the star of the morning. Henry was invaded by a powerful and perverse fascination that dwelt in the thought that this small, dancing creature would be enslaved, would endure long months of bewildered weakness until she became a mother. The more elusive she seemed the more he burned to possess her. She stirred and re-awoke in him bygone mystical dreams, which took upon themselves new significance: "I shall take her in my arms and compel her to materialize, to become mere flesh of this earth. I shall fashion a woman out of this flame; I shall mingle my being with that of this sinuous snake, this Melusine. An essential particle of my body will inhabit her unreality, will slowly come to life, to birth and to the light of day, and this child will be myself and this small elusive Anne. He shall unite our two essences, issuing forth from mystery like Arthur the Breton King, the mystical forefather of the Tudor race, born of the Sorceries of the enchanter Merlin, like Alexander the Great, conqueror son of the divine serpent who loved his mother Olympias. Had not Eve herself, with the aid of the Tempter, created a strange descendance under the Tree of Knowledge?" For Henry, for that marvellous son who should at last spring from his loins, the serpent of fable had become a woman.

He promised her that he would be faithful and that he dreamed of no happiness save with her. Was she angel or demon? He could not determine, and in that very doubt dwelt enchantment. His desires, his thoughts, his dreams were as undefined, as conflicting, as they were overwhelming. He revelled in a tumult of confused and shattering breakers. He drew a deep satisfaction from concealing his love, and experienced a very delirium of joy at the thought of eventually disclosing the secret, of showing Anne to his assembled Court, of crowning her to the clash of bells. He swayed back and forth between two visions, setting the one against the other, rejoicing equally in sunlight and in the darkness of those shadowy chambers where lovers meet, where they lie together in so voluptuous a gloom that it seems almost tangible and soft as velvet. Henry promised that Anne should be Queen; then he temporized, appalled. She shrugged her shoulders, insulting him freely, and he realized with surprise that her insults caused him pain. He became very unhappy and envied her boldness, her virtue which he thought heroic; Anne dared to tell him that he was afraid, a fact that he had never admitted to himself, and an impulse arose in him to kill her. But he could not do it; and thenceforth his desire for her waxed greater. Between them was the bond of a secret shared, a secret more shameful than any illicit love, more exquisite in that it was spiritual sin. When Henry's thoughts dwelt upon her, he shuddered.

Anne's Withdrawal.

She left him to shudder and withdrew to Hever, nor did the Boleyns interfere. She had them by now completely subjugated and they served her without opposition. Henry would ride to see her at Hever and she would refuse to receive him. Returning to his castles, to Windsor or to Greenwich, he would take up his pen and compose long letters. He envied those scribblers of Italian sonnets; Thomas Wyatt, so insincere, but who knew so well how to mingle upon paper falling leaves, the heavens, the stars and his desires. He would sit composing amorous verses, tearing up his efforts and beginning anew. He found his words heavy, stiff and unskilful and his lucubrations those of a village swain. He would cover the sheets before him with hearts in which he enshrined an A. and a B., surrounding them with a

garland and flanking them with his name and rank:
Henry, the King. He no longer claimed to be loved for
himself; let her take him for his crown, for his power, so
long as she took him. He adopted the humble motto of
the faithful lover: "I seek no other," and cut it in the bark
of trees. He would as gladly have cut it in his living flesh.
But Anne refused to return to Court. She was fearful
of the contempt of the courtiers and she was fearful that
Henry would take her by force. Possession has been
known to break a witch's spells and, moreover, Anne
knew the effect of absence. She divined the sufferings
of this virile lover compelled to chastity, the visions
that haunted his unquiet nights. For now he shrank from
contact with Mary; Anne had made too deep an
impression to permit of his taking refuge in illusion and
he marvelled that he had formerly been able to do so.
It was Catherine's bed that he sought at night.

Anne mistrusted her own powers of resistance; she
had thought of him so incessantly that he had entered into
her soul. Love is not necessarily a desire to yield; the
desire to take may also be love. She had no admiration
at all for Henry, but there may be an attraction in an
inferior mind, and had not Percy, who had formerly
pleased her, been even weaker than Henry? He had wept
at her feet. She laughed at Henry but she felt compassion
and that curious gratification which a woman draws
from the indulgence of contempt and even of hatred.
What young girl has ever been able to forgo the
pleasure of seeing a man abased. Delilah, even while,
and perhaps most of all when, she betrays, finds fulfilment
in the arms of Samson. The Amazons never destroyed
more than one breast.

Henry Outwits Wolsey.

She would have liked to be established blatantly, with splendour, but Henry was not the man for such methods. He feared to turn the entire Court against them both, and Anne was not slow to understand that in the event of a revolt he would sacrifice her. She therefore agreed to subterfuge. "If I were to announce my intention of marrying you," he told her, "one and all would unite to oppose it and we should be unable to obtain the divorce. Later on we can speak openly, but we must begin our campaign by acquiring allies; we must entice all those who hate Catherine, and while keeping our ultimate aim concealed, induce them to think that they are working for their own ends." Anne made no objection.

Wolsey was not resigned to the loss of the tiara, to the fact that he had been duped by Charles, and Henry approached him immediately: "Let us punish him, let the nephew pay through his aunt: you must deliver me from Catherine. Charles has betrayed you and we will cease to support him; I am perfectly prepared to accede to your wishes and to form an alliance with Francis. I will even consent to marriage with a Frenchwoman, with a princess of your choosing whom you yourself will bring to England and who therefore will always be in your debt." Wolsey, who was ageing and harassed by his own rancours, wrote to the Pope asking for the divorce, and Anne, with Percy's defection to avenge and other ancient affronts into the bargain, smiled to see her old enemy fall into the trap. She began to think that Henry had been no fool in his refusal to entertain any thoughts of violence and admitted that there was much to be said for subtlety. The most fulfilling revenges are those that ripen slowly; and gradual suffocation is better than sudden death.

Pope Clement VII was a dubious Medici bastard, who had risen to eminence by pliability and shrewdness. Beneath his abundant black beard he harboured less faith and devotion than diplomacy and a personal desire to humble Charles. "He will understand," said Wolsey, "the urgency of a divorce and will furnish the necessary pretexts. Both he and his predecessors have handled more difficult cases. Reasons of State must inevitably prevail. And in this instance the position borders on incest; there is a verse of Leviticus, a Scriptural precept to be invoked. Therefore all should be easy." Henry himself kept Anne informed of the proceedings, visiting her for that purpose. Spring was at hand. Catherine spent her days at her tapestry frame, but her tired eyes bore the trace of tears. Huddled at her feet the princess Mary divined a hidden danger and her heart was consumed with bitterness.

Anne Takes the Stage.

Henry, there is little doubt, was unsuccessful in concealing from Wolsey the depth of his passion for Anne. The old roué must have paused a moment to consider whether, in deposing Catherine, he was not preparing a bridal bed for the little Boleyn. But Henry assured him that his feeling for Anne was nothing more than a caprice, a fire of shavings that would burn itself

[125]

out quickly and Wolsey knew that the best way to dispose of a caprice is to satisfy it; he was mistrustful of chaste emotions. Anne was compelled to sacrifice her pride and allow it to be believed that she had become the King's mistress, that she was no better than her mother and her sister and had accepted the offer of their leavings. She returned to London from Hever and was present at festivities. Wolsey entertained her and Henry at a masked ball at which she removed her mask, while Wolsey, smiling indulgently, reassured the French ambassadors and discussed their princesses in connection with Henry's approaching betrothal. Anne defied the contemptuous glances of the women; she despised them for their stupidity in judging by appearances and for not seeing through them to her real objective. As she moved among these women she thought of her secret and her heart glowed with a delicious excitement. The Cardinal's musicians played the newest airs and Anne regarded the divorce as almost an accomplished fact when an unexpected obstacle arose.

A High-handed Fashion of Treating the Holy Father.

Pope Clement VII and the city of Rome had recently been attacked by a formidable army which had been raised in the name of his most Catholic and obedient nephew the Emperor Charles, by Bourbon, the renowned French traitor. Bourbon himself fell before Rome and his brigands remained without law or leader. They hurled themselves into the town and massacred five to six thousand persons in a single night. The Pope took

refuge in Castel Sant' Angelo and the more active among
the cardinals managed to reach its walls and were
hauled up in baskets amid a flutter of scarlet robes. The
victorious troops included Catholics and Lutherans and
among them they came to an equable understanding;
the Lutherans sacked the churches and the Catholics
looted the palaces, and while both of them massacred
men indiscriminately they agreed upon a more methodical
division of the women. While the female laity were
violated by the Catholics, the followers of Luther raped
the nuns. It cannot, however, be denied that some did
both.

These events were hailed with dismay in London, by
Wolsey, by Henry and, privately, by Anne. None of the
three could fail to realize that the bearded Pope,
besieged in his castle, was in no position to anger Charles
and thereby run the risk of getting his throat cut. For the
present, at any rate, the divorce must be postponed.
Catherine rendered thanks to God—the entire populace
of Rome had been slaughtered to preserve the rights of an
innocent Queen.

An Unfortunate Journey.

Five or six weeks having elapsed, Wolsey offered to go
to France in order to conclude a new alliance and arrange
a new betrothal for Henry. Henry having warmly
approved the project, Wolsey set out in pompous style
accompanied by his crucifers and by his numerous suite
clad in black velvet. Henry found his departure a relief;
he would no longer be compelled to dissemble, he would

be able to see Anne at the hours she appointed, while submitting to her notions of chastity. In his spare time he was busy compiling a learned pamphlet on divorce, with the aid of Wolsey's episcopal friends, who collected the necessary data.

Throughout the summer Anne and he enjoyed their idyll. They left Wolsey in Paris, negotiating, discussing the divorce, asking for a new wife for Henry, betrothing the young Mary to a son of France and generally involving himself. In the autumn he announced his return and Anne determined to humiliate him from the first moment of his landing, to lose no time in letting him realize that his sun was setting.

She was at Greenwich with the King when Wolsey's messenger came to announce the Cardinal's arrival: "His Eminence desires to know in what place your Grace will deign to receive him?" Anne forestalled Henry's reply: "Tell the Cardinal to bear in mind," she told the messenger, "that etiquette demands that an ambassador should wait upon the King immediately upon arrival. The Cardinal, being merely an ambassador and a very humble subject, should act in accordance with custom."

Wolsey was astonished. What was this woman that she should dare to speak in such terms? It was very obvious that the King's fancy had persisted. He saw Henry and reported the successful issue of his mission: the alliance concluded, the betrothal arranged. Henry's little eyes shifted and became inscrutable: "The betrothal must be cancelled." "For what reason, your Majesty?" "Because I love Anne Boleyn and because I intend to marry her." "Is it possible! Remember the greatness of England, the grave interests involved, the inevitable anger of Francis. Think of the vileness of the Boleyns, of Anne's own past and of her dubious amours . . ." Henry looked sulky. Wolsey knelt at his feet, sobbing and kissing his hands, adjuring him in grandiloquent words. Henry sighed with boredom, staring down distastefully at the old actor in petticoats who grovelled against his knees. He longed to say: "A truce to fine phrases and let us give eloquence a rest! This is not a case of the happiness of peoples or of the greatness of any land. I want this girl and you want to keep your power. Do you think my passion will give way to yours? I am the stronger and the younger of us two: yield or I shall strip you of everything."

Diplomacy.

Wolsey yielded, saying to himself in the meanwhile: Let us gain time, and Anne read his thoughts. She determined to try to do without him, selected an envoy from among the laity and sent him to Clement VII. In this she showed her ignorance of clerical resources: her lay messenger was completely outwitted. So she permitted Henry once more to ask his Cardinal's advice, realizing that it takes a priest to deal with priests. Two bishops were therefore dispatched to Clement VII and they humbly begged him to come to a decision. But the Medici had a wily mind; he wished to offend neither Henry nor Charles and refused to pronounce judgment. Charles had permitted him to escape from Rome and he had taken refuge in a small fortress, but even there he hardly dared to breathe lest Charles should decide to

evict him. "A divorce?" he enquired of the English
envoys. "By all means; there are certainly excellent
reasons. But consider the danger of my present position
—have some pity! I give full powers to Cardinal Wolsey
as my Legate; let him judge in accordance with his
conscience!" He would gladly have added: "Let me wash
my hands of the matter"; Passiontide was at hand, when
the Church related the story of Pilate.

Wolsey mistrusted the Pope's suggestion, but Henry
plagued him: "The Pope has given you full authority;
you have only to pronounce judgment." But Wolsey
told himself: "I must hold my hand, even at the risk of
my life." He explained to Henry that the Pope had set
a snare: "If the judgment were pronounced he would at
once revoke it. He would say that, as your minister, I
had acted by your orders. Ask him to send us an Italian
Legate, a Cardinal specially chosen for the purpose and
invested with plenary powers." Clement VII agreed and
Wolsey suggested Cardinal Campeggio. He knew that
Cardinal Campeggio, being an invalid and a martyr to
gout, would be a long time in reaching England. Meanwhile he offered up fervent prayers to God: "Lord, how
long must I be troubled with this girl?"

The Sweating Sickness.

But Wolsey's prayers remained unanswered and at the
end of May London was stricken by a terrible epidemic of
the sweating sickness. In every house and at every street
corner people were seen to break out in a sudden sweat,
to fall down, lie groaning for an hour or two and expire.

They appeared to dissolve into water through their pores, to melt like wax in the sun. They suffered little: a headache, a slight nausea, and those who remained out of doors perished of cold while those within doors died of heat. A few recovered, as though waking from a dream; life itself assumed a dreamlike quality. The flesh, the muscles, all that combined toward the strength and beauty of the body had become illusions that faded before the eyes.

The bodies of the dead lay in heaps in the streets; it seemed like the end of the world. Wolsey left London and disappeared. Nobody knew where he had hidden himself; perhaps he hoped by subterfuge to outwit Death. Henry, in a panic, sent Anne away, to the cool shade of the woods at Hever. She went, but she bore the vile taint in her blood; she took to her bed and sweated. God or the Devil saw to her recovery and in a few days she was cured. Wolsey had been premature in his rejoicings.

Henry himself had a change of heart; the sweating sickness terrified him and he also retired into the country. The sweating sickness threatening and then striking his palaces reminded him of the fragility of human greatness and of the vanity of fleshly passions. He prayed, spent his mornings on his knees in church, received Holy Communion every Sunday, took refuge in the performance of his duty and in virtue and clung to the feet of Catherine. Many times, like the plague-stricken, he sweated, but with fear, and he began to have doubts of his theses on divorce and upon the sinfulness of his first marriage. Leviticus decrees: Thou shalt not marry thy brother's wife; but, on the other hand,

Deuteronomy, which is no less holy and no less authoritative, says: Thou shalt marry her . . . If so many innocent Londoners had died it was doubtless in order that their King should return to the paths of righteousness. God frequently sacrifices the bodies of the vulgar for the salvation of a soul elect. The sickness dealt particularly harshly with the dissipated . . . Compton died, Henry's old boon companion who had been the perverter of his youth. Carey died, the ignoble Carey, Mary Boleyn's accommodating husband. All those connected with Henry were being wiped out, his servants and even his apothecary; fortunately his physician was spared and Henry clung to him like a leech. He insisted upon being examined and dosed; he only left his doctor to seek his confessor and at night he lay meekly in Catherine's bed. She cared for him and consoled him and became for him once more the kind and trusted friend of earlier days. In his gratitude and under the spell of his impulse towards virtue, he experienced, despite his terrors, a certain renewal of passion for his wife.

At the end of a month the sweating sickness disappeared and Wolsey emerged from seclusion. It was glorious July weather and Henry began to venture on to his terraces, hurrying in at the slightest signs of sweating. He gradually realized that people had ceased to die, that the dead were all buried, that life had resumed its normal sway and that the world was still fair. He stroked his own body, astonished to find it hale and hearty and powerfully material. He rode again, shot with the long bow and endured fatigue without even a headache. He begged his physician to keep his distance, deserted his confessor and left Catherine and her daughter to their prayers. He moved to another palace, summoned Wolsey to attend him and sent a messenger post-haste for Anne.

To him she seemed yet more exquisite after so much anguish. Life could still hold for him an element of the unreal. He was not very certain of being on the solid earth and wondered had he left it for a lovelier land in whose Elysian fields women assumed the ethereal imponderance of spirits. Anne, however clinging and winsome she might be, remained for him unalterably the virgin who is immune from carnal approach and who preserves her mystery. She was kind to him, but as a fairy or a nymph might be kind, a being nourished by the sap of the forests, a creature entrancing but still inhuman, with whom any physical merging is impossible. He would stroke her hair, her cheeks and her body; she conceded him all things save the final act, the simple act that fulfils and appeases. His lips caressed her, he lived upon desire and the anguish of a consuming and delicious thirst.

WOLSEY'S LAST STRUGGLES

(1528—1530)

A Cardinal's Legate Who Takes his Time.

CARDINAL Campeggio's arrival was imminent and Henry advised Anne to leave London and retire to Hever. She was highly indignant at the idea that he could be ashamed of her, that her irreproachable purity should be in question, and she was even more alarmed that Henry should renounce their nightly meetings and lest Wolsey should seize upon the opportunity of supplying the King's bed with another woman who might calm his senses, soothe him and remind him of the blessedness of peace. Then she reflected and came to the conclusion that it might be opportune to test her power, even when absent. She jibed at Henry for his cowardice and for his eternal scruples and departed to enjoy the autumn scents of Hever.

The decrepit Campeggio at length made his appearance. Henry received him with great ceremony and the respectful demeanour of an obedient son. The Londoners once more beheld the Pope's cross borne proudly aloft by a priest mounted upon a mule. Campeggio was lavish in blessings. He was accompanied by his son, a tall lad who supported his hobbling steps. The son in question was perfectly legitimate, Campeggio having entered holy orders late in life, being inconsolable because of his wife's decease. For twenty years the future Cardinal had been a professor of law at Padua; he was therefore well qualified to evolve a plausible judgment. But his haste in the matter was no greater than Wolsey's; these old men seemed to feel that eternity was at their disposal and were averse to hasty pronouncements. It was necessary to study the case and to listen to both sides. Henry thought it unnecessary that Catherine should be consulted, but Campeggio stuck to his point. He hoped to find gentle means of persuasion; she was, after all, only a woman. He therefore visited her and asked her whether she would not care to leave the world and take the veil. What better future could she expect? For her the age of passion was past, together with that of child-bearing. God was undoubtedly summoning her to the cloister and Campeggio described from personal experience the joys of the ecclesiastical life. He described it as the refuge of the sensitive and disillusioned; Catherine thought the Italian over-bold. There could be no fitting comparison between a humble professor of law and a Queen, an Infanta of Spain. She replied that she would take the veil when Henry entered a monastery and Campeggio, for all his subtlety, could offer no hope of such a contingency. Catherine therefore refused any concession.

Campeggio collected reinforcements and returned to the charge accompanied by Wolsey and four bishops. Catherine sent them away empty-handed and perfectly satisfied to be so.

Henry sent for Campeggio: "If she is willing to be a nun I am perfectly prepared to become a monk. We will both take vows of celibacy, and later the Holy Father will release me from my vow. She will remain bound while I shall be free, and as England must naturally have royal heirs I shall, always of course with the Holy Father's permission, choose another bride."

Campeggio found the suggestion ingenious but over-involved and in any case too undignified. It is not advisable that a Sovereign Pontiff or even a king should publicly cut capers. "Then," suggested Henry, "I shall imitate the holy men of the Old Testament. I have very frequently read in the Bible that the Lord permitted the patriarchs to have several wives at the same time. Sarah, for instance, being old and sterile, Abraham took Hagar as his concubine and Hagar gave him a son. Jacob had two legitimate wives, who, moreover, were themselves sisters; to these he added also two concubines, being doubtless of a great virility, and from them descended the twelve tribes of Israel. David had a number of wives and Solomon a well-populated harem, and these were the forebears of the Saviour's own lineage. Why should not I also have two wives? Must the teachings of the Bible only be obeyed when they forbid and not when they authorize? Catherine could continue to be the official Queen, while Anne could bear me a son. We could all live together in perfect harmony." On Campeggio expressing some astonishment, Henry reminded him that the celebrated Luther, who was, after all, a man of great erudition, allowed the husband of a sterile woman to go and sow his seed elsewhere; that he even permitted the wife of an unfruitful husband to take another father for her children. That he held it a sin to deny to man or woman the right of reproduction, or to deny to unborn souls the opportunity of coming to birth. "But Luther," retorted the Cardinal, "is a heretic." Henry held his peace, but he began to think that even heresy might have its good points.

First Expulsion of Catherine.

There was much talk at the street corners. The gossips were indignant that a girl of no account should presume to make trouble in the royal household and attempt to supplant the Queen. The sterile women and those who were plain felt themselves particularly threatened. Henry convened some of the nobles and London's principal citizens at Bridewell. He treated them to a lengthy moral homily in which he explained that his union with the Queen was irregular and forbidden by the most sacred laws; that in permitting its consummation an error had been made and that for twenty years he had been living in sin. He added that such a position could not be allowed to continue and that he had determined upon the sacrifice of putting away Catherine and taking another wife. "My heart will bleed, but God's law must be my first consideration." This rigmarole was delivered with the unction of a sermon, of a call to repentance, in a stream of mellifluous eloquence. Henry revelled in the joy of preaching, he wept over himself, became the dupe of his own play-acting and saw himself as a martyr. A few days later he begged Catherine to leave him and withdraw into the

country. It was December, the great log fires heated
his blood and he wanted Anne to be near him. Catherine
submitted; she enjoyed submission, having a particular
vocation for suffering. He watched her depart down the
leafless avenues and sent for Anne, who was becoming
anxious, but two months of separation had not cooled
the ardour of her stout swain. She refused angrily to
return, reminding him that he had dismissed her. Henry,
infuriated, threatened the Howards and they hurried to
Hever, flinging themselves at Anne's feet until she
graciously yielded.

He spent an entire fortnight alone in her company
and then remembered that he was Catherine's husband.
Christmas was at hand and he did not wish to be in mortal
sin. Feeling himself authorized by the Bible to follow
Abraham's example, he went to join Catherine at Greenwich, taking Anne with him. The two wives thus lived
side by side in two separate apartments and he spent the
days with the younger and the nights in the bed of the
more mature. Doubtless Catherine reaped some advantage from the memories of his daylight hours. He
settled into this three-cornered domesticity, in which
he was prepared to enjoy a tranquil happiness; but Anne
was no lover of compromise.

Winter succeeded autumn and in February Clement
VII fell ill; it was devoutly hoped that he might die,
but he lingered and finally recovered. Campeggio
at length promised to pronounce the divorce. He
had in his baggage a Papal bull already signed which
he showed to Henry. "Publish it," said Henry, but
Campeggio and Wolsey refused; they still nourished
hopes that Henry would tire of Anne. Such a thing

may happen suddenly, on any fine morning and when the lover himself least expects it.

Catherine before the Tribunal.

Anne threatened and Campeggio and Wolsey must needs feign obedience. On June 21st they summoned a tribunal. Considerable trouble had been expended in its staging; Campeggio and Wolsey, clad in their scarlet robes, presided. Henry sat at their right hand upon a throne; Catherine on their left, also upon a throne. The bishops were preparing to listen to the pleadings when Catherine spoiled the performance. When her name was called she rose from her throne and passing in front of the cardinals without so much as a glance, fell upon her knees at Henry's feet. There she made a short speech, her eyes streaming with tears. She refused to recognize the authority of her judges and accepted only that of her dearly beloved husband. She had always obeyed him, had borne him children, had welcomed all his friends and had come to him a virgin. Having spoken, she rose and left the hall. An esquire was sent after her and this obedient wife utterly refused to return, informing the messenger that at her next meeting with Henry she would not fail to excuse herself.

It is doubtful whether Wolsey or Campeggio was much surprised, but Henry was completely disconcerted. Finally, however, he recovered his wits and embarked upon his customary arguments: that Catherine was a saint but that the Lord must be obeyed. . . . Catherine's initial virginity he forgot to mention, but he sent to the subsequent sittings of the tribunal a succession of nobles who remembered her marriage to Arthur and who related the little husband's delight and his boastings. Why should it be considered a cause for astonishment that a youth of fifteen years should be adequate as a husband? Aged statesmen, beginning with Howard, dwelt lasciviously upon their early exploits, stimulating the tribunal with the details of their amorous apprenticeships.

The cardinals, less than ever in a hurry, spent an enjoyable month in listening. Anne was fuming while Henry counselled patience, but nevertheless he was duped. The estimable Campeggio it was who tricked him. On the twenty-first of July he declared that the time for a vacation was at hand, that nobody could be expected to exercise their judgment in the hot weather and that the session was therefore closed. There was a great outcry at Court, where all Wolsey's enemies, hoping that he would destroy himself, had rallied around Anne. In the Privy Council Brandon caused a sensation; he struck the table with his fist, declaring that cardinals had always been unlucky to England. "But not to all Englishmen," Wolsey retorted. "But for me, at the time when you married his sister, the King would undoubtedly have had you beheaded."

Which was true, but, none the less, Wolsey was losing ground.

The Fall of Wolsey.

Henry avoided Wolsey, fearing the influence of the ageing minister. Two months elapsed. Henry and Anne went north, hunting. In September Campeggio announced that the Pope forbade the resumption of the trial, having decided to judge the case himself. Campeggio waited on Henry to take his leave and Wolsey accompanied him to the palace. The entire Court expected that Wolsey would be arrested, but with one glance he recaptured his master. After dinner Henry escaped from Anne, sought out Wolsey, carried him off to his study, kept him there till late and finally accompanied him to the door with an urgent invitation to return.

The evening was an unqualified triumph for Wolsey, but with night Anne resumed her empire. In the chastity of her chamber she awaited Henry: "Your Grace must choose: either him or me . . ." "When I see him, I am unable to withstand him . . ." "Well then, swear to me that you will not see him . . ." "He is to wait upon me to-morrow morning . . ." "He must find the room empty; to-morrow we go hunting." She allowed him to sleep for five or six hours; then, at the break of day, she woke him, helped him to dress and together they mounted and made off into the dew-drenched forest under the light of the paling stars. Henry never saw Wolsey again.

Campeggio had departed, surprised to find the door open, but at Dover a shock awaited him. Anne firmly believed that his baggage contained the bull of divorce signed by Clement VII. She sent officers after him, who burst into his bedroom, hurling his luggage to right and left. They accused him of being a common thief and of having stolen valuables from Wolsey. Capes and rochets flew through the air, his personal linen, the bandages for his gout. They found neither the alleged valuables nor the bull. Campeggio had had his doubts of diplomatic immunity and the bull had been burnt quite six months previously. He hastily repacked his possessions and embarked, thankful to escape uninjured.

Wolsey was again in office; Henry demanded the Great Seal and ordered him to depart. All London rushed to the river banks in the hopes of seeing him pass by. They expected that he would be taken to the Tower and that they would soon see his head fall beneath the axe. His barge went downstream through a horde of vessels over-loaded with the curious; between two dense hedges of jostling, heaving howling onlookers. In the neighbour-hood of the Tower the yells became more deafening, but Wolsey's barge did not stop at the Tower; he did not land until he was far from London, at Putney. On the bank he found a horseman awaiting him; a friend of the Boleyns', of George and of Anne, Norris, one of the esquires of Henry's little company. Norris had just arrived at a hard gallop; his horse was in a lather and Wolsey wondered what sinister errand had prompted such haste. It was a letter from Henry, kind, almost affectionate. Wolsey wept as he kissed it and fell on his knees in the mud. Norris, feeling unable to remain standing before so much misfortune, knelt down beside the Cardinal. Then Wolsey mounted his mule and rode off towards a humble manor which he possessed in the neighbourhood of Esher.

Henry took Wolsey's money and Anne annexed his palace and York House became Whitehall. In any case she was sick to death of living with Catherine. She ran through the galleries delighted with the furniture, the plate. Henry followed heavily after her, dragging his

ulcerous leg and listening to the echoes of her rapturous
cries. Finally he would rejoin her and closing the doors
behind him would kiss her hands, the skirt of her gown.
She remained the virginal bride, besieged by the
Minotaur; she offered him half-pleasures, prolonged
but unfulfilling.

A Provisional Cabinet.

The dismissal of Wolsey did not further the divorce;
quite the contrary. There was no longer any leader in
England and Anne was immersed in her revenge. She
rejoiced in Wolsey's misfortunes and sought a means to
add to them and this sterile pleasure caused her to neglect
essentials. She was not more than twenty-two years of
age and largely a prey to her nerves. Meanwhile
Catherine remained the official Queen, the legitimate
wife and the companion of Henry's nights.

Henry was astonished at his own daring in having dismissed his former master; he forgot that young Anne had
been at his shoulder, urging, prompting and almost
compelling him to action. Now at length he ventured
to draw breath, he savoured his freedom, feared it and
enjoyed it. He would have liked to assume the reins of
government, a measure of which he had dreamed for ten
years, but at the moment of doing so he was assailed by
doubts of his own adequacy, finding in himself unsuspected limitations. He dared not declare himself absolute
sovereign. But he carefully avoided appointing an out-
standing minister. He compiled a provisional cabinet; in
other words, a cabinet of nonentities. During this

interregnum he hoped to gain courage to study matters of State more deeply, to recruit devoted, or at any rate docile, agents, to constitute an administration and finally to declare himself, seizing absolute power. This plan compelled him to adjourn the divorce and an unexpected situation developed: Henry and Anne setting aside that love which had so lately caused the downfall of Wolsey and concentrating exclusively on politics.

Henry was busy weaving his schemes, and they sufficed to absorb him by day and possibly also obsessed his thoughts by night. He appeared to have delivered England to the extremists. Wolsey being removed the Lords of the Council were able to think themselves masters, and Henry stood aside and gave them their heads. Among them were soldiers and bishops, Howard, Boleyn, Brandon and even some of Catherine's friends. Those of the military element were very clamorous; in so much as they were all enemies of Wolsey they appeared to be linked in a lasting alliance, but Henry knew well that they hated one another, and they began to mutter as soon as they had shared out those fragments of the spoils which Henry consented to leave them. The kill devoured, their former appetites awoke and they eyed each other hungrily. This was a situation which had been foreseen by Henry, whose policy was to loose them at each other's throats till they were exhausted by their private quarrels.

He hoped, however, that these quarrels would remain unobtrusive, that they would limit themselves to concealed hostilities, avoiding open warfare. A pitched battle clarifies a situation, clearly indicates where lies the greater strength and designates a conqueror, and Henry had no use for a conqueror. The palm might, for instance, fall to Howard, whose bulldog grip would afterwards be hard to unloose. Anne herself was not anxious for the undue advancement of her arrogant uncle Howard. It was necessary to impose upon these birds of prey hovering round the council table a certain measure of verbal moderation, an appearance of respect for the grandiose terminology of toleration and union. With this aim in view it became necessary to introduce into their midst a man of such probity and simplicity that each one of them would be compelled to dissimulate his passions and make an outward show of virtue. Henry therefore fetched from the outskirts of London, from Chelsea, that lovely, peaceful Thames-side village, his old companion, the gentle Thomas More, the friend of letters and of the arts, the good husband, the good father and the dutiful son, and it was upon this sedentary philosopher that he conferred a semblance of authority. In order to give himself leisure to mature his schemes, he organised chaos, paralysis and torpor.

Thomas More.

What had More in common with the Howards and the Brandons? He was the guileless Daniel in the lions' den. He had none of the qualities of a leader of mankind. He was devoid of passion and wished to see the earth possessed by kindness, nobility and altruism. Above all other things he valued peace, had avoided any overt clash with authority, had achieved a good position and a comfortable income. He deeply reverenced religion and the crown and it was his habit to sing at High Mass on

Sundays. But he also delighted in reading the classics, forgetting the pagan convictions of their authors. He lived with his wife, his aged father, his three daughters and his sons-in-law in perfect harmony. He had dreams of social reform and had written a phantasy, tracing a picture of the ideal constitution of the fair realm of Utopia. His ideal was based upon the suppression of private property, since the greed of possessions slays the soul and precludes happiness. Yet he retained his house, his goods and his income, being too wise to attempt the realization of his dreams. He had little comprehension of the hearts of men, was aware of the fact and shrank from any effort towards reformation. He lacked the requisite violence for an apostle, and did not confuse his phantasies with his faith. He studied astronomy, the movements of the planets, and spent his nights in contemplation of the stars. He corresponded with the leading scholars and philosophers of Europe, loved the arts, including painting when its subject was chaste. He entertained Holbein and commissioned that artist to paint him together with his entire family. His beauty was essentially that of his spirit; physically he posesssed a large nose, a wide mouth, the massive structure of a yeoman scholar. His eyes were small but kindly, humorous and a trifle vague, from visualizing dreams of unattainable purity.

Henry, torn by uncertainties, welcomed his guileless-ness. Despite his nobility, More was very human, but he had retained only the higher qualities of mankind. Yet the most debased of men could recognize in More some-thing akin to their better selves, some aspirations for-gotten since childhood. No man is so corrupted as to have utterly lost even the nostalgia for altruism and virtue, and More, precisely because he was no extreme ascetic, because he had not at that time divorced virtue from comfort, afforded to others an agreeable suggestion that rectitude is repaid by paradise on earth.

Henry would therefore visit him at Chelsea; he would talk to the painter Holbein and commission him to paint portraits. He would listen to his friend More inveighing against capitalism and take pleasure in allowing himself to be convinced. In that peaceful home his passions found repose, he forgot Anne and his nights of frustration, his voracious appetite for power and for gold. He discussed the Eucharist, the Latin poets, conjugal affection and the human soul.

Belabouring the Wounded Lion.

And this man was the innocent shepherd whom Henry imported into his Council, whom he installed as leader of his wolves. To him he gave the Great Seal, appointing him Lord Chancellor, and the whip that Wolsey had wielded for fifteen years became an innocuous crook. Moreover, More detested Wolsey; he was incapable of understanding that tyranny may sometimes be required and that greatness must involve compulsion. He allowed the nobles, Brandon as well as Howard, to harry their enemy to demand his impeachment and prepare the indictment. Wolsey was accused of usurping the King's majesty, of having given his signature precedence over Henry's, of having written: *Ego et Rex Meus*, "I and my King"; even of having sought to slay that King from whom he held all his power. "Have we not often seen him," ran the accusation, "constantly whispering in his Grace's ear, bending close to speak in an undertone? Since we know that he was infected by a shameful disease, his breath must necessarily have been contaminated and his intention was to infuse venom into the royal brain."

They evolved such absurdities and the learned More believed them, but Henry intervened and objected. He found the nobles lacking in tact and thought their indictment set him in a dubious light. Why must they suggest that he had been a mere puppet in the Cardinal's hands? And why these allusions to a questionable malady: Henry thought of the ulcer that ate into his leg, and considered it decidedly unnecessary to draw public attention to the state of his blood. He decided that it was high time to curb the meddlers and to bring More out of the clouds. Anne, for her part, was also reflecting. She came to the conclusion that she was weary of revenge and that she preferred to concentrate upon her principal objective: Anne was determined to be queen.

Henry was still afraid to stand alone and he sought for a useful tool among Wolsey's secretaries. He realized that only Wolsey had known how to rule and that he must grasp the heritage of his system and his weapons. Hence, perhaps, his indulgent treatment of the old Cardinal and the letter delivered at Putney by Norris. Wolsey, on his side, understood clearly that he was expected to furnish men. On the day of his departure he had sent his jester, Comus, as a present to amuse the King. Comus had wept bitterly at leaving Wolsey and the archers had been compelled to take him by force; the poor fool had no understanding of life. Presently Wolsey sent the King a more valuable gift; he gave him Thomas Cromwell, who was reputed his evil genius, who since the disgrace of his kind master had spent his time in weeping, and above all in mourning his own fall from prosperity. Henry promptly sent for this Cromwell, who obeyed without pausing to dry his tears; no archers were required to bring him into the Presence. Thomas Cromwell swam with the stream.

Travel Enlightens the Youthful Mind.

Cromwell was possessed of an acute business sense. He had been useful to Wolsey in delicate transactions and had been entrusted with certain arrangements with the Church. Wolsey, as an observant Legate, had noticed that English monks, particularly in rural communities, stagnated in idleness, dirt and vice. It occurred to him that in an era which was witnessing the rediscovery of classical civilizations, of Plato, Homer and the treasures of Greek literature, there would be no harm in suppressing a few of these religious and bestowing their fat acres upon scholars and professors. Coming to an understanding with the Pope, he began closing monasteries and founding colleges, by means of some convenient transfers of funds. But the workman is always worthy of his hire, and Wolsey considered it only fair that a portion of the moneys should remain in his hands. The operations were therefore entrusted to Cromwell, who, at the merest hint from his master, reserved for Wolsey a large share of the spoils, surreptitiously keeping some pickings for himself, since early experiences had impressed upon him that it is never wise to be poor.

Wolsey made no parade of Cromwell, whose appearance was the reverse of prepossessing. He was of extremely low birth, having risen from surroundings which, though not beggarly, were obscure and unsavoury. His father, indeed, had been almost of middle class, a manufacturer of cloth in Putney. But his factory had not been his principal business; he had borrowed and lent money and tampered with shady transactions, in addition to which he had been brutal and quarrelsome and too drunken even for Putney standards. Cromwell the son was worthy of his sire. From his earliest years he had grasped the fact that the prizes of life are reserved for the shrewd. Fruits which might have seemed gross or tasteless to scions of an ancient race appeared succulent to the palate of Thomas Cromwell. London was only a few miles from Putney and London offered vast resources: women of the stews with willing lascivious bodies, riotous houses where one drank and gamed amid rich and pungent odours. He had little to spend; the father was often in difficulties and was also probably parsimonious. The adolescent Cromwell picked up what he could and the law found him brazen. He was at that time much too young to deal with it adequately, and it very soon had him in gaol. There he knew poverty and blows and had time to reflect. He decided that England was an inhospitable country to paupers who happened to be endowed with brains. The fog and the mud got on his nerves and he therefore quitted his ungrateful homeland and crossed the sea. He wandered on the Continent in search of sunshine; that had been twenty or twenty-five years ago.

He became a soldier in the German forces and learned the charms of pillage and of rape with no authorities to annoy him. Then he decided that brutality was too crude and realized that if you can acquire loot by force, big fortunes are only made by shrewdness. He determined to study the intricacies of finance and got employment in a Venetian bank. He gained refinement, not of his senses, perhaps, in spite of the mild air of Venice and the pearly skins of her courtesans, but certainly of the intelligence. The serenades of Venice may lull the sensuous to indolence, but Cromwell kept a firm hand on his faculties and concentrated exclusively upon mental issues. He inhaled the stimulating breezes from the East that blew across the lagoons and watched the ships loaded with exotic spices anchor alongside the Schiavoni. He read the latest books, discovered Machiavelli, saw that Venice was still feeling her way and he understood Florence. At any rate he understood her neatness, her taste for accuracy if not her beauty. He remained a barbarian, but was seasoned, toughened by the sunshine. Fully aware of all he had acquired, he turned his face once more toward England. He was determined to dominate; he contrived to approach Wolsey, and Wolsey understood his value. Now Henry had summoned him and Cromwell knew that the bulky man would be as wax in his hands: he knew that he had achieved greatness.

A Jack of All Trades.

Cromwell lacked the manners of a courtier. His face betrayed his strength, his insatiate appetite for life. In the gutter from which he had originated it is essential to terrify at first sight, to show that one can kill and will dare to do so. Courtiers must wear a veil and wrap themselves in courtesy; they may handle pitch, but they must be clad in silk. Cromwell bore no outward signs of the mire; the beast of the forest, the wild boar, even when wallowing in the mud of its lair, does not suggest defilement—but in the appearance of this emancipated being could be clearly read his desires and his passions. His investigating nose seemed to scent the most savage of human odours. His deep-set eye, sunk in its orbit, was never raised towards sky or clouds but remained inflexibly focused upon its prospective prey. His skull was huge and round, a skull to defy fists or weapons. His complexion was florid, rubicund with blood, but one felt that beneath the upholstery of flesh, at the cheek-bones and at the jaw, there was an aggressive structure. His short neck offered no facilities to the noose; moreover, he habitually hunched his shoulders.

Henry's first reaction to him was one of repugnance. He had never been in contact with a strength so primitive and crude. Then he realized the energy of this spirit and drew reassurance from its vileness. Cromwell, come what might, could never become his master, but he would squeeze England between his thick hands and offer it to his King. He would crouch obediently at the foot of the throne, gnawing the bones he was given and, if need be, enduring such blows as came his way: he would be an enslaved Wolsey. Anne also drew near and overcame her disgust, mustering a smile for this man, and between them they concluded a tacit bargain: Cromwell understood that if he contrived to rid her of Catherine she would deliver over to him the heart of the King.

As Wolsey had formerly done, Cromwell sensed the secret impulses of Henry's mind. He knew that Henry did not wish that the indictment drawn up against Wolsey should be pursued. Cromwell intervened and induced the nobles to abandon their foolish project. He still feigned a great devotion to Wolsey, while dreading any possibility of his return. But he was not called upon to attack him; the hatred of Wolsey's old enemies sufficed: the Howards were there, and Anne.

Wolsey had received a gracious letter from Henry promising the return of his property and hinting at further favours, and Anne had sent him a jewel as a present. Wolsey, delighted, had moved to nearer quarters, from Esher to the Charterhouse at Richmond, not far from the royal palace. He doubtless hoped that Henry, disconcerted at being so long unsupported, would visit him privately or invite him to return. But Henry was no longer unsupported; Cromwell was at his side, and Anne soon persuaded him to agree to Wolsey's dismissal. The matter was arranged between her, Uncle Howard and Cromwell. The latter, one day, paid a visit to his old master and approached Wolsey with apparent anxiety. "Your Eminence, my lord Howard has intentions on your life. I have seen him and he has spoken to me privately. 'Since you are his friend,' he said, 'advise him to make good his escape, for if he delays, I shall kill him with my own hands.'" Wolsey was terrified; he felt himself surrounded by treachery, he beheld in his mind's eye Howard's ravaged face, his sunken eyes glaring from beneath his lank black hair, his gnarled hands. . . . He

set out toward his archbishopric of York in the wild
country on the Scottish border.

Cromwell's Inspiration.

Cromwell, still kept in the background as an adviser
too vile to be openly acknowledged, realized that his only
hope of real advancement lay in serving Anne and in
obtaining for her that well-nigh impossible thing: the
divorce. Cromwell and Anne, probably without having
concluded any definite pact, formed a united front.
Their plan was a very simple one: to obtain the Pope's
consent, and should he prove obstinate, to follow
Luther's example, break with the Holy Father and wrest
England from the Church of Rome. Cromwell, his
appetite whetted by the destructions of convents accomplished under Wolsey, dreamed of expelling all monks
and raking in all their property. He knew Henry's
cupidity and fully realized that before the prospect of
acquiring so much gold, the royal theologian would find
admirable arguments against the religious and glow with
indignation at their corruption.

There came a day when Cromwell murmured in
Henry's ear: "Since the Pope refuses to grant the divorce
your Grace should attack him openly and abolish his
power over the English Church." "But the English
Church cannot remain without a Head." "What better
Head could it have than your Grace?" Why accept
orders from the Bishop of Rome, a bastard Medici, rotten
to the core, a coward, selling justice to the highest
bidder? Who could doubt that Clement would have

broken Henry's marriage had it been an English army that menaced Rome? Clement had been elected by simony in defiance of all accepted laws. Clement was unchaste, he was ignorant of theology and, moreover, completely indifferent to the subject. He was allowing the spread of heresy in Germany to put souls in peril. Henry must understand that the Lord had appointed him to a divine mission. He alone could interpret divine law. He alone could regenerate the Church, restore its purity, save those who had been misled. He, Henry, was the light of the world. The nights brought Anne to Cromwell's assistance: "Only Clement, out of cowardice, opposes our happiness. Challenge him—elect yourself Pope of the English Church. You yourself shall judge in the name of God and send away your obstinate old wife. Think how the years pass; I am now twenty-three and you are forty. Do you intend to go on waiting for me until death?" And in order to stimulate him she would offer him her lips. Henry gave his approval to Cromwell's suggestion and appointed him to a place on the Council. There he laboured hard to make Henry Pope of England, but the task was to take time, many weary months.

Anne and Cromwell would willingly have imitated Luther and his adepts, but Henry had little liking for appeals to the populace, to ignorant crowds. Being himself a theologian, he wished to set against the Pope only scholars of his own temper, experts and all the professors of Western theology. This procedure had been suggested to him at an earlier date, and Anne and Cromwell, disappointed by Charles, brought it forward again. Cromwell, indeed, thought it highly practical. He knew that science, even theology, was very poorly remunerated, that professors frequently have large families to support or else very material passions which science cannot gratify and which they secretly dream of indulging. He felt certain that a little money adroitly distributed would easily convince these oracles, and he sent messengers to all the European universities. He obtained excellent results, but the process took time.

Death of Wolsey.

In the autumn of 1530, Anne, in search of amusement, decided to gratify an ancient grudge and to have Wolsey delivered into her hands.

During the four or five months that he had spent in the retirement of his archbishopric of York, the Cardinal's mind had turned toward holiness. He had made a pilgrimage from village to village, saying Mass for the peasants and making his chaplains preach to them. He reconciled family feuds, distributed generous alms and built castles. Three hundred stonemasons were in his employ. He was to be accused of conspiring and was denounced to Henry, with the suggestion that he probably had allies in Scotland or might even be in touch with Charles. Henry knew him to be formidable and trembled. He gave orders for his arrest, and that he should be brought to London, and Anne exacted that Wolsey should know that he owed his death to her, because he had formerly insulted her. She entrusted the task of seizing him to her erstwhile betrothed, Percy

Wolsey was in the country when they came to inform

him that a messenger from the King was approaching the house. He rose to his feet and left his dinner, and beheld Percy, who stood motionless, cutting him off from the staircase—Percy, more dead than alive, devoured by his hopeless passion and now also a prey to his almost lifelong terror of his old master, before whom he had wept so fruitlessly. Wolsey realized that he was to be led to his death and became even paler than Percy. He made an attempt to recover himself, had his belongings packed and mounted his mule.

In London Anne, Howard and the rest of them, doubtless including Cromwell, were preparing an indictment. They also prepared an apartment in the Tower and Henry was awaiting the prisoner with impatience. He no longer knew whether he loved or hated Wolsey and blamed him for not having died on the day of his dismissal. He was now an unwelcome and alarming ghost that must without delay be banished from the earth. A messenger from Percy reported that the victim was leaving York. Then it was learned that Wolsey was ill. Terror had laid him low. This unbridled lover of life and of all its splendours was panic-stricken at the thought of the axe. His heart, his bowels failed him. He was compelled to interrupt his journey and spend a fortnight, half of November, at Sheffield Park, as the guest of Talbot, a relation of Percy's. Then he set out again, dragged himself as far as Leicester, where he collapsed, saying: "My bones will lie here." Henry, astonished at the delays, feared that his victim might evade him. He dispatched the constable of the Tower, Kingston, gaoler of the State prisoners. When Wolsey beheld that sombre countenance he released his hold upon life. He declared for the last time that he had never desired anything but Henry's well-being and his glory. "Had I served my God as faithfully He would not have rejected me." But he had doubts of his salvation. Two days later he died at dawn.

THE GLAMOUR OF THE CROWN

(1530—1533)

It Is Unwise to Wait Too Long.

WOLSEY being dead, it was time to dismiss Catherine. Anne never left Henry's side; all the winter they had been hunting; they would hurtle through the forests, tiring seven or eight horses beneath them. Henry would watch her galloping ahead of him, rising in the saddle, thrusting through the undergrowth. They rode through mud and snow, were sometimes drenched by the rain, their faces were whipped by the wind. Anne seemed more than ever possessed, her flesh more vital, her eyes wild. She would halt at crossways and bend her bow, and the does would be driven toward her in order that she should pierce them with her arrows. When they returned in the evenings, Catherine awaited them and Anne would be compelled to withdraw into the background. The struggle had endured for five years and Anne hated Henry for having been too weak to overcome those who opposed his wishes, for not having dared to have his will of her. She felt herself being inwardly consumed; her own fire devoured her, was turning to madness, was withering her. Her thoughts dwelt on the quiet sleep of the dead—then she would rouse herself and reproach him for allowing himself to be duped and would once more demand the crown.

Henry was cooling off; Anne's resistance had humiliated him. There is always danger in making the imaginative wait too long. They have their dreams and are able to feed upon them. They may, if they have dreamed long enough, renounce reality and, fearful of disappointment, make their escape. Anne no longer had for Henry her sinuous charm; he found her insults less attractive. She was beginning to repeat herself, to be tinged with vulgarity. He would have agreed to part with her if by so doing she could have lived in his memory as purity, eternal youth, incarnate grace.

A Pope in Doublet and Hose.

The priests were beginning to protest, to wail for their Pope, so Cromwell lost no time in making them feel the lash. With the coming of spring he convened them, informed them coldly that they were all traitors in that they had served Wolsey and gave them to understand that if their lives were spared it was only thanks to the King's mercy. He added that such mercy called for their gratitude and for a corresponding sacrifice. The priests offered money which Henry accepted, informing them, however, that they had a further obligation; that the laws of the realm now forbade obedience to the Pope, and they were begged to lose no time in recognizing as their only master: "Henry, Protector and Supreme Head of the Church and Clergy of England." There was a wave of horror, the priests thinking partly of their own freedom while speaking exclusively of the rights of the Church. Henry and Cromwell insisted, sending George Boleyn to the Assembly. The Assembly thereupon pretended to agree and finally produced a compromise. They said that they recognized Henry as their Head: "in so far as was permitted by the law of Christ." This was highly unsatisfactory, since the law of Christ, in the event of Henry weakening, might well prove to be merely the will of Rome. Only a half-step had been achieved.

Catherine had remained at Windsor Castle and Henry, if he went there, could not avoid the sight of her. She was still playing at being Queen. Anne demanded her expulsion and Catherine accordingly departed with her exasperating pose of holiness. She joined her daughter Mary, who was now seventeen. Ugly, shrivelled and violent, as stubborn as her father, she lived a life of prayer and virtue and condemned her father's adultery with all the passionate ignorance of a virgin. She read Spanish books and prepared herself for martyrdom. Hers was a sombre youth, seasoned by the bitter salt of tears. For several months Catherine wept beside her, but in the autumn they were separated.

A plot was being hatched against Anne; she had wounded all her enemies and even her relations by her harshness and her arrogance. She opposed Howard, determined to rule her clan. Brandon told Henry one day that she was deceiving him and was no virgin, having formerly given herself to Thomas Wyatt. The priests, threatened in their Pope and in their freedom, turned towards Catherine, hailing her as a martyr. They surreptitiously incited parish priests, monks and deacons and

a murmur arose. The clergy swarmed on the roads. At
various pilgrimage shrines miraculous images, it was said,
had begun to weep and to bleed. A young priest who
was Henry's nephew, Reginald Pole, and whom he
cherished for his prowess in theology, crossed the
Channel and began writing pamphlets against the new
Jezebel.

In the spring the Pope, having adjured Henry to take
back his wife, found himself refused his subsidies. Farewell, English gold; farewell, the rich harvest! The
clergy in England were deprived of power; they wailed,
but like all Churchmen confronted by arbitrary force,
had no alternative but submission. One man only
attempted to protest and that was the upright Thomas
More, the ingenuous champion of principle. He refused
to remain a member of the government and resigned his
office. Henry accepted the return of the Great Seal with
a scowl: he did not like criticism.

Anne allowed the summer to go by. Henry's glance
was straying. Other women, younger, unfamiliar,
friends of Brandon and of Howard, pious maids of
Catherine's household, began to hover around the King
and Anne realized that the game of chastity was played
out; it was time that she bore him a son.

The Journey to Calais.

She could not, however, give herself suddenly,
capitulate abruptly, thus revealing her misgivings. She
must at all costs remain the huntress, the capricious
Artemis who chose Endymion while she allowed Actæon

to be slain by her hounds. Henry was permitted to kiss her elusive hands. She would laugh and bend over him, whispering reminders of earlier promises. August was drawing to a close, great golden clouds lingered in the sky and the birds broke again into tentative song. The air was full of autumnal scents. Anne would take Henry's head in her hands, would press it against her breast, making him listen to the beating of her heart: "Will you not have compassion upon so great a love?" Did he not understand the intensity of her sufferings, that she was overwhelmed by desire, that she could no longer control her passion? And indeed, exacerbated by constant caresses, her whole being vibrated like a taut violin string.

He begged for another seven or eight months, but she offered to give herself to him. When, however, he approached her rapturously, she suddenly withdrew her offer, demanding a guarantee. She must be recognized by a foreign Court and publicly received by the King of France.

She was already practically Queen. She took precedence over the princesses of the blood royal, over Mary Brandon, over Henry's own sister and the dowager Queen of France. Henry gave her the marquisate of Pembroke, which had been a Tudor appanage, formerly the residence of his grandmother, Margaret. It was a fog-bound castle on the Welsh coast, a rocky coast beaten by the waves, a mystical country saturated in legends of the knightly King Arthur and of the fair Iseult. Anne was also provided with several small crowns.

Francis was in need of money and therefore agreed to a meeting with Anne. But he did not promise to bring his wife, Queen Eleanor, sister to Charles and niece to the unhappy Catherine. Henry, however, attached little importance to this Eleanor. Francis had been compelled to accept her as the price of his freedom from imprisonment in Madrid, and nobody in France paid her much attention, Francis himself less than any other. Henry requested that she be left at home, saying that he abominated Spanish fashions. But he fully expected, and so did Anne, that Francis would be accompanied by his sister Marguerite, the poetess, the spinner of tales, the heretic. She was no Infanta; she wore Paris dresses and understood many things. Anne had formerly been one of her household, and looked to her now for support, but Marguerite had a social sense and she did not make her appearance.

Henry hesitated on the brink of departure. He was not over-pleased that a chit of a girl whom all the French knew and had perhaps despised should thus be seen to be keeping him in leading strings. He affected a contempt for Francis and his friends because of their frivolity, but he dreaded their laughter. He instructed his agents to demand that all light-minded persons be excluded from the meeting and only those admitted who were of weight and consequence and respectful of the majesty of kings. Francis agreed.

They crossed the Channel at the end of October and established themselves at Calais. Francis was awaiting them at Boulogne and Henry went there to pay him an initial visit, remaining for three days. There were tournaments and balls but little enthusiasm; the great days of the Field of the Cloth of Gold were no more. Thirteen years had passed, bringing many reverses. The

frivolous had all been excluded and Henry was bored.
He returned to Calais for All Saints Day, and Francis
came there to join him while the bells of the city tolled
for the dead. Francis was requested to lead Anne out
to dance at a ball, as he would have invited the Queen,
but he refused, fearing a loss of dignity. Anne, however,
evolved a subterfuge; she went to the ball masked and
Francis did likewise. He seized Anne by the hand, pretending to be ignorant of her identity; Anne removed her
mask and Francis feigned surprise. On the following day
he sent a gift of diamonds to his partner. Jewels being
offered only to queens, Anne expressed her delight. That
night, in the conventional room which had been assigned
to her in the castle of Calais, she opened her arms to
Henry. She humbled herself and allowed him to possess
her. The gentle wash of the waves was audible through
the windows, the tapestries waved in the night breeze,
and a dying log fire glowed upon the hearth.

They remained more than a week at Calais. Francis
had gone and the chill air of November emphasized the
silence. They had lived so long in a dream that reality
surprised and alarmed them. Anne was at length a
woman; Henry had delivered her from her own un-
balanced fancies and revealed her to herself, finding her
interior rhythm, giving her serene happiness, the
pleasure of ceasing to think, of allowing her mind and her
nerves to be lulled to sleep, of being no more than a
physical vessel, utterly fulfilled and submissive. For her
there were now order, peace and repose. The sky was
tranquil and colourless, the sea more grey than the sky
with faint ripples and reflections and a few drifting sails.
The nights unfolded themselves, long and blissful. The

lovers were surprised to find no more hatred between them, to sleep in mutual trust, happy in each other's arms. At last they set out homewards, rocked by a lazy sea.

The Secret Marriage.

They awaited the coming of the gift from Heaven, the son, the Messiah whose birth should be Catherine's undoing. In January Anne knew that the child was in her womb, that he was already beginning to live.

Many years had elapsed since Henry had last been a father. At twenty-five such joys are taken lightly; at forty they constitute a deep gratification. Henry, slow of mind, still doubted; Anne, the fruitful and submissive wife, was no longer Anne. He had fed too long upon imagination and could not believe that the Divine Huntress was his, that their two bodies had merged and taken on new life.

It was high time to think of marriage, otherwise the predestined child could be no heir but would come to birth a bastard. They sent for a priest and had him brought one morning to the Palace of Whitehall. Servants of tried discretion erected an altar in an attic and they summoned two intimate friends and Norris, the man who had knelt in the mud beside the disgraced Wolsey. The unworthy priest, having been heavily bribed, hastened to forget that Henry was already married. He joined their hands and blessed their rings.

But Anne was awaking from her dream condition. Unsettled by her own happiness, by her hopes, by the child she carried, she became once more capricious and

cruel. She flaunted the immodesty of the newly wed;
her sudden laughter was heard again and she lived
surrounded by a horde of bold and frivolous young men.
She had always taken pleasure in awakening their lusts
and now she avenged herself on them for Henry's
deficiencies. She also punished them for their disrespect,
for, despite their fear of the King, they treated her as a
semi-harlot. There were five or six of them: Norris,
the witness to her marriage; her brother George, whom
she had made Lord Rochford; Wyatt, her former suitor,
the poet from Hever who had so basely consented to
desert her. She offered them women, her sister
Mary, her cousin Madge Shelton, a swarm of willing
wantons.

She hated Wyatt while knowing that she had never
ceased to attract him. He had remained in Italy for a long
time and had there experienced many adventures; then he
had returned, resumed his sonneteering. On a day in
February he was waiting in Anne's room, together with
his companions, when she thrust her small, vivid head
from between her bed-curtains. "Wyatt," said she, "I am
hungry; I have a craving for an apple. Do you know why
that is? The King says he knows. The King says that I am
pregnant." Wyatt went very pale and Anne laughed.
"The King is mistaken, I am sure he is mistaken." And
her head vanished behind the curtains.

The Divorce.

The marriage must be made public but not until the
divorce had been pronounced. In spite of the example

set by the holy Patriarchs, Henry dared not continue to keep two wives. Supreme Head of the Church of England, he might himself have dissolved his first marriage, but he preferred to depute that task to a prelate and he required a new man for the purpose. The chief English see, that of Canterbury, being opportunely vacant, whom should he appoint to fill it? Where should he find a docile and broad-minded priest? He consulted Anne and Cromwell and all three of them promptly thought of Cranmer, a suave Cambridge don who had formerly given them good advice and who had helped them in rousing the European universities against the Pope. Cranmer impressed all three as being the man they required.

Cranmer had remained in Germany at Nuremberg and, unknown to Henry, had become half a Protestant. The excellent Cranmer found it hard to believe in Transubstantiation, and it seemed to him a very severe saying that priests should be debarred from marriage. Why should a God of infinite goodness deprive his most virtuous children of innocent pleasures designed, moreover, for the propagation of life? Cranmer in his youth had been a married man. On becoming a priest he had thought to renounce the flesh, but at Nuremberg he fell a prey to the demon of carnality and united himself in marriage to an amiable German, the niece of a renowned and arch-heretical doctor.

Henry, who was in total ignorance of his aberrations, wrote to him urging his immediate return. Cranmer hesitated. He knew that Henry believed in the Real Presence and held that all priests should lead celibate lives; he could not therefore hope to impose his Grete.

King Henry VIII
by Hans Holbein

Catherine of Aragon
Artist Unknown

Thomas Wolsey
Artist Unknown

Anne Boleyn
Artist Unknown

Jane Seymour
by Hans Holbein

Anne of Cleves
by Hans Holbein

ETATIS   SVÆ ·21

Catherine Howard
Artist Unknown

Catherine Parr
After Holbein

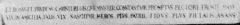

Thomas Cromwell
by Hans Holbein

Thomas Cranmer
by Gerlach Flicke

A man of single heart would have remained with his wife, but Cranmer was not prepared to face indigence. He was offered the premier see of England, carrying with it an enormous income. He swore to Grete that he would so arrange matters that she would be able to join him later and share in his glory; and mingling his tears with hers he left her.

Henry was careful not to appoint Cranmer himself; he arranged that he should be nominated by the Pope, and Clement accepted Cranmer unsuspectingly and duly sent him the pallium. Cranmer, in return, must swear obedience to the Pope, an oath, however, which he intended to ignore. It was a position calculated to trouble any conscience, but Cranmer's subtle brain evolved an ingenious solution. On the vigil of the day appointed for his vow of obedience to the Holy See, he collected several witnesses and informed them, in strict confidence, that his impending oath would be null and void. This statement having been duly recorded, Cranmer appeared in his cathedral and, in the presence of his flock, calmly took all the necessary vows.

March was drawing to a close and the royal infant was expected in September, so Cranmer mustered bishops and priests for the purpose of discussing the divorce. Howard, accompanied by several gentlemen, sought out Catherine and advised her to submit. She refused yet again and talked about God. Howard informed her that her protests were futile, since Henry and Anne were already two months married. In May she was visited by Cranmer and a party of nine carefully selected bishops and was told that they constituted a tribunal which would proceed to the judgment of her case. They summoned her to submit and to appear before them, and Cranmer was particularly eloquent. Catherine replied by her usual speech, refusing categorically to appear. Cranmer withdrew, deeply pained, announced that she was refractory and settled the affair in her absence in ten days.

There was no divorce, but a simple annulment of the marriage. According to Cranmer and his learned colleagues, Catherine, despite twenty-four years of faithful cohabitation, had never been Henry's legal wife. The two parties had both been misled by an error. It was a pity that their daughter Mary had insisted upon living for seventeen years and thus perpetuating the error in question. Henry informed Catherine that she was no longer Queen, but merely the widow of the lamented Arthur, and therefore Dowager Princess of Wales. He forbade her household to pay her royal honours and dismissed those who persisted in doing so.

Anne Boleyn Crowned.

Cranmer remained in London, assembled a conclave of priests in his Palace at Lambeth, and presented them with the news of Anne's marriage. None of these prelates expressed surprise or murmured a word about polygamy. Not one suggested a further ceremony, which could only have been detrimental to the child. It was even stated that the marriage in the attic had taken place in November, and on the first of June Anne was crowned.

She set out from Greenwich Palace in the royal barge, going upstream and landing at the Tower. It was a venerable custom that all princes should sleep there the night preceding their coronation. She was met at the landing stage by Kingston, the Constable, the same whom she had formerly sent to Sheffield to arrest the dying Wolsey. Kingston detested Anne. He was a heavy, churlish fellow, an old soldier, recruiting officer to the King and also a shrewd ambassador, a conservative of strict morality and deeply attached to Catherine. Anne was accompanied by several maids of honour, her cousin Bryan and her other cousin, Madge Shelton, who was being courted by Norris. She slept little that night and lay listening to the crowd in the streets. She thought of the dark dramas that had been enacted in the Tower, of the ghosts of the murdered little princes.

Dawn comes early on the first of June. Her maids chattered as they robed her and dressed her black hair. The trumpets rang out; below, in the courtyard, the procession was forming. A very quiet horse had been provided for Anne; she mounted carefully and set out beneath triumphal arches of flowers. The gossips crowded the streets, the apprentices and their masters had left their benches; they gazed, but silently, without doffing their caps. Anne's fool, who capered in the procession, shouted: "Keep your heads covered, the air is chilly in June!" And so she made her progress, slender in spite of her pregnancy, trembling with suppressed arrogance and rage, the envy of women, the desire of men, but equally detested by men and women alike. She was the accursed as she reared her slim neck and smiled. At Westminster, where Henry awaited her, she took her seat on the throne. Cranmer in his golden mitre advanced, she knelt before him and he placed the crown on her head. Her cousins pressed forward and pinned it to her hair. The cold fires of the diamonds shimmered above her eyes; she knelt in the coloured rays of the Abbey windows, in the light of innumerable candles amid a mist of incense.

The Princess Elizabeth

Then came summer, its silent fruitful fields, its slow-running rivers, its cool, shadowy halls. Anne lay dreaming among her cushions. She let herself relax, becoming purely animal, a prey to those submerged reactions that saturate the tillage in March when the ears of wheat are forming. Henry spent the nights on the towers of Greenwich or Windsor, watching the stars, attended by his astrologer, who, compass in hand, noted the celestial conjunctions and promised him a son.

Henry's love had undergone a transformation; he now thought only of the child. In giving herself Anne had been her own undoing and the fire which she had for so many years instilled into Henry's veins was dying down, was all but quenched. The mystery that had dwelt in the woman was now enshrined in the unborn babe.

Can there be a purer impulse than the hope of paternity? Henry allowed it to suffuse his being, welcomed it, trembling amid ecstatic dreams. But joy in this world is seldom entirely spiritual, and one day when Henry was particularly joyous a woman chanced to catch his eye. She was young and she smiled and Henry was so joyous and so pure that he immediately took her.

Anne was growing anxious, she sent forth her spies, she by no means shared Henry's credulity. She had no belief in astrologers; the child might be a girl—at the mere thought she felt herself to be dying. She had once again begun to hate Henry; her brief carnal response was past and she saw him as he was, heavy, worn, impure of blood. The ulcer on his leg was spreading, he was slow-minded, cared nothing for poetry and loved only ancient music. The young men laughed at him: Norris, Wyatt and her brother George, and she was bound to this ageing tyrant. He had awoken her body only to disappoint it, to arouse it and to give her a terrible thirst for youth.

She insulted him, throwing his infidelities in his teeth. Formerly he had accepted her insults with humility, but formerly also she had been the goddess, the moon-ray that is pursued from leaf to leaf. To-day he had possessed her, she lay on her cushions wounded, unwieldy by reason of his act, utterly despoiled of her dominion. He roughly ordered her to hold her tongue; who was she to complain when Catherine had been silent?

In September she felt that her time was at hand. She saw Henry, his broad face with the tiny narrow eyes padded round with fat, leaning over her; he was expecting his son and was confident of his happiness. Anne thought him foolish and rather nauseating; she found herself almost hoping that she would disappoint him, the prospect of his joy seemed unendurable.

She heard a cry and felt the touch of hands about her body; they were taking the child from her and someone murmured: "A girl!" She opened her great black eyes and stared at the broad face. She laughed to see it changed, deflated. Falling back among her cushions she closed her eyes again.

She heard the whispers of her attendants and Henry's

protests and thought to herself: "If only I could die!" In her mind's eye she beheld him clearly with all his bulk and his stupid violence and quailed at the prospect of living perpetually beside him, day after day, until old age and death. He had approached the bed and was leaning over her once more, calling her 'sorceress,' and she said to herself: "Now he can see all the blemishes of my face, all the lines channelled in it by suffering, and I am unable to rise up and hold my own—to put on my mask of deception, the mask that baffles him, that allures him and makes him dream." She could feel his breath upon her hair, she looked at him and then she closed her eyes and wept.

Never before had he seen her shed a single tear, and now he silently watched them stealing from beneath her closed lids and trickling down her face to her neck. His heart was touched and he also felt near to weeping. He flung himself upon her, fumbling among her lace pillows, and took her in his arms. Anne's head fell backwards, her eyes remained closed and her tears continued to flow. Henry kissed her cheeks, drinking those pitiful tears. "Anne," he told her, "I will never, never leave you. I would rather lose my throne and beg my bread from door to door."

X

THE FUMES OF BLOOD

(1533—1536)

Painful Reflections.

H ENRY'S tears ceased flowing and his emotion
subsided. He sought his own apartments and
reflected. Why had he felt impelled to promise
Anne that he would never in any circumstances leave her?

Such moving and dramatic scenes should be avoided;
they stirred the depths and brought unwelcome elements
to the surface. Henry had no desire to see himself too
clearly, he had less than no liking for self-analysis. He
was neither clairvoyant nor altruistic, but loved an
existence that was comfortable, warm, powerful and
vague. He was a musician, with a taste for the indefinite,
but chance will occasionally tear aside veils; chance or a
temporary, imprudent impulse; and Henry had suddenly
acquired the knowledge that he had for some time past
desired to leave Anne. Desire was possibly too definite
a term; it was rather a vague inclination, a smouldering
hope. He had visualized himself as alone and free, with
Anne vanished, Anne become no more than a memory,
or at the most a shadow as unobtrusive as Catherine. And
in these imaginings he had undeniably found pleasure. He

[175]

was now compelled to face the fact that he wanted to send her away. He had sworn never to leave her and he knew that such an oath had been born of the very fact that he had feared to break it.

"And why, after all, should I hesitate to leave her? I have never loved her with any real affection. I only coveted her with my mind and with my body and she kept me in suspense and caused me much suffering. Possibly I was able to arouse her physically; I can remember the response of her sinuous body and the tender fulfilling nights at Calais. But I know very well that I never touched her heart, that she despises me and has often mocked me to her maids, her brother and the young fools who surround her."

With a simplicity of which he was now ashamed he had managed to persuade himself that she was the bride elected by Heaven to give him a son, to provide an heir to his throne. He could not now refrain from laughing at his delusion. Anne had been the chosen instrument of Satan, sent to him in order that he might imperil his soul. Her very chastity, her artifices, her demi-virginal expedients now appeared to him to have been merely diabolical. There was more purity in simply yielding to desire, in a woman who gave herself frankly and generously. Bessie Blount and Mary seemed saints by comparison. They exhaled the honest fragrance of new-mown hay, the scented beauty of short summer nights. In their beds a man might sleep without remorse, almost without any consciousness of sin. Anne was accursed; the gossips of the street corners were right.

Was not the very fear that now beset him significant, and also the immediate despair that had invaded his being as soon as he knew that the child was a girl? He felt a conviction that Anne was damned, that no son of his would come from her womb.

A Tactless Prophetess.

The clergy were growing turbulent. Monks and other Catholic agents flocked the streets, and incited the people of the countryside, terming Anne a prostitute and Henry Anti-Christ, and speaking of the Lord's anger and of the hour of chastisement. A little seeress produced appalling prophecies: God had appeared to her and had announced that Henry would be hurled from his throne and would perish by a shameful death. She was not as yet prepared to specify the date, but asserted that his end was near. She began by placing it a month ahead, then she corrected herself and postponed it for three months, and finally accorded him six.

She was the humblest of peasants and had been a servant on a Kentish farm. She suffered from mysterious ailments. Then she alleged that the Blessèd Virgin had appeared to her and had inspired her and thereupon she began to prophesy. She made various pilgrimages and crowds began to follow her, and one day in the presence of several thousand pilgrims she suddenly announced that she was healed of her sickness, but that the Lord must be requited for His mercies and had commanded her to proclaim the truth to men. She beheld trees and swords in the heavens and ascribed to them symbolical meanings. Certain monks surrounded and acclaimed her and interpreted her dreams. Fearful that she might go astray, they put her into a convent and explained to her that she had been sent to bring back Catherine, the pious Queen, to the throne and to win back England for the Holy Father in Rome. Her revelations became exceedingly definite and exclusively political and it was then that she prophesied Henry's downfall and summoned the impious king before the judgment-seat of God.

Henry was scared; he was not easy in his mind. This little peasant might be genuinely inspired. But he clearly understood the policy of the priests: to predict his downfall in order to encourage a rebellion, call in the aid of the Scots and of Charles's armies and thus, proclaiming a Holy War, succeed in imprisoning him, possibly in killing him, and placing the crown upon the head of his daughter, Mary. Such a proceeding would be an infamous parricide, but the service of Heaven sanctifies all means—Cromwell quieted his fears and arrested the seeress.

Anne, Cromwell and Archbishop Cranmer were closely united. They all knew that if Mary came to the throne not one of them would be left alive, and it was always possible that Henry might die or be killed in an accident. They compelled the Commons to pass a law that pronounced the Princess Mary to be a bastard and secured the succession to the little Elizabeth. This step seemed calculated to assure the future: Anne would be regent, Cromwell would complete the pillage of the churches and Cranmer would impose Protestantism on England. Nobody would retain any belief in the Real Presence and priests would be given permission to marry. Cranmer had already summoned his Grete from Germany and now kept her at his side. Children were being born

who were mysteriously concealed in the purlieus
of the vast archiepiscopal palace.

A few months later Anne was again pregnant, or at
any rate, she believed herself to be so. The Heavens had
smiled upon her once more and were shedding the dew
of their approval upon the earth. Henry recovered his
energy; he permitted Anne and her two allies to send
the prophetess to her death; he had allowed himself for
too long to be terrorized by the demented creature.
Twenty times at least during the past winter he had
thought himself dying, but the fatal six months had at
last elapsed and the prophetess had patently lied and
must pay the price. She was burned at the stake in the
pale April sunshine and confessed before she died that
her voices had deceived her.

Six monks who had been arrested with her died by a
different death, being duly convicted of high treason.
The fire in their case was considered too merciful and
they were dragged to Tyburn, where they were hanged
by the neck until they had tasted all the pleasures of
strangulation. When they were seen to be almost bereft
of breath they were cut down, stripped, disembowelled
and the executioners tore out and chopped up their
entrails. When their cries had ceased and life was
extinct they were yet further mutilated: they were
quartered and their remains exhibited to the people.

Three days earlier Henry had consented to the imprisonment of his old tutor Bishop Fisher and the too
learned Thomas More. They were accused of having
listened to the seeress. But their crime was, in reality,
of much more serious a nature: they represented to
Henry his conscience, the memory of his innocent

years. They disapproved of all his unjust actions and the mysterious inner voice that spoke to Henry in his hours of remorse had always the accents of Fisher or of More. He envied them and admired them, but, tortured by jealousy, he was unable to let them remain alive.

Cromwell undertook to deliver him from these importunates, these living mementoes of a too virtuous past. He summoned them to Lambeth, to the palace of his friend Cranmer, and there required them to subscribe to the acts recently passed by Parliament repudiating Catherine and her daughter Mary and recognizing in their places Anne and Elizabeth. They refused: Fisher with violence, since he was of a great age, in no way attached to life and had given himself entirely to God; More less vehemently, thinking of his wife and daughters, of the pleasure he experienced in reading the poets, in contemplating the stars and learning the secrets of the universe. Both were arrested and taken to the Tower.

The End Justifies the Means.

Catherine was inflexible; she refused to admit that her daughter Mary could be a bastard. She felt that almost the whole of England had been roused by the priests and was now awakening. She knew that the nobles in the north were preparing a revolt and that Charles was contemplating an invasion. Henry and Anne imprisoned her in her chamber, dismissing all her attendants. She realized that they had thoughts of putting her to death, but what was death that she should fear it? All her life she had thought only of paradise. She also hoped that God might intervene and overthrow Henry; that she might see Anne assassinated, Cranmer burned as a heretic and the traitor Cromwell hanged, drawn and quartered.

Nearly all the nobles of the Court were against Anne; her own uncle, Howard, weary of her despotism, was deserting her and treated her openly as a harlot. He had conceived a new combination: he had betrothed his only daughter to Henry's bastard son by Bessie Blount. The little Richmond was a likeable child and Howard was bringing him to his father's notice, in the secret hope that one day he would be proclaimed heir to the throne. Then Howard's daughter would be Queen, he himself probably prime minister and Protector of the Kingdom, omnipotent. But to achieve such an end Anne and little Elizabeth must be disposed of.

As yet nobody dared openly to stab the favourite. Catherine and her friends chose a gentler method and laboured to provide Henry with a new mistress.

To the Pure All Things are Pure.

Henry's old friends sought to alarm him, urging him to avoid irritating the fanatics and advising him to sacrifice Anne. Was this faded girl worth the risk of downfall or death? Why not repudiate her and return to the normal path, reinstating Catherine, the unblemished spouse? Catherine was undeniably plain, but the poor woman expected nothing but a measure of outward consideration: "She will remain far from your bed, living between her prayer-stool and her embroidery-frame. She will appoint comely ladies and will permit you to caress them. Has she not always done so? She knows a Queen's duties of obedience and respect and that a royal husband is not to be treated as a lover. The virgins prepared by her will be all that can be desired. There is surely some good in Catholicism since it trains women to be submissive."

A little girl emerged from obscurity, an unassuming creature with nothing striking about her but duly coached by Catherine. Henry stroked her cheeks and set her upon his large knees. She made his summer pleasant, fulfilling and peaceful . . . The little girl sent letters to Mary bidding her be of good cheer.

Catherine was confident of success and the northern nobles were maturing their plot, but they lacked discretion, and Percy, the erstwhile and eternal adorer of Anne, surprised and betrayed them. Their leader was brought to London and was tried by the Lords, but the trial clearly showed Anne that she was accounted already lost, dispossessed. The Lords of the tribunal, heretofore so abjectly submissive to Henry's lightest wish, dared to raise their heads and, despite the most glaring evidence of conspiracy, acquitted the arrested leader. An attempt to overthrow Anne was not reckoned a crime.

To Anne there remained only one hope: the son that she bore within her. But what was she to do if Henry really lost his head over the little girl with whom he had been provided? Anne had long ruminated the murder of Catherine and Mary; in her family, poison was a frequent expedient. Two or three years earlier the Boleyns had tried to kill Bishop Fisher by means of a drug administered in soup. They had contrived to bribe the cook, but Fisher had escaped and only a few of his servants had perished. Henry had not dared to wreak vengeance on the Boleyns, but he had had the accommodating cook boiled alive.

Anne, however, feared to strike her two enemies even secretly, so she went to Henry and demanded their heads. But Henry was not amenable and Anne's rages appalled him. For Catherine he had always harboured a deep respect and in his eyes she still remained a saint. Mary was of his blood and in her childhood he had adored her—can a father ever be justified in striking at his own progeny? What would the Lord say? There had, of course, been the example of Abraham . . . "Either they must go or we," Anne would reiterate: "If we do not kill them we ourselves shall die." And she would offer to strike the blow for him. He had only to go to France, leaving her full authority. She would act immediately and they would be free.

As he still withheld his consent she became violently excited and flew into such a fury that she suddenly miscarried. The longed-for Messiah had forsaken her body and she remained utterly dispossessed. It might have been thought that Satan afflicted her and Henry departed to seek refreshment in the arms of his new attraction. Anne would have liked to make an end of the girl, but here again she dared not yield to her impulse. However, she dispatched her customary spy, her brother George's wife, Lady Rochford, to point out to the damsel that the air of the Court might prove unwholesome, that she was in considerable danger and would be wise if she went elsewhere. The girl, believing herself to be already as good as dead, ran to throw herself into Henry's arms. He immediately had Lady Rochford arrested by his guards and, despite Anne's protests, lodged in the Tower.

On the Continent a new alliance was being concluded to Anne's undoing; Francis, for motives of self-interest, was making advances to Charles. Clement VII was dead and the new Pope, Paul III, intended to recover England. This Paul III was a very able man who had begun his career under the Borgia Pope by imprisoning his own mother and selling his handsome sister Julia to Alexander VI. By these means he had become rich and also a cardinal. He was now old and wise and would have thought only of the Church but for a rather terrible bastard bestowed upon him by the God of Love and of whom he wished to make a prince. Charles acquired his friendship by promising Parma to this hopeful. Paul III, Charles and their ally Francis did their best to win over Henry: "Leave Anne and we shall all be your friends."

Anne Retaliates.

Anne parried the thrust. She could see that Henry was becoming bored with his new favourite; the novelty of a body is not everything, there must be some mental companionship to enrich the intervals, and Anne had not lost her mental attraction. But she would have liked to find a sorceress who would anoint her body and endow it with a new enchantment.

"Oh, too familiar body," she would say aloud as she

gazed at herself in the mirror, "body bereft of all mystery, body whose savour he knows all too well, who can restore to you the freshness of the young leaf, or the magic of the unattained? Must I then perish because he craves new embraces?" She was nauseated by Henry's crudity, but she sought to find for him the pleasure that he desired. From among her ladies she made her choice and sent her cousin, Madge Shelton, to his bed—a good-looking girl, little troubled with brains, whose body had been conditioned and initiated by the caresses of the young esquires of Anne's little court, particularly by those of the elegant Norris. Henry was very appreciative of Madge's physical attractions; this was the fourth time that he had sampled Howard blood and he promptly dismissed Catherine's little friend. Madge brought him back to Anne and he enjoyed the body of the one and the still alluring mental companionship of the other. His happiness, however, exasperated Anne, who was now as bitter as gall. She frequented sooth-sayers, who had told her that Catherine and Mary had cast spells upon her and that while these two sorceresses remained alive she would never bear a son. Believing Henry to be once more her slave she yet again demanded their lives, but Henry was a thrall no longer.

Executions.

In the spring there were a number of executions. Three Carthusians and two priests loyal to the Pope were dragged to Tyburn and there hanged, drawn and quartered. They put the severed arms of the Carthusian

Prior over the doors of his monastery as a warning to the monks. These, however, had the courage to bury the arms, whereupon they were seized and suffered a lingering death.

Then Henry rid himself of his two dear friends Fisher and More. He had hoped that during the winter Fisher would die of the cold and had given orders that he should be deprived of his furs. Remembering his own childhood and his grandmother, Margaret, he would have preferred to avoid direct action; but Fisher persisted in remaining alive. On the fifth of May he was led before the tribunal and condemned. The Pope, in the hopes of saving him, had made him a Cardinal. Henry sniggered when he was informed of this fact. "Let Paul III make haste and send him the hat; we shall see that he lacks a head on which to wear it." On the first of June More appeared before the Court. He made an attempt to defend himself, courteously stating his case. He enjoyed political debate and allowed himself this last pleasure. He was condemned, as a traitor, to death by mutilation.

On the eighteenth of June three monks were quartered at Tyburn. On the twenty-second Fisher was beheaded and his poor old body stripped and exhibited to the populace. A few days later they brought More the news that he was to die, but that the King in his mercy had spared him mutilation and that he would only perish by the axe. More received this boon with a jest, reflecting upon the days when Henry had come to observe the stars in his simple Chelsea home, and went to the scaffold. He was very ill and had to be assisted up the steps, but he died without one angry word. His head was duly placed on a pike upon London Bridge, but his favourite daughter, coming by night, contrived to steal the head and bore it away.

Meanwhile Anne was busy giving balls. She had managed to dispense with Madge and had won Henry back to her arms. They were now united by the blood they had shed, by the odour that arose from the stakes where their victims agonized, by the terrors that obsessed them both. In Anne's bed Henry was less fearful of the shades of Fisher and More. He trusted that God would not see fit to smite him; he himself was chastising the enemies of dogma. In May he had burnt fourteen German emigrants who were so criminal as to assert that infant baptism was worthless and that adults should be rebaptized.

A Counter-attack by the Just.

Henry was once more suffering from boredom and Catherine's friends produced yet another female diversion. They chose her this time both refined and chaste. Her name was Jane Seymour, she was not very handsome but she had a virginal charm and dignity. She had formerly been one of Catherine's maids of honour and her family was of sound provincial nobility. Cromwell had a secret hold upon both of her two brothers.

This time it was no passing fancy that was offered to Henry, but a love that was pure and respectable. Jane was one of those girls who take life seriously, are determined to ignore the fact that they possess physical passions and await patiently the coming of a husband. But Jane was already nearly twenty-five and the husband had not yet made his appearance. She respected Catherine and regarded Mary with the deep devotion due from a well-brought-up young gentlewoman to a princess of the blood. She seemed so quiet that Henry relapsed into shyness and dared not declare himself. But in the course of the summer he made a progress in the southern parts of the kingdom and paid a visit to Jane Seymours' parents. He said nothing definite while implying a great deal. It almost amounted to a formal declaration.

Fruitful Nights.

There is a risk for a woman in attempting to preserve chastity if the object of her pursuit is a married man. At the Seymours' castle Henry recovered his former good spirits; he enjoyed September and its cooler days, its early morning mists and the dew on the fields in their autumn greenness. It is a gentle month in which the passions acquire a just balance.

But the pleasures of the day-time are only a prelude to happiness and at night Henry returned to Anne. She would lie beside him, silent in the darkness. Possibly also under the influence of the autumn season or perhaps pursuing a secret policy, she was docile and submissive. His hand would go to seek her among the cool sheets and she would seem to be asleep. She would be lying curled up, limp with warmth and drowsiness. Her relaxed form would seem gentler under his caresses, would seem to him almost innocent. He would touch her lightly, furtively, fearful of waking her, while she controlled her nerves and compelled herself to remain languid. He would possess her, believing her to be still asleep, enchanted to find her body so pliant, so quietly feminine, so different from her soul. He rejoiced in the darkness, in the silence and in her closed eyelids. But even in possessing her he was unfaithful to her. Was she Anne or Jane? He hardly knew; she seemed rather to be a stranger, a new being, a sombre harmony.

She allowed herself to be taken, repressing her recoil, and October with its abrupt changes of weather, its west winds, its flying leaves, its heather and its autumn tints found them still wandering across hill and dale from one estate to another. By day he left Anne; went hunting; let his thoughts dwell upon Jane. At night he hardly spoke to Anne but waited until she slept.

She became pregnant and a few days before All Saints, her suspicions being confirmed, she informed him of the fact. The old enchantment resumed its empire and she was once more sacred; within her enigmatic and rebellious body slumbered a part of his victorious self. Her complaints, her tears had for him the grace of April showers that are heralds of fruitfulness. In her weakness she was as appealing to him as a child and forgetting Jane Seymour he cherished Anne, caressing her fecund and sheltering body. Anne was once more begging for the death of the two importunates, speaking in the name of her unborn child and quoting the words of a seer: "So long as those two women remain alive you will never become the mother of a son."

Death of Catherine of Aragon.

Anne kept Mary immured and Mary prayed and played upon the virginals. She fed upon pride, penances, obstinacy and music. Nobody knew whether she possessed any senses.

Henry dared not sign the death-warrant; he sought for some indirect means, some ruse that would succeed in beguiling God and men. A few days after All Saints, inflated with the joy of his coming paternity, he enquired whether there was nobody who would rid him of his former family.

Three centuries earlier, Henry II of England, incensed against the Archbishop of Canterbury, Thomas à Becket, had also cried: "Who will rid me of this man?" Thomas à Becket had been murdered at the altar and Henry trusted that the Boleyns or his faithful Cromwell would not fail to recollect this anecdote and would understand.

Twenty-eight days went by and it was learned that at Kimbolton Castle Catherine was ill. She was suffering from violent pains of the stomach and bowels. There was also vomiting and her doctors were doubtful of her recovery. No one dared to express astonishment at her illness. She had never at any time enjoyed robust health, her many pregnancies had exhausted her and everyone knew that her life had been a torture. Henry had been saying for several years past that she was dropsical, like her mother, which was a falsehood, and that she would not live long, which was likely to be true. But the vomiting ceased and Catherine recovered and Henry and Anne became deeply depressed.

Their depression, however, endured only a month. Almost immediately after Christmas Catherine fell ill and began to vomit again. It then became clear that she was not to be spared and Mary sent an urgent request to her father that she might be permitted to go to Kimbolton and see her mother for the last time. He temporized and replied that he would think it over. Charles's ambassador succeeded in reaching Kimbolton where Catherine, in a dying condition, had not slept for several days. She thanked him for having come: "I shall at least have one friend beside me; I shall not be left to die alone, like a beast."

She lingered for another seven or eight days and the ambassador was compelled to leave her. A Spanish lady who had formerly accompanied her from Spain and who had since married an English gentleman contrived to outwit the guards, to reach her side and assist her. Mary was far away; she was praying.

On the sixth of January, the night of Epiphany, Catherine felt herself growing weaker. She began to repeat prayers; her Spanish friend and her chaplain were with her. She had plaited her grey hair round her head and was smiling, visualizing the end of her sufferings and their reward. Toward two o'clock in the morning the priest wished to say Mass. He saw that the agony was beginning and desired to give her that last consolation; but she restrained him, reminding him that the Church forbids the saying of Mass before four o'clock in the morning. He obeyed. Four o'clock struck at last. The servants had already prepared an altar in the room and Catherine gave the responses and received Holy Communion. Then she waited, commending her soul to God. She reviewed her life, her childhood under the Spanish stars, the cypresses of the Generalife, the white rocky peaks of the Sierras, the green fields of England and its fogs; her solemn nuptials, her children in their coffins, her many sorrows. She closed her poor, large blue eyes, dulled by too many tears and she seemed to feel against her lips the forehead, the hair of her daughter, the only being whom she had ever loved with a perfectly pure and selfless affection. She detached from her neck a small gold cross and asked that it should be given to Mary. Her visions were becoming confused; the heavy form of Henry seemed to approach, to overwhelm her. For twenty years he had caused her suffering and it was doubtless by his act that she now lay dying. But she was unable to hate him, for he was her child and her master. She could hear his laughter when he had been a little boy, dressed in white, and see him as he was then, dancing a jig. But she banished these earthly memories from her mind and brought her thoughts back to God. She died at two o'clock that afternoon.

Henry and Anne were awaiting the news almost in silence. Finally a messenger appeared: They were free. Henry assumed a solemn air, summoned several of the courtiers and spoke of the happiness of his people. The Pope and the Emperor, he was careful to point out, had now lost all conceivable pretext for complaint. Peace would be declared.

Anne beckoned the messenger to her and emptied her purse into his hands: "Now, at last, I am Queen," she said.

XI

THE SWORD

(1536)

The Shattering of a Hope.

THEY enjoyed one day of triumph, with no thought of donning mourning clothes. They both dressed themselves in yellow, the colour of joy, of light and of sunshine and Henry stuck a little white feather in his hat. There were festivities at the Castle; Henry sent for the baby Elizabeth who was two years of age, held her up in his arms and presented her to the courtiers, while Anne, pressing both hands to her belly, tried to feel the movements of the coming child, the promised son. Mary, a captive at Hunsdon Castle, wept for her mother and prepared for death.

Anne, however, divined that she was surrounded by mystery; she perceived signs of a secret joy upon the faces of her enemies. Brandon, Carew, all those against whom she was fighting, appeared to her to smile. Even Cromwell averted his eyes from hers, and her gaze dwelt thoughtfully on that round head, that long snout and those piercing eyes. She knew that he, before any other, was quick to divine his master's unexpressed desires. If Cromwell was withdrawing himself, then Henry meant to leave her.

She sent for her brother George, her advisers, her party and they told her that in Catherine's death dwelt her greatest peril. Henry, who, until then, had not dared to repudiate her for fear of thereby being compelled to revert to Catherine, was now free to divorce her and marry Jane Seymour. Anne realized that they were telling the truth and she ceased to scheme for Mary's death. On the contrary, she even attempted to conciliate her, to obtain her forgiveness. She asked Mary to return to Court and to resume her rank as a princess of the blood; she promised not to humiliate her or to make her bear her train. Her aunt, Lady Shelton, who was Mary's gaoler, transmitted the messages, but Mary refused.

Anne now had her moments of despair, but then she would remember that she carried a prince. In less than six months' time the child would be born and he would save her from the abyss. She would visualize Henry's delight, the ridiculous pride he would display. His heart would be touched and she would know how to be gentle, to stroke his brow, to assume the innocent ways of the spouse chosen of God. She would become confident, laughing in anticipation of her triumph and then, struck with fear of her own joy, would fall silent, trying not to think, inviting sleep. A spasm of happiness or of fear might prove fatal to all her hopes and leave her once more bereft of her son.

Catherine had not yet been buried, but they had quickly thrust her into her coffin. The two Spanish physicians who had attended her wished to perform an autopsy, but they were not permitted to do so. She was embalmed by one of the kitchen scullions, a man whose duty consisted in opening sheep and beeves in order to remove the suet and obtain fat for making candles. This man reported that her heart was quite black and shrivelled. Of the stomach, he had nothing to say; what knowledge had he of human stomachs?

The two Spanish physicians desired to leave England and take refuge under Charles's wing, but Henry prevented them, at first kindly: he had been so much touched by their zeal that he wished to retain them in his service to attend upon his person. One of them escaped, but was pursued and recaptured and taken to the Tower, where he vanished into the silence of a dungeon.

It was the season of the great January hunts and Henry rode through fogs and frost. Anne remained in her bedchamber, brooding her prince, her hope. On the twenty-fourth of January she was informed that Henry had fallen from his horse. She believed him killed and fainted, but he soon returned, uninjured.

He seemed to hate Anne and had again sent for Jane Seymour, compelling Anne to receive her. One day Anne opened a door and beheld the chaste Jane seated upon his knee. Anne was becoming desperate and on the twenty-ninth of January, on the very day when Catherine's body was being removed, she miscarried. Henry was uncertain whether to mourn or rejoice, but all Anne's enemies were triumphant: she was lost.

Morose Reflections.

Henry was withdrawing himself from her; he was meditating and Cromwell watched him, seeking to read his mind. One day, discreetly and as though alarmed at his own words, Henry murmured that Anne was perhaps a sorceress; that she must surely have made use of a spell to attract him. But spells can be broken; the Church has her exorcisms and those who employ magic are given over to the fire. Cromwell understood that Henry desired Anne's death.

Henry avoided simple emotions and direct thoughts and found pleasure in non-comprehension and uncertainty. In his heart he had no genuine belief in sorcery, but he pretended to believe until he almost deceived himself; or, rather, he duplicated his personality, giving himself two souls. He would imagine spells and enjoy the terror they caused him. Fears which had occasioned such vivid suffering when they had originated from some genuine cause, such as the sweating sickness, the plots of his nobility or the knife of an assassin, aroused in him a voluptuous pleasure when they were born of his self-conceived phantasies, of prodigies woven in his own mind. He would be thrifty of his thrills and try to prolong them. Alone in his chamber, or riding silently through the woods, he would evoke the recollections of his love for Anne. He would remember her laughter which had seemed to him so strange, so ambiguous. He would think of her almost as of one departed, enfolding her memory in his dreams. She had for so long remained to him almost imaginary that he seemed to have shaped her according to his own desires. Now he regretted that she had yielded herself to him; of Artemis, of the wood-nymph he had made a woman, but in the act of possessing her he had destroyed her. She was now no more than a blemished picture and perverted his memories of herself.

Scenes would recur to him which he had thought forgotten, a gesture which had not formerly struck him as unusual, a casual word which had now acquired a profound meaning, a meaning which he was careful to leave obscure, lest in being defined it should lose its significance. He would repeat the word to himself in an undertone, refusing to understand it, seeking in it a mystery. He would shudder but persist until his shudder was intensified and sent a chill down his huge spine. Sometimes the word would evade him; who could deny the enchantment?

Always, in her presence, he had felt himself shackled. It had been for her youth that he had so deeply desired her, but she had remained for him an inaccessible spring. For over twelve years his longing had consumed him. He had wished to feel as she did, as did those young men who had surrounded her, as did her brother George, Norris and that delightful company of lads who played with her, whom he had thought to love and of whom he had become jealous. He had tried to model his spirit on theirs and had failed. Now he was not so sure that he even desired to do so; what he desired were impossible things: to absorb their youth and carelessness into his own deep powerful life. But it was all no more than a fantastic dream, and if he wished that Anne, George or even Norris should remain for him such stuff as dreams are made of, it might be necessary to destroy their bodies.

Then his dreams would vanish and Henry's obsession would change. His heavy flesh, his senses would vibrate and the shapes that he had visualized, those vague, diaphanous forms, would become once more definite, warm and living bodies. He would hold Anne in the grasp of his coarse hands; would hear the voices of George and of Norris. They would seem to have absorbed all the substance and richness of life, would hallucinate and harry him. They were there before him, laughing and despising him. He reviewed all the humiliations which they had dared to inflict upon him and to which, in his fear of suffering, he had deliberately closed his eyes. Once more he endured the full measure of all his shame. Anne leant and whispered a few words in her brother's ear; those greatly beloved countenances would draw close to one another. They were alike, united by blood and perhaps by some other bond. Norris would appear, different, a stranger, even more cruel. Then others, all those who surrounded Anne. Mark, her favourite musician, the squires who sued for her favours, the girls who waited on her, Madge Shelton whom she had thrust into his arms. She must indeed be a fairy, since all those whom he saw around her drew from her this rich sustenance of supernatural life. All those faces, whether male or female, assumed a starry splendour; Henry was dazzled, enchanted and then wept with anguish: their bodies appeared to him to merge together . . .

In order to escape from the dreams of his solitude he would go and seek Anne in her chamber; he would move among them all, seeing them with his physical eyes, uttering casual words. Sometimes his visions would be dispersed as though at the breaking of a spell. He would look at Anne, at Norris and at George and be surprised to find them so dull, so commonplace. But a word or a smile, even the rustle of a garment would suffice to plunge him once more into his frenzy. Sometimes Mark would play on the lute or would sing. Henry had long been attached to this Mark, had kept him in personal attendance and made him a gentleman of the bedchamber. Mark's voice and his music had made the heavens bluer and the clouds more lovely. But now Henry had a horror of his voice; it stifled him, filled him with too violent desires and he would leave the room and go in search of silence.

Then Jane Seymour would be thrust upon his notice. She was quite devoid of halo or of mystery and gave no rise to dreams of any kind. She was a normal girl, without much brains or heart, entirely precise and circumscribed. She appeared insensible to scents, to the urges of springtime, to the influences of its breezes. She played correctly on the spinet and employed her needle in embroidering small, prim flowers. She had a receding chin, a mouth closed to kisses, a brow pure to excess and well-set eyes devoid of fire or passion. She was pale as though the sun had never warmed her skin, and her blood flowed peacefully in her veins. Henry knew that she would be virtuously fruitful. But could he take any pleasure in begetting a son by her, in perpetuating himself through so dreary and tepid a channel?

He tried to bring her to life and using the most customary of temptations, he offered her gold, hoping she would prove covetous and develop the fancies of a Danaë. She returned his purse: a girl of noble blood was not for sale. She entertained him with moral lectures, urging him to recall Mary to Court and to restore her to

[199]

her proper rank. She spoke like a parrot and Henry rallied her, telling her to think of the children she herself would bear him and not of that tiresome rebel. He decided to allot her apartments in the Palace and compelled Cromwell to give her his quarters. He had hopes of going up to her bedchamber at night, of amusing himself with her body, of perverting her and thus forgetting her rival. But she checkmated him: a girl of noble blood must not live alone. She brought with her one of her brothers, her sister-in-law and, in fact, installed a family party in the little lover's bower. She had chosen from among her brothers the more serious, a fellow as steady and as limited as herself. She avoided Thomas, an incorrigible philanderer who loved life and whom Henry frequently met in Anne's apartments.

March and April went by and Henry still slept beside Anne. He would listen to her sleeping, would gaze at her neck, at her long hair. He knew now that he meant to destroy her and she also understood that her death was near. She no longer even wished to be pregnant: her entire body was done with life. On the twenty-third of April Henry publicly flouted her and her clan. He refused to give George the Order of the Garter and conferred it upon Anne's enemy, Carew.

Cromwell Takes Action.

Cromwell felt that Henry wished to kill Anne and he therefore set about preparing for the murder. He formed a special judicial Court including Anne's uncle, Howard, her father, Thomas Boleyn, Brandon, five or six others and himself.

Six days elapsed and on the thirtieth of April Cromwell arrested the musician, Mark. He was taken to a house in the suburbs of London where a small squadron of torturers awaited him. There he was informed that he had been Anne's lover and that there existed proof of the fact: he denied it. The torturers approached and set about their business. Mark's flesh was sensitive, he screamed and begged for mercy. They promised to desist if he made confession. "Have you ever been the Queen's lover?" "Have pity . . ." "Seize him again—" "No, no, I was indeed the Queen's lover." "How many times?" "I don't know." "Make an effort of memory . . . was it twenty times?" "No, no." "Ten times." "No, never, not once, I lied." "Very good, give him some more." "Spare me, I implore you . . ." "Five times? Answer us——" "Well, then . . . three times." "Scrivener, write down that he has said 'three times.' And you were not the only one? There were others?" "Yes, yes—many others." "Who were they?" "I don't know." "Yes, you do know, and the greater the number the lesser was your own guilt. Who were they? Do not compel these men to proceed. Who were they? Norris?" "Yes, Norris . . ." "And Brereton?" "Yes." "And Weston?" "Yes." "And perhaps George Boleyn himself, the Queen's own brother?" "Oh, never . . ." "Yes, indeed, his own wife has denounced him. And you were a witness, were you not?" "Yes, yes, I was a witness . . ." He was left all day in the mysterious house while Cromwell bore his avowals to his master. Henry gazed at Cromwell with haggard eyes: then his visions had been true, his dreams had taken solid form. While Cromwell was speaking he watched them come to life and float before his eyes merging into one another.

The First of May.

He was at Greenwich, on the hill, and it was the lovely night of the first of May, that night which he had used to spend in the woods, delirious with the scent of the mosses and of the flowing sap. Beneath his balcony the young men went by singing, and he could hear the voices and the laughter of girls who were going to seek their lovers among the trees. His pages also were running wild in the park, shaking the branches, looking for the little tree which they would uproot in the early morning and bring back in triumph. The idyll of springtime filled the air. Henry listened to the singers; their voices were uncertain and they sang out of tune, but distance, the rustling of leaves and the sound of the flowing river turned their careless notes into heart-rending and exquisite dissonances. Henry would have liked to shed innocent tears; he felt himself to be powerful, simple and generous. He let his chamber robe fall from his shoulders and allowed the night air to bathe his limbs. Then he approached the bed where Anne was awaiting him. He was weary of dreams and weary of visions; he possessed her slender body in all simplicity. It was their last night together.

In the morning they clothed themselves in new garments of green satin and as soon as they were dressed they went to the window. There was blowing of horns and they beheld the swaying branches of the may-tree as it was borne towards them. The squires, the pages, the lackeys and the maids all were in green, down to the humblest kitchen scullion. In the gallery waited the lords and ladies of the Court and they also were newly clad in green. The walls were decorated with boughs whose young green leaves stood out against the sombre green of the tapestries. Beyond the windows were trees, and yet more trees.

There followed a great banquet and then a tournament and Henry sat in the tribune beside Anne. He had chosen George and Norris as champions, the two beings that so constantly obsessed his mind. He wished to look upon them for the last time, to be close to Anne, to merge them together. For twelve years they had been the hub of his existence. And now they made their appearance, mettlesome in the May sunshine, sparkling with youth, and Henry felt old and tired. But he told himself that already they were but half alive; a few more gambols and they would cease to be.

As soon as the celebrations were over he rose. He was going to London and he begged Anne to remain at Greenwich. "Only one more day, and she will know!" he reflected. He dared not stay near her and enjoy her panic; he dreaded her cries, her fury—a spell is quickly cast! Norris was no sorcerer, so he commanded his attendance; Anne watched them both depart.

On the way to London Henry called Norris and made him ride beside him, like a friend. Then he told him in an undertone that he had been accused of betraying his sovereign and being Anne's lover. Henry implored Norris to tell him the truth, to comprehend the torment endured by a loving husband in doubt. He appealed to the goodness of Norris's heart, giving him to understand that he would be forgiven. He let himself be carried away by his imagination, playing his part with passionate conviction. Norris listened in silence; he understood the game; the strange melodrama that must end with his death. He admitted nothing; and in London Henry had him arrested and taken to the Tower.

Henry shut himself up at Whitehall. He visualized Anne in her bedchamber at Greenwich. Towards ten o'clock at night he had her informed that Mark and Norris had been arrested. He was preparing to go to bed when his son, Richmond, came to bid him good night. Henry clasped the boy to his breast and wept. "Be happy," he told him. "I am going to have that harlot arrested; she wished to poison you, you and your sister Mary." He was left alone, still dreaming of Anne's terror. She must be realizing by now that she was lost; she must be envying the free boatmen who rowed down the Thames; she must know now that flight for her was impossible.

Anne's Arrest.

On the following day Cromwell, Howard, and all the members of the Privy Council arrived at Greenwich. They sent for Anne and informed her that the King was aware of her infidelities. She replied that she was innocent; but her uncle Howard cut her short, indignantly. At two o'clock in the afternoon she was made to enter a barge and Howard escorted her to the Tower, while the lightermen crowded the banks to watch her go by.

Kingston was still Constable of the Tower, that burly soldier whom she had formerly sent to arrest Wolsey, and he welcomed her arrival with delight. He already had within the custody of his walls, Mark, Norris and George whom Henry had caused to be seized in the Palace and who had been brought to the great prison at midday. Kingston was a firm Conservative, admired honourable behaviour and had pitied Catherine. To Mary he was devoted as to all Catholics and he hated young folk who were frivolous, disrespectful and immoral. In his view Anne was merely a prostitute, a brazen woman and possibly a witch, who, having defied the Divine laws, was now at last to reap the just punishment of her crimes.

Anne in the Tower.

Anne looked at Kingston and then at her Uncle Howard who accompanied her. Both these men desired her death. They escorted her across the drawbridge and both were thinking: 'She will never again leave this place: she will be tried, executed and buried within these walls.' She was trembling a little, but she managed to remain smiling.

She asked Kingston: "Where are you leading me; to a dungeon?" "No, madam, to the apartment that you have already occupied; that in which you slept on the eve of your coronation." She bowed her head; almost she would have preferred a secret dungeon. The apartment to which she was going held too many memories. When she entered it she saw again the glorious June morning when she had awoken so joyfully, listening for the first chime of bells. She had still hopes of influencing Henry, of being able to move him; it might suffice if she could merely contrive to see him, or if she could arrange for George to plead her cause. She enquired: "Where is my brother?" but no one troubled to reply; they preferred to leave her a prey to groundless hopes.

She was met on reaching the apartment by Kingston's wife, a lady who was the worthy partner of her husband: virtuous, respectable and a consummate hypocrite. She curtsied low but set her spies at the doors and behind the arras. Anne was allowed to retain four female attendants; and of these some betrayed her. Kingston and his wife noted down her every word, reporting them to Cromwell who in turn bore them to Henry. Nobody informed Anne of what she was accused: it was hoped to take her unawares, to confuse her and extract a confession. She was known to be imprudent and excitable to the verge of madness. She might even, out of defiance and out of contempt for Henry, accuse herself of imaginary crimes, lie and destroy herself. Feeling that she was spied upon she remembered God and ordered that the Sacred Host should be exposed in the little oratory that adjoined her bedchamber. There she would shut herself alone with her Saviour, fixing her eyes upon the protecting Presence, feeling herself surrounded by its mysterious Grace.

Then she would return to sit among her women and would talk: never had she betrayed the King. He must only be testing her and would soon recall her. She would resume her crown. When she woke in the night-time she would be astonished to find that she lay alone, surprised at not feeling the great sleeping bulk at her side, at not hearing the sound of Henry's breathing.

She would think of her sister, of her mother who, like herself, had given him their bodies and suffered the caprices of their master. She would visualize their embraces, the more horrible now for having been so trustful and so loving. She would picture Henry, almost a child at the knees of her mother Elizabeth, his young body caressed, soothed and then awakened to unsuspected mysteries. She herself knew the touch of Elizabeth's hands and had felt them upon her as a little girl; she also had been lulled to sleep upon those knees and had rested her head upon that breast with its familiar perfume. She would merge herself in thought with Elizabeth and Mary and would feel in her flesh the wounds he had inflicted upon the two of them. He had set them aside, trampled them and had given them rivals within their own household, compelling them to hate, the one her sister, the other her two daughters. And now he was about to kill her, the youngest, the only one of them to be chaste, who had kept herself from any other man. He knew this to be a fact, but he would be inexorable.

She would summon her women and stupefy herself with words, swearing that she had never been anything but faithful. She had possibly sometimes been flighty and thoughtless. Yes, Norris had at times appeared enamoured of her and one day she had said to him: "If I were to become a widow . . ." But Norris had cut her short, exclaiming: "Sooner than have such a thought I would have myself beheaded." Men in love were by no means always courageous: Percy and Wyatt had been sufficient proof of that fact.

She was attractive to men and had condescended to perceive it; but where was the woman who lacked such vanity? One day, when she was reproving Mark, her musician, he had declared that in her lay his only happiness. "I do not dare to ask that you should vouch-safe me a word; even a glance from your eyes will suffice me . . ." Bold words, perhaps, coming from a mere musician. Were those possibly the words he had confessed under torture?

Others also had thought her fair, but could anyone think that extraordinary? Brereton had told her so and so had Francis Weston. Weston, like Norris and like Henry himself, had also been in love with Madge Shelton. But Madge had never been able to keep a man. One day Anne had been speaking of her to Weston who had said: "There is a woman in this palace whom I love more than she." And she had known very well of whom he was speaking. She should, of course, have told him to be silent, but she had always delighted in making men desperate, so she had asked him: "And who can this person be?" And Weston had replied: "Yourself."

Behind the door, Kingston and his wife were listening, scandalized, raising their eyes to heaven and invoking the saintly Catherine's spirit. Then they noted down the sentences, particularly the names, and Cromwell, reading with satisfaction, would slink off to Henry. "Proof of two further lovers," he would announce, and Weston and Brereton were promptly arrested. Wyatt was also seized on the grounds of his former passion, and Cromwell added to the others Francis Bryan, a cousin of Anne's who had always opposed the Boleyns but who had a taste for politics and was in Cromwell's way. Weston, Brereton and Bryan further enriched Henry's visions, and there was also one Richard Page.

THE SWORD

Henry Away from Anne.

Henry now lived on dreams. He visited Jane Seymour and was entertained at balls and feasts. But he scarcely perceived the faces that surrounded him and the music he heard was an indefinite murmur. Since it was still May and the nights were amorous, he would have himself rowed in his barge on the river. Other barges, loaded with musicians, would follow. He would let his finger-tips trail in the water, cold as it flowed downwards to the estuary, clean and sweet like the Oxford meadows or the forests of Wales; warmer as it came from the sea at the turn of the tide, salt and heavy with the essences of unknown lives. The barges would follow the river toward the bridge; sailing vessels would go by, one could smell the odour of their keels, the barge would glide beneath the walls of the Tower. Henry would not even raise his glance; she was there, she still lived, it seemed to him that she must sense his nearness. In the dark the great bulk of the fortress appeared to rise up, to oscillate, to throb. He visualized Anne's slender neck, her strange eyes. Perhaps everything would vanish from before him: the courtiers, the musicians, the entire universe. He would bend over Anne's mouth and would fall asleep for ever. But a cool breeze would arise and he would hear the creaking in the forest of masts and rigging, the flutter of the standards on the battlements. A shiver would rouse him; he would think that he could hear her laughter. What being was she dreaming of, alone in her prison, what young and graceful body devoid of ulcer or blemish, what partner unmarred by the grossness

[209]

of age? They were all there, under lock and key. Henry in his turn began to evoke them, George and Mark and Norris and the other four. They were praying, weeping perhaps, for courage ebbs with the coming of darkness. And then, death was always a terrible thing. He alone could allow them to live, could rescue them from their anguish and restore them to the light of day. But no; he would let them perish. He loved George and he loved Norris. He also loved Anne. Mark's voice had delighted him and brought him peace. All that he most cherished upon earth was there, but he was weary of cherishing and of disillusion.

He would order his oarsmen to return to the Palace, sinking deeper into his melancholy and his loneliness. He would glide along the river, wrapped in his mantle, with closed eyes. He had called down Death upon these all too beloved beings; Death was hovering over them with extended wings. He had only to command and almost without his knowledge Death would sweep down and strike them silently and surely. Once more sounds of singing drifted to him across the water, the drunkards were being thrust from the ale-houses and came staggering down to the river banks. In their beds the women stirred from sleep and, remembering Anne, signed themselves with the cross.

Henry would again seek out Jane Seymour; he would kiss her and give her the jewels of betrothal, but his life in reality was still centred on Anne. Then he would shut himself up and sit writing verses, but remembering how she had always laughed at his poems he would tear them up or burn them. He could no longer distinguish dreams from substance and would ask himself whether he and Anne had ever had any real existence, if their life itself had not been some strange phantasy. He began to write a drama based upon their history, seeking to imagine Anne's lamentations. He would write for long stretches and then lay down his pen; this was not the manner in which she spoke. He had never really known her, she would die with her mystery unsolved. One evening when the Bishop of Carlisle entertained him to supper, Henry showed that prelate his drama.

The Five Young Men.

The judges met. On the twelfth of May Norris, Mark, Brereton and Weston faced a jury. Mark, still shuddering at the memory of the torture, pleaded guilty. Doubtless Cromwell had led him to believe that if he did so his sentence would be merciful, that he would be spared the drawing and quartering and would merely be beheaded. Norris, Brereton and Weston maintained their innocence. All four alike were condemned to death. Boleyn, Anne's father, was a member of the Court; trembling for his own neck he had actually requested that he might be among those who would judge his son and daughter.

These last were reserved for a higher tribunal. Henry was unable to endure the idea that Anne should be publicly dragged through the streets, that she should be soiled by the stares of the populace. On the fifteenth of May the judges met in the Tower and Anne appeared before them, arrogant and queenly. Cromwell accused her of adultery and incest. Witnesses deposed that she had on one occasion remained alone with her brother in her bedchamber, that George had been observed to lean across the royal bed. Howard was among the judges and Percy who had loved her. They pronounced her guilty, decreeing that she should be burned alive or beheaded, according to the King's pleasure. Howard, pallid beneath his black wig, pronounced sentence and Percy, overcome with faintness, was compelled to leave the hall. Anne walked out lightly, her long neck erect.

George was brought before them. The accusation of incest seemed absurd and there were those among the judges who thought he would be acquitted. But George knew Henry; he knew that he would not be allowed to live, and he sealed his own fate or avenged himself by a final insult. The judges alleged that he had said of the King a thing so calumnious that it could not be spoken in the judgment hall, before the populace who stood and listened at the barriers. They whispered the outrage from ear to ear, fidgeted on their chairs and appeared to suffer. "I must, however," said George, "be informed of my offence." It was written down on paper, and handed to him with every evidence of alarm. He unfolded the paper and burst out laughing: "It seems that I am accused of having said that the King was a wretched bedfellow, being impotent." The judges veiled their faces and hastened to condemn him.

The Death Agony.

On the sixteenth of May Kingston informed George, Norris and the other three that they would die on the morrow and should make their peace with God. A scaffold was erected on the green of Tower Hill, quite close to the prison, and the five were led to it. Mark repeated his confessions and his tears and was then beheaded. Brereton and Weston affirmed their innocence before kneeling in turn and placing their necks on the block. George expressed repentance for his follies and his loose life and asked for the prayers of the populace; Norris died in silence.

Anne still hoped that Henry would be merciful. He had sent Cranmer to her on the preceding day; his gentle Anglican bishop. Cranmer had explained to her mellifluously that Henry desired to divorce her, to pronounce the little Elizabeth a bastard, doubtless with a view to making young Richmond his heir. But a quiet divorce was required, by mutual consent, and Cranmer begged Anne to accede to the King's wishes. He let it be understood that she would then obtain mercy and would also be permitted to leave England. She consented to the repudiation and told her women that evening that she would go abroad and make her home at Antwerp. Cranmer had been most carefully ambiguous; he adored mental reservations and subtle diplomacy. Doubtless he had intended to convey that Henry, who could send Anne to the stake, would be content with the axe.

On the seventeenth she realized that they were killing George and her four friends. She heard the bell tolling, the voices of the crowd, their prayers. On that same day Cromwell pronounced the divorce and in the evening Kingston came to tell her that she was to die on the morrow.

She was frightened of the axe and preferred the

sword, a lighter, more romantic weapon. Her neck was so slender that a sword-stroke would easily sever it. The London executioners seemed to her too brutal and she asked that a Frenchman should kill her, the headsman from Calais. In France she had spent a happy, careless youth; at Calais, amid the chills of a cold November, Henry had so passionately loved her.

She slept little the night of the eighteenth, keeping her chaplain in the adjoining room. She rose at two o'clock in the morning, summoned the chaplain and began her prayers. The oratory was dark; the little monstrance shone between the two candles; the host within it was luminous and seemed alive. When day broke the chaplain began to say Mass. Anne approached the celebrant and received Holy Communion, swearing that she was innocent. After she had received her God she renewed her oath.

She had expected to die at nine o'clock but the executioner failed to appear. It was said that he had been delayed at the mouth of the Thames. Henry had weakened, he wished to feel that she would live one day more, one long beautiful spring day. Night fell again, she talked with her women and with Kingston and encircled her neck with her fingers. "The man with the sword will have an easy task," she jested. "What name do you suppose history will bestow on me? There have been William Long Nose, John Lackland and Robert of the Short Boots; I shall be called Anne the Headless." The nickname struck her as funny and she laughed, but her laugh no longer had the strident ring that had so moved Henry; it was resigned, almost tender.

She beheld once more the night and its stars, she

inhaled the odours of the river and from afar, blown to her across the roofs, the scent of flowering meadows. She thought of the castles she had lived in, of Hever where Wyatt had made her the lady of his sonnets and where her mother was now in tears. She had prayed so much on the previous day, had thought so constantly of death that she was no longer able to meditate; she sought for diversion in living things, in the enchantment of the hour, in the fleeting present. A sea wind arose and the new day broke with a wan grey light that seemed to chill the heart. Anne heard the cries of birds and of men. The scaffold had been ready for twenty-four hours and now Kingston brought her a score of gold pieces in a purse so that she might bestow her final largesse.

She summoned her women, for she wished to be beautiful. She made them gather her long hair into a net, drawing it far above the nape of her neck and placing upon it the pearl coiffe which she loved. She still desired to be crowned as with stars, to scintillate. She chose a wide robe of scarlet silk and a grey overdress. She had selected them as being cut low in the neck and she also removed her necklaces.

Henry was at Whitehall, but he had sent Jane Seymour to the country to the house of his friend Carew. He wished to be alone. He had ordered Cromwell to allow the London populace to surround the scaffold at the moment when Anne was to die; but he had also commanded that no foreigners be admitted and that Anne must be silent or must only speak briefly. He was haunted by the fear that she would yet find words with which to wound him for ever. Since he had spared her the fiery stake of the sorceress, she must not be allowed to cast spells.

A Fair May Morning.

Towards half-past eight o'clock Kingston went to Anne's apartment; she rose when she saw him—she was ready. Kingston informed her of the King's desire and she promised that she would speak little; her daughter and her parents were in his power and might become the victims of his vengeance. She no longer thought of him with any hatred; he had vacated her body and her heart and become a stranger. The door opened and Anne descended the stairs, followed by her four attendants.

Kingston led the way and they reached the courtyard where a very low scaffold had been erected. The populace surged forward, thrust back and hustled by the guards; only the front ranks could see anything. Anne beheld her enemies, Cromwell's round shaven poll, Brandon with his flowing beard. They had brought with them young Richmond, overgrown at seventeen, worn by premature excesses and already marked out by consumption.

The grass grew in the courtyard and Anne for the last time felt beneath her feet the innocent life of the earth; beggars knelt on either side of the way she must walk and she gave them her twenty gold pieces. Then she mounted the scaffold which was strewn with straw; the headsman and his assistants were waiting. Kingston handed over his prisoner to their charge; he was careful to observe all formalities.

Anne advanced to the balustrade and in a weak voice she spoke to the people. All countenances were turned toward her; the vast crowd seemed to swell and she felt that they had compassion for her. But it mattered little to her; her thoughts were far away in the spring meadows where, of a sudden, flowers are born.

She was thinking also of Henry; she thought him grotesque and could almost have laughed. She mocked him discreetly in a manner that escaped the comprehension of the crowd, but she knew that Henry himself would understand when his comely Richmond should ingenuously repeat her words. "I have not come here to preach to you but to die." She asked for no prayers for herself, but only for Henry, who doubtless had great need of them. "Pray earnestly to God for the King," she said. "He is kind, he is good and has been very good to me. My judges also have tried me justly and by the law I am justly condemned. I am indeed very happy to die." She saw her judges redden and felt some amusement, but she kept looking back over her shoulder. On entering the courtyard she had perceived the headsman with his two hands crossed over the hilt of his tall sword and she guessed that he now stood behind her. To her he was more living than the teeming crowd and she felt the weight of him upon the nape of her neck. From the corner of her eye, furtively, she watched him.

Her women gathered round her. She removed her pearl headdress and her dark head became visible in the sunshine; now her eyes alone continued to sparkle. She knelt down. One of her women blindfolded her with a kerchief and thus her eyes were no more seen. She laid her head upon the block, thinking that she would never again behold the day and she murmured: "Lord, have mercy on my soul." Then she heard the headsman draw nearer and pause, she knew that he had raised his sword.

It whistled through the air, she cried out: "God!" and knew no more.

The small head with its long, slender neck sprang into the air and then fell upon the straw. There was the dull sound of its falling. A gunner who was watching from the battlements shouted an order and there followed the roar of a cannon. There was only one shot and men and women fell to praying. Three years ago they had watched her ride through that courtyard on her way to her coronation to the sound of bells and cannon. Now a very narrow coffin was brought, perhaps an arrow box supplied by the archers of the Tower. In the coffin they laid the Huntress's body and carried it off to the chapel. A stone of the pavement had been pried from its socket and into the hole beneath it they thrust the coffin.

Henry, in a fever, had been straining his ears; around Whitehall the streets were deserted and the servants of the Palace held their peace. From the east came sounds that seemed to Henry overloud; that tore at the strings of his heart: could it be possible that he had delivered her over to all those eyes?—she whom he had so often grudged to the very light of day, wishing to shut himself away with her, to revel in her, and in that mystery which slumbered in her being, of which she herself was ignorant but of which he had sensed the enchantment? And now the day had come when he was defiling her, the crowd was to take its pleasure of her downfall, was to sate itself with her blood. The headsman was to touch her body and her head would roll in the straw.

The time passed so slowly and there were vast harmonies in the May morning! Henry's ears throbbed and he felt exhausted. At last he heard the long-awaited signal of the cannon. His desire was accomplished and Anne was dead.

He became conscious that he had closed his eyes. He opened them and the day appeared to him less fair; the blue of the sky itself seemed crude. Again he listened, seeking to recover those marvellous harmonies that had been his exquisite torture, but now he heard nothing but vulgar shouts. It seemed to him that his limbs were heavier and that the world had lost its beauty. He had slain the sorceress.

In order to avoid people and the reports of his judges he walked to the river bank and entered his barge. He had himself rowed to Carew's house, where Jane Seymour was awaiting his arrival. But it was not Jane Seymour that he sought; he had drunk of too heady a wine to be able to slake his thirst at her simple spring. He wanted the river, the clouds, the gentle breezes, a bird's flight across the heavens, the vast soothing light of day.

XII

THE SIMPLE PLEASURES OF DOMESTICITY

(1536—1537)

The Third Marriage.

AT forty-five years of age, when the passions begin
to diminish in violence, consolation is sought in
the charms of peacefulness and order and of all
those material possessions which one has considered
desirable. And yet, on review they seem singularly
colourless and appear even to have a foretaste of decay.
Lasciviousness having palled there is a tendency to substitute gluttony, for it is not easy to live without vices.
The palate and the tongue acquire refinement and assume
unforeseen subtleties. But these pleasures of the belly
render the circulation sluggish and lead the way to
torpor.

Henry, his heart tormented by the thought of his
blood-guilt, had at length rejoined the virtuous Jane and
had borne her off to the Palace at Hampton Court. He
had allowed her to believe that Anne was culpable and
she therefore approved the execution. She would have
approved it, however, even had she known that Anne
had been faithful to Henry. That brazen woman had
dared to seduce a married man, to thrust herself into the
place of his legal wife and to oust her from the conjugal

bed. Anne had been immoral and had therefore deserved a thousand deaths. Henry spent the evening with Jane, speaking to her tenderly but with little passion. Of passion, for the moment he was surfeited; he only desired repose and sufficient distraction to prevent his thoughts from dwelling too much on the other one. Jane kept herself surrounded by her relations and her chaperons, the guardians of her precious virginal honour. They played at quiet games. Possibly, if Henry had insisted, Jane would have consented to open her arms and to allow herself to be intimately caressed, but he contented himself with licit pleasures. It was their last evening as betrothed lovers and they might well be satisfied to enjoy its purity. Jane, for once, had put away her embroidery; she had short, plump fingers roughened at their tips by her needle—she would on occasion mislay her thimble.

When Henry felt that sleep was at hand and that he might hope to capture it without thinking too much of Anne, he rose, kissed Jane and went off to his bed. Possibly he was accompanied by a bedfellow. Sometimes he would select an esquire or a confidential servant. Or a friend. That night he may well have chosen Nicholas Carew, from whose house he had earlier fetched Jane, or perhaps he selected one of the Seymour brothers, Edward the virtuous or Thomas the philanderer. Carew and the two Seymours had been ecstatic since the moment when they had heard the cannon from the Tower. Carew had always been opposed to Anne and the two Seymours had supported the claims of their sister. They aimed at being brothers of the reigning Queen and had an eye upon Boleyn sinecures; Carew was their lifelong confidential friend. The two Seymours were barely twenty years of age and both for Henry had the charm of novelty. Edward was grave, Thomas exquisite. Carew had a long lean countenance, a weedy beard and a long nose. Henry asked himself whether he dared sleep. Sleep led to dreams and he feared to dream of a severed head, staring eyes and a mocking mouth.

He therefore spent a restless night, but consoled himself by reflecting that the following day, when night fell, he would have Jane to bear him company. That simple creature with her stolid brain and lack of imagination would banish nightmares by the mere fact of her presence. It is wise to mistrust a taste for the unreal, for poetry, for harmonies of an undue richness. It is wiser for a man to take refuge in prose. A virtuous housewife is not to be despised.

He rose while the night was still very dark. He had perhaps been dreaming, but he tried not to remember. Many rooms in the Palace were already lighted and outside he could see shadows go by through the small diamond panes of the windows. His servants and his gentlemen of the bedchamber bathed and perfumed him. They attended to his leg, bandaging his terrible ulcer and curled his sandy hair which was beginning to turn grey and was growing thin. It was a minute and voluptuous toilet and he emerged clad from head to foot in white. On his legs were marvellous stockings specially woven in Italy, but the finer the mesh of the stocking the closer it clings to the flesh and the more visible is a bandage, and so the entire Court could stare at that accursed ulcer. He had been too proud of his mighty legs and God had accordingly smitten him.

As soon as he was ready, when he was resplendent in

satin, gold and gems, from his slashed shoes to the plume in his hat, he passed into the adjacent chamber which had been prepared as an oratory. He had given the same orders as for his marriage with Anne. What was the use in making any difference? He had wedded Anne in a room at Whitehall and now he was marrying Jane in a room at Hampton Court. Whitehall was in London and Hampton Court in the country and both palaces had come to him from Wolsey; both were ancient loot and it is pleasurable to associate present happiness with the memory of past victims. He was, however, unable to be married before the two witnesses who had attended the ceremony with Anne. Norris was beginning to decompose in an unknown grave in the Tower.

Jane awaited him in sumptuous bridal robes. She did not look her best, being too pale for the white dress and the unkind light of early morning. A more subtle girl would have painted her face, but Jane's charm lay largely in her ignorance or contempt of artifice.

Henry was now twice divorced and twice a widower. Jane was a maid and there was no obstacle to their marriage. The priest said his Mass, the same that Henry attended daily. He blessed their rings and Henry put one upon his own finger and the other upon the already plump hand of Jane. With the coming of day they went forth married and began their peaceful existence.

He would not consent to her being crowned; such pomps tend to mar the simplicity of domestic life; moreover, he feared the comments of the irreverent populace. Clowns cannot be expected to appreciate subtle distinctions; they judge of princes and of the great by their own low standards and they might be surprised that their King should marry again so soon. In country districts there are demonstrations if a widower is unduly hasty in seeking consolation. They had already sniggered at the crowning of Anne. And then, in any case, these pageants were costly affairs; they could not be repeated at three-yearly intervals and Henry, usually so prodigal towards himself, was occasionally subject to attacks of avarice. Jane was too sensible to exact such expenditure and, finally, why must an archbishop intervene? Henry, Head of the Church of England, Lord of souls and Vicar of God in the Kingdom, had sufficiently anointed Jane in the bestowal of his ring.

When they had spent an idyllic week in the country he took her to London and showed her to the Court, and since it was essential that the Queen should have a crown, he chose one from among those of Catherine or of Anne. He had not given up to anyone the personal estates of his two deceased wives, but had claimed them as a thrifty family man. Such an one when he remarries has need of jewels and he even retained their dresses and mantles. Catherine, with singular ignorance of his nature, had thought herself entitled to bequeath some furs to her friends, but Henry had kept a firm hold on them and had used them for his own garments and to trim those of Jane.

The new Queen was not very brilliant at her first reception; she stuttered when she attempted to speak to the ambassadors. But far from being displeased, Henry excused her; this one at any rate had no desire to mock him. On Whit Sunday he showed her to the people, but quietly and without undue display: he escorted her, wearing her crown, to hear Mass at Westminster.

She had a well-formed body, agreeably developed with a healthy, cool skin. She lacked passion, but Henry was content without it. Does any husband of forty-five wish for burning ardour in a wife twenty years his junior? This one seemed pure but devoid of an ignorance that could only at her age have been misplaced. She showed a desire to please, a seemly responsiveness, was equally agreeable whether roused or left to her slumbers. She was as submissive as a very young girl and worshipped Henry as a god because he was her King. The days were delightful and the nights tender; he had the pleasure of being master without brutality.

She was likely to be fruitful, for her body was quiet and placid. She resembled those ewes that simply and with little suffering people the meadows with snowy lambs. But Henry, for once, lacked confidence in himself. There had been disquieting features in Anne's pregnancies and miscarriages. Had she perhaps only conceived by enchantment or by horrible unions with those five who had perished on the scaffold? It was whispered that little Elizabeth was Norris's daughter and George Boleyn had accused his King of impotence. Was he naturally afflicted or did some infection corrupt his blood? Or had he been emasculated by sorcery, by an evil spell? Had the spell been broken? Should he perhaps have burned Anne?

But he was no longer so sure that he desired a son. Any child of Jane's must remain mediocre. He would sit and stare at her shallow face; she was not of the blood of which kings are born. And in any case, even should she bear a son, how many years must elapse before he came to manhood, before he developed a soul of his own?

When he emerged from childhood Henry would be old, very old indeed, or very possibly dead. The future seemed to hold such gloomy perspectives that Henry shrank with fear, a fear he refused to entertain. What would be the use to him of this child whom he would never understand, who to him must remain a stranger? The gulf between generations can never be bridged; Anne and George had been respectively only fifteen and seventeen years his juniors, and yet never had he been able to reach them. He felt weary of desire and almost weary of life itself.

Richmond.

Why not be satisfied with his bastard, Richmond, who was already nearly a man, whom he knew and loved and who was endowed with so many gifts? Richmond was handsome, learned and brave. He read the poets, he respected Henry and loved him, and every evening he came to kiss him good night, revealing to him his candid and transparent spirit. Richmond was all that he himself would have liked to be; Richmond loved the flesh, loved life, but was pure of all stain. In the beautiful eyes of this Knight of Faery, this Prince of Romance, dwelt all the melancholy of the love-child, of the bastard, of the unwanted, neglected child reared among strangers. Henry had for many years never given him a thought; his mother, Bessie Blount, was nothing but a loose woman. She was always gay and slightly eccentric and had kept the prestige of having been the King's mistress. Of this she made full use and, being widowed of her prolific Taillebois, had refused Lord Grey, the King's cousin, whom she considered too old and too stingy. She had married one of the richest and handsomest young men of the Court, Lord Clinton, who was eighteen years her junior, and in Clinton's arms she forgot Richmond.

Henry now loved Richmond with all the love that he had so long denied him, the more so that he knew him to be ill and feared to see him die. In the evenings Richmond shivered with fever; in the mornings he was flushed and his eyes were too bright. Henry recognized the curse of his race, that of which his brother Arthur and his father, Henry VII, had perished, the ill that stalks in fog-bound countries. He dared not send him to be governor of Wales. Richmond had spent one year in France, the climate of Paris seeming fine and dry to Londoners; but he had lived there too precociously, indulging his passions. In winter he was sent away to the South, to the Channel coast where the sun sometimes shines and where the air is warmed by currents from the Gulf Stream. He should have remained chaste, but as a matter of policy the little Howard had been put into his bed and absorbed his strength while he waned upon her childish bosom.

But Henry hoped on and prayed earnestly to God, refusing to believe that the boy could slip through his fingers. He felt that he could chain him to life by loading him with gifts and making him rich. He would say to him: "Do not leave me; I will give you England."

He might very well be appointed heir to the throne. Mary and the little Elizabeth had lost their rights and legally were not less bastards than he, and he, moreover, was a male. And in any case why should not a bastard inherit? William the Conqueror, a bastard, had made

England, and from that bastard the English kings held their throne.

Mary, however, was a determined obstacle. With the death of Anne she had thought herself saved and all her rights re-established. She wrote to Cromwell asking him to intervene. Henry refused to see her, left her at Hunsdon Castle, but he sent her his blessing. He judged it excessive to put her to death, but he wished her to acknowledge her illegitimacy and to yield precedence to Richmond. Howard offered to go and see her, to use every endeavour: the old schemer was confident that he could impose reason upon a helpless little prisoner of twenty years old.

He took two bishops with him and departed for Hunsdon Castle, but Mary resisted all persuasion. She was the King's humble slave but also the servant of God, and God had made her legally a princess of England. Howard insisted and then lost his temper, violently shaking his battered, wrinkled old head. Mary, puny but vibrant, glared at him with her piercing eyes. "If you were my daughter," the old man declared, "I would knock your head against the wall!" She was not his daughter but his future Queen, and was not in the least afraid of his anger. She was well aware of the vileness of his soul; that he slept with servants, with a kitchen wench, that he would summon this drab to torture his wife, and that the pair of them would tread her underfoot, crushing her breast until she spat blood, and then disseminating the rumour that she was crazy.

Howard foamed with rage and threatened. But Mary repeated that she would swear nothing. They could get rid of her secretly and shamefully by poison, as they had disposed of her mother. She was ready. The old murderer had to retreat with his bishops; he returned to London and urged the King to kill her.

It was easy. Anne's trial and execution furnished a convenient precedent; there was nothing to prevent a tribunal from condemning Mary as a traitor and sending her to the scaffold. Howard would have relished so energetic a measure, but Henry hesitated, and Cromwell offered to arrange matters more mercifully. He began by depriving the princess of all rights to the succession; the Lords and the Commons, skilfully coached, declared that Henry was absolute master of his throne, as concerned both the present and its future disposal, and was free to appoint his own successor. Then Cromwell informed Mary of the risk she ran, letting her know that the axe awaited her. Martyrdom, to Mary, would not have been unwelcome, but the Emperor Charles, who had been told how matters stood, advised her to obey, or to feign obedience. An act extracted by force was not binding before God, and the Church had always admitted of mental reservations. Mary must live in order, some day, to save England and bring her back to the true Church. For a long time Mary hesitated, then, one night, she made her decision and signed an act of complete submission which had been drawn up and sent to her by Cromwell. Henry and Jane then visited her and embraced her and Jane made her a present of a ring.

It only remained to make Richmond Prince of Wales, but in the meantime Richmond was dying. Henry had doubtless acted unwisely in sending him on the nineteenth of May to the Tower to be present at Anne's execution. He should have preserved the lad from her terrible eyes.

Richmond dwelt on the horror of that comely severed head, he could not sleep at night and began to spit blood. Nothing checked his illness, neither the warm June sunshine, the scent of the new-mown hay nor the hope of being King. Life seemed to him too vile, too different from the poets' dreams, and he let it fall from his hands.

The shade of Anne must be haunting Richmond, who was Henry purified, the son she might have borne. She was drawing vampire sustenance from his youthful blood and in him finding consolation for the loss of Norris and George. She was throttling him with her slender hands and on the twenty-second of July he died. Anne had taken him to her kingdom, perhaps to dark enjoyments, and Henry once more repented that he had not burned the sorceress. He would now have inhaled with sadistic pleasure the odour of her roasting flesh.

Howard in Disgrace.

Jane cradled Henry in her arms. Why must he weep? Could not she conceive a child? Henry dared not refuse to assist her to this end and found it an excellent distraction from tears, an admirable antidote for dreams. The body, when tired, falls more easily asleep and enjoys a deeper repose. But there was certainly nothing seductive about Jane; daily she appeared to him to grow plainer. He cast an eye upon the various new attendants whom she had assembled as maids of honour to provide her with a regal escort. They all struck him as more lively than Jane, gayer and less insipid, and he began to murmur to his friends: "I remarried too hastily. I should have waited and made my choice . . ." But these regrets did not prevent his nocturnal exercises; he would blow out the candle, close his eyes and muster his memories.

He vented his fits of ill humour upon his friends. Howard in particular exasperated him: he now blamed him for having persuaded him to kill Anne, for having dared to sentence her, he, her uncle, who should have been her defender. Poor Anne had indeed met with nothing but ingratitude! Howard also had been the one to thrust Richmond into his arms and was therefore guilty of his present distress and melancholy. What had been the use of making him love Richmond? Howard must have been well aware that the boy's health was precarious. He might have remained far from Henry's eyes and then his death would have been unmourned. Henry felt that Howard never failed to cause him suffering. And why should Richmond have been so early married? His precocious matrimony had worn him out. And that law which the Lords and Commons had voted giving the King the right to appoint his successor: what was the use to him now of such a law? Whom could he appoint? Where could he find an heir? These people were making him ridiculous.

Howard, with his knotty hands and his wrinkled old murderer's countenance, was creeping altogether too near to the throne. He was undeniably fifteen years Henry's senior, but he was sound of wind and limb and probably had every intention of seeing Henry buried. He knew the King's ailments and all about the ulcer; he had learned a great deal in the days when he had fawned on Anne and had skulked in the shady corners of her bedchamber. He was doubtless aiming at being one day prime minister to some infant king, Regent or Lord Protector. Nothing humbled him: one of his brothers, a man still young and handsome, had recently eloped with and married one of Henry's nieces, who, some people regarded as heiress to the throne. Henry had promptly arrested the ambitious bridegroom and had flung him into a dungeon in the Tower, where he had been left to die of boredom far from his princess. Henry accused Howard of having buried Richmond stingily and begged him to retire to one of his castles, to vanish.

He could, of course, have had him beheaded, but felt that it would be an excessive remedy for his transient mood of boredom. Howard was possessed of great talents which might yet prove useful. He alone in England knew how to command an army. For forty years he had held the Northern frontier, beating the Scots a half-dozen times, easily drubbing those kilted barbarians. And Henry was uneasy on the score of Scotland, his nephew, James V, being on too good terms with the Pope and with France. James might declare himself the legitimate heir to England and in the name of the Catholic Faith invade the Kingdom and tumble Henry from his throne. It was therefore wise to save Howard against a possible rainy day, for Henry, fearful of battles, had need of a captain. Finally, it required considerable energy to execute a man of Howard's calibre, and Henry felt very tired indeed. He sought to tone himself up by eating enormously, but all that he swallowed turned to fat. He began to despair of the future and of himself, and in October he told his friends that he felt certain that he would never beget an heir. He lived a constant prey

to accesses of vague melancholy. And so he permitted
Howard to live.

The Pilgrimage of Grace.

Henry, however, was not given time to remain bored.
Fate intervened to arouse in him a passion that always
retained its pristine vigour: that of fear. One night in
October, as he lay beside Jane, gloomily making the best
of her virtuous embraces, he heard the sounds of an
approaching multitude; whereupon a servant entered
his bedchamber announcing a messenger who begged the
King for an immediate audience. Henry ordered that he
should be admitted, and the man flung himself into the
room and fell upon his knees, breathless and sweating.
Henry, with his hair standing on end, thrust his head from
between the bed-curtains and listened to the stammering
report. He gathered at length that the men of Lincoln
were in revolt, demanding the re-establishment of the
Roman Catholic Faith. They intended no personal harm
to the King and only desired to throw themselves at his
feet. But Henry mistrusted these respectful rebels; he
knew too well whither such prostrations can lead.
Jumping out of bed, he summoned his Council.

Cromwell was not gratified. He sunk his long nose
into his triple chins, and looked sideways. This Lincolnshire revolt had been provoked by his policy. For nearly
a year, in order to please Henry, fill the royal coffers and
line his own pockets, Cromwell had been waging war on
the monks, suppressing their monasteries and annexing
their lands. All in the name of morality and the glory of

[233]

God, of course. Commissioners, of his appointing, travelled from monastery to monastery, prying into the life of the monks, investigating. A skilful police officer can always produce criminals when they are useful to the minister employing him. Cromwell's men discovered in the monasteries every one of the seven deadly sins: pride, covetousness, lust, gluttony, envy, sloth and anger, and in so far as concerned the horrible sin of lust, they discovered in addition manifold variations. According to them nuns bore children, monks seduced their penitents or indulged in culpable practices among themselves: Cromwell's myrmidons blushed to their very eyes when making their reports of these alleged infamies.

Cromwell suppressed three hundred small convents and nobody would have grumbled, with the exception of the religious, had he conferred a portion of the spoils on the laity. The nobles had reckoned on acquiring lands, the peasants had expected a reduction of their rents. But the King kept the lands and increased the rents, and the beggars who had been fed by the monks were in yet worse case. When they came to fetch their food they found the doors closed against them and the officials of the government belaboured them and threatened to hang them from trees. Thereupon nobles, peasants and beggars immediately revealed an ardent devotion to the monks and the Faith. The lion having claimed a monopoly of the prey, the disappointed wolves and jackals rebelled.

The monks preached a crusade as Christian martyrs. Cromwell offered them pensions, but they disdained to accept them. The simple populace began to murmur and it was again rumoured that the Virgins of the great sanctuaries were weeping. The monks talked of Henry's arrogance and of the outrage to the Holy Father, and they carried banners bearing the effigy of Christ bleeding from the Five Wounds. The Lincolnshire peasants followed them like sheep; most of them were ignorant of their destination. They were going on pilgrimage and thought to gain paradise. Behind them was the secret support of the nobles and they numbered in all some twelve or fifteen thousand. There was talk of marching on London and demanding Cromwell's head.

Henry indeed would willingly have given it to them, but that Cromwell knew the art of replenishing the treasury. Also, Henry felt that if once he weakened and gave way to these clericals and their vile horde of supporters, if once he allowed his fear to be suspected, his nobles would all emerge from their lairs, would march upon him, realize their former project and, killing him, would elect Mary as Queen. He therefore raised an army in the South, in the civilized counties on the Channel coast, finding recruits who recked little of religion and who were fully prepared to tackle the clergy. He gave the command of them to Brandon, a stupid general but one who had no fear of hard knocks. Cromwell, the former soldier, might have been a better tactician, but in a war no noble would have followed this plebeian's son.

After Lincolnshire the wild North rebelled and Yorkshire and Lancashire raised the standard of the Five Wounds. A few bishops and several nobles joined them, together with Wolsey's old enemies and those who supported Mary and Charles. But the affair was half-hearted, the result little more than a rabble.

Brandon muddled along helplessly with his raw forces

and Henry was soon compelled to recall Howard, promising him vast Church lands and assuring him of his friendship. Howard quickly forgot his transient disgrace; he was anxious to divert himself at the expense of the tumultuous army of pilgrims; he eagerly and joyfully scented blood. But the poor wretches might give him trouble, and it would be wise to begin by allowing them to exhaust themselves. He himself had no longer the vigour of his youth and he now preferred cunning to force, was veering towards the tiger or the cat. Henry, prompted by him, made an offer of peace, or at any rate of an armistice, but his terms were too excessive. He demanded that they should hand over ten ringleaders and the pilgrims had no intention of handing over anyone at all. They for their part exacted the dismissal of Cromwell and of all the anti-papist bishops. They even mentioned Mary's claims; they still felt themselves to be strong and they behaved accordingly. Henry feigned extreme benevolence, assuming the demeanour of a tender parent and they proved themselves sufficiently foolish to believe him. The whole affair seemed ended in mutual embraces and they returned to their homes.

But Henry meant to have his revenge and he was egged on by Cromwell and Cranmer. Howard was training his army and in February it was ready for the fray. During the four winter months the pilgrims had almost all dispersed, but perceiving that Howard was on the point of striking, their leaders, the monks and nobles, recalled them. Some of them obeyed, but in a disorderly multitude, and Howard fell upon them, harassing them, outmanoeuvring them and reducing them to panic. They flung down their holy standards and fled, and Howard captured some two hundred of them, whom he hanged, drew and quartered. There were executions in every county of England and every Northern town had its share of the holocaust. The pick of the prisoners were taken to London to provide entertainment for the cockneys of Westminster and Saint Paul's. These were dispatched at Tyburn. One pious lady of high birth was burned at Smithfield. Two nobles who had been prominent leaders were sent North and exhibited to the peasants throughout their journey. One was killed at Hull, the other at York, and their corpses were left to rot on the ramparts. Cromwell was then able to resume his pillage of the convents.

The Pregnancy of Queen Jane.

Spring was once more at hand, a green English spring, of sudden showers, blue skies and fleecy clouds, and Henry had emerged from his melancholy. Fear, followed by the desire for revenge, had given him back the joy of living. His imagination had had play; he had visualized himself as conquered, pursued, assassinated, and such nightmares, when they are not realized, restore to the body all its pristine vigour. Even Jane seemed more attractive; she smiled and, if phlegmatic, was alive, and the ghost of Anne, wreathed in horror, was gradually fading. The presence of death stimulates desire; blindly, the man who feels threatened seeks to perpetuate his life, to infuse it into a new creation. As March approached Henry, in the midst of massacres, learned that he was again about to become a father. The miracle dated from those terrible days in January, from the time when, with the aid of Cromwell and of Howard, he had been weaving his schemes and nervously baiting his traps. His nights had now proved to be as productive as his days: he had conferred fruitfulness upon Jane's body; he had once more sowed his seed. He caused his triumph to be proclaimed from the housetops; every bell in the kingdom was pealed. Jane's tired face filled him with tenderness and he took pleasure in her pregnant fancies. He also took pleasure in the barbarous executions, in the fear of all his subjects, in the coming of the spring sunshine and in his sensation of renewed youth. He had many intense gratifications and he felt himself light of heart.

The King's Catechism.

The monks hid themselves, and Cromwell sent forth new Commissioners, methodically pursuing his policy of pillage. Gold poured in to provide magnificence, to pay for games, tournaments and masquerades. By the coming of May and the anniversary of Anne's death, all the small convents had been stripped and Cromwell turned his attention to the big ones. He silenced some of the more influential abbots by threatening them with axe and rope or by offering them a share of the spoils. The alternation of these procedures met with a certain measure of success. A few of the more powerful religious yielded to their sovereign's orders and resigned themselves to devouring their own flocks. Monks and nuns were thrust forth into the world, nor did all of them repine; the life

[238]

of the world has certain attractions when one possesses the means of livelihood, and since they had only yielded to compulsion Heaven could hardly hold them responsible.

On the Continent Charles and Francis continued their wars, while Henry looked on and enjoyed tranquillity. Pope Paul III thundered and threatened, but nobody even troubled to listen to him: the secular princes were otherwise fully engaged. He had summoned to his side Reginald Pole, Henry's cousin, who had formerly been his ward. The Pope made him a Cardinal and Pole did his best, intriguing, protesting, seeking to influence the princes. He also wrote books in which he attacked Henry, labelling him tyrant and antichrist. Henry replied to this, book for book. He was also engaged in preparing for England the articles of her new religion: ten articles to which Englishmen must swear belief under pain of being burned at the stake. Henry sought for persuasive arguments that would win souls; he desired, so far as was possible, to avoid the death of the sinner. He would shut himself in his closet and there indulge in meditation, resting his ulcerous leg after the activities of the chase. His ideas lacked boldness; he feared the innovations of Luther and of the other too ardent reformers who dared to doubt everything and who, after striking at the altar, might possibly end by aiming at the throne. Henry clung to the seven sacraments while recognizing the Eucharist, baptism and penance as more important than the four others. On the other hand, he was determined to abolish purgatory, which was proving a stumbling-block to Cromwell's confiscations. If the monasteries and convents had received so many gifts and so many dying bequests, it was in order that they might pray for the souls of the donors, draw them out of the fire and hoist them up to paradise. But if it were possible to demonstrate by argument that such souls were safe in heaven and subject to no penance, then the prayers of the religious would become superfluous. They would cease to pray or to need payment for praying, and the properties bestowed could revert to the King. Let nobody suggest their being returned to the donor's descendants; such an operation would be far too complicated! Henry dreamed of these properties, pored over Cromwell's ledgers and evolved pregnant arguments.

The Kingdom has an Heir.

August and then September found him still engaged in this noble employment. Jane now had renounced all exercise; she lay dreaming, absorbing sunshine and shadow while ripples of happiness passed across her countenance. Henry would stroke her hair and impatiently await the night when he would lie at her side, laying his hand upon her and feeling the movements of his child in her womb. He marvelled at the tranquillity of this woman's pregnancy. Neither Catherine nor Anne had ever contrived to give him these placid aspirations, had ever allowed him such fulfilling peace. Jane seemed to partake of the autumn and of the ripening of the fruits of the earth. On the trees, on the trellises, apples and pears were beginning to weigh down the branches and Jane's breasts were also growing heavy. Henry sought for dainties to offer her, sending to France for rare delicacies: strawberries artificially forced out of season, and cunningly flavoured

quails. He made no attempt to consult the astrologers;
the year appeared to him so auspicious that he was sure
of having a son. All passions seemed appeased, all storms
and all suffering. He savoured his happiness almost
without thinking about it, as a thing that was his due and
that nothing could take from him. At length came the
moment when the fruits fell from the trees; the dull
sound of their fall to the ground could be heard and the
rustle of dry leaves detached by their falling. Jane felt
that her time was hard upon her and the child was born
in the dead of night, making her joy and Henry's more
intimate. Henry supported his wife in his arms; one of
her women told him: "Your Grace has a son," and Henry
almost wept. The Lord had been merciful. The light
of the candles flickered on Jane's pale face and she fell
back weakly; she seemed utterly despoiled. The child
wailed as they washed it and presently Henry took it
naked in his arms; he was astonished to find it so frail
and so light. All the future of England depended upon
its tiny body. Henry was overcome by a sudden sadness;
to himself he seemed as pale and as weak as Jane, his
part upon the world's stage seemed played out; he felt
a faint premonition of death.

Henry   Bereaved.

Life appeared to have automatically fallen into pleasant
lines: Henry was to enjoy all the happiness and peace of
bourgeois domesticity. He was to divide his time
between Jane and the baby, listening to the rocker's
lullabies and enquiring minutely after the infant's

digestion. Jane would supervise the kitchens, their diet would be palatable but plain, and Mary also would have her place at their table. Mary was now twenty-one years old and the birth of a prince had obliterated her political importance. Her cheeks were becoming greyer and her eyes more penetrating; one felt her to be weighed down with medals and scapulars. She was doubtless destined to become an old maid or might possibly be dispatched with a small dowry to some German princeling. She would sit embroidering beside her young stepmother, now no longer either complaining or conspiring. A reliable person was bringing up little Elizabeth. Henry was sometimes stingy in the matter of gowns and wearing apparel; but there must of course be economy, even in a palace. His days would pass very agreeably: a few quiet rides, the ulcer on his leg being carefully wadded, a little dicing with his equerries, a little music and theology and two or three hours of discussing business and giving orders to Cromwell; regular meals, a comfortable bed, Jane's body, not over-lively but soft and plump; virtuous pleasures.

Henry evolved this scheme of existence as he paced the avenues of Hampton Court. He no longer thought of the past, neither of Catherine nor of Anne; being now happy and favoured by Heaven, he believed himself to be the soul of kindness. He would pause near the apartments assigned to his son and listen blissfully to that infant's cries. Three days after his birth he had him pompously baptized, naming him Edward after his merry grandfather, who had been so beloved of women. Several times a day Henry went upstairs to visit Jane: he was the most attentive of husbands.

This wholesome felicity lasted for a week, but on the eighth day Jane fell ill. She had insisted on leaving her bed and had caught cold; it was also said that she had eaten too abundantly, the greediness and the fancies of her pregnancy having persisted. She was feverish and being terrified of death her fear lowered her resistance. After a couple of days of uncertainty she died. When he beheld her cold, insensible body and realized that never again would he see her smile, Henry decided that he had loved her deeply and asked himself whether he would be able to survive her.

XIII

FROM SHADOWS TO REALITY

(1537—1540)

A Diminishing Sorrow.

HE wept a great deal, for this was the first occasion upon which death had dared to strike him in his partners. Of Jane's five predecessors not one had ever been ill. Bessie Blount and Mary Boleyn had been splendidly healthy; Catherine and Anne had only died with his assistance, and Elizabeth Boleyn had flourished until lately, when she had died of the shock of her children's execution. But Henry could feel no regrets for Elizabeth, for was not her very death a treasonable criticism, implying an unjustifiable sympathy for her offspring? Thomas Boleyn, for his part, had shown more tact; he was ensconced at Court, hoping for further preferment.

Why should Heaven, in giving Henry a son, temper its favours by depriving him of his wife? What could be the meaning of such qualified generosity? Had Jane perhaps been too lowly to endure her glory; had she died of being Queen, of giving an heir to England? She had drained her cup of happiness at a draught: certain princesses of legend, Danaë, Semele, had perished of being the chosen of Zeus, of bearing in their wombs the seed of the gods . . .

To assist and console him Henry had two particularly tender individuals: Cromwell the adventurer and Howard the assassin, both of whom advised him to lift up his heart. England had need of him and could not afford to lose so good a master; therefore why wear himself out weeping beside a coffin? They persuaded him to leave Hampton Court and return with them to London, to Whitehall. The Princess Mary undertook to remain near Jane's body and there to fulfil the regulation three weeks of prayer. She took pleasure in religious ceremonies and in solemn mourning, and she assumed such grave family duties as one to the manner born.

Whitehall was a cheerful palace, Wolsey's suave creation, and, moreover, for Henry it housed romance, since it was at Whitehall, in an attic, that he had been secretly married to Anne. He wept for a few days longer, then fell to dreaming and evoking memories. Then, since he found these memories painful, he determined to distract his mind and think of the future.

He might have taken a mistress, but he did not feel adventurous, the days of the three Boleyns were past and gone, and he had acquired a crop of habits and moral convictions. But to live alone seemed to him out of the question; the gentle Jane, without his realizing it, had filled an immense place in his life and he felt himself fated to remarry and utterly incapable of a bachelor existence.

Mary of Guise.

It did not strike him to select an English woman again, a girl of modest rank whom he would raise by marriage to his own level. Misalliance is generally the outcome of passion and being devoid of any violent desires his thoughts automatically turned toward a princess. In spite of his mourning for her he remembered Jane's insipidity and certain of her limitations, and it seemed to him that a French woman was likely to give him more satisfaction. It had been the atmosphere of Paris that had pleased him in Anne and even in Mary Boleyn. In the event of the new bride proving frivolous he would be very well able to put her in her place.

Cromwell therefore began to make enquiries. Francis I still had an unmarried daughter, but as she was only fourteen years of age Henry might be considered slightly paunchy for her. Moreover, France was mistrustful of the English climate. A French princess who had married James V of Scotland had died of consumption within three months of her landing. Cromwell would be compelled to look a little lower.

He thought of Mary of Guise, the pretty widow of the Duc de Longueville. The Guises were not of royal blood but merely cadets of the family of the sovereign Dukes of Longueville. They were poor and very numerous and lived on the King's favour, but they were possessed of irresistible charm. They won both battles and hearts. Violent, acquisitive, passionate, adventurous, tragic and seductive, tampering a little with sorcery, the Guises were the Boleyns, more refined, more powerful and more capable. Henry had pleasurable thoughts of this Mary of Guise. His taste for the unknown began to stir, his nostalgia for the indeterminate. He knew her to be betrothed to his nephew the insolent James V. The King of Scotland got on his nerves, because of his comparative youth, of his predilection for Catholic priests, of his mistresses, and his bastards. This James, having once seen Mary of Guise, had fallen in love with her and had for her sake thrown over another betrothal. Henry would have felt it an achievement to rob him of his prospective bride.

An unmarried girl would perhaps have accepted Henry, but Mary, being a widow, knew the advantages of a husband thirty years of age. James offered romance and Henry represented boredom. He might be jovial, but he was also bulky and of tainted blood; he was a skilled musician but disdained frivolous ballads, and his prudence in the battlefield was well known to be excessive. Henry was not likely to appeal to the French, his only prestige being of a grim description. Mary of Guise had no wish to be the protagonist in a new tragedy and she gave her preference to James.

Francis, with a view to consoling Henry, thereupon suggested a Bourbon princess; but Henry ascertained that James had refused her and that he was being offered James's leavings, so he threatened an alliance with Charles that should wreck France. James V, however, retained his Mary.

Christina of Denmark.

At Brussels, in Charles's household, lived a little widow who, it was thought, might console Henry. Her name was Christina and she was the daughter of the Emperor's sister and of the King of Denmark, Christian II. Her mother was dead and her father held a prisoner upon

an island in the Baltic Sea. This Christian II was said to
be mad. He had been brought up to extreme democracy,
having been sent to board with a bookbinder in Copen-
hagen; and there he had acquired a hatred for the
aristocracy, whom he had proceeded to treat with a very
high hand. In the course of a single morning he had had
ninety-four Swedish nobles beheaded, and even then had
considered his executioners too dilatory. The nobility
had turned him out and had given the kingdom to his
uncle. When he reappeared he was arrested for high
treason and imprisoned in a tower from which he could
barely perceive the daylight. He was given a dwarf for
company.

Charles had supervised Christina's education and she
had already once served his political turn. At fourteen
years of age she had been thrust into the bed of the last
of the Milan Sforzas who was known to be dying, and in
exchange for his bride the Sforza duke had, at his death,
some six months later, bequeathed his duchy to the
Emperor Charles. Christina had put on a black dress and
had returned to Brussels. But Henry had no opinion of
the handsomeness of Charles's relations, while Catherine's
looks were an unpleasant memory. This Christina, who
was Catherine's great niece, might easily have the misfortune to resemble her. On the other hand, he felt it to
be salacious to sample the same blood twice while skipping
a generation, and he found in this case an agreeable
parallel to the demi-incestuous mixtures he had indulged
in with the Boleyns. But he made it a condition that this
girl should be pretty. His ambassador wrote assuring him
that she was charming, that her skin might be thought
less white than that of Queen Jane, but that she resembled

Madge Shelton, that accommodating cousin with whom Anne had so obligingly provided Henry. Christina was tall but plump; she had a gay smile and three dimples, one in each cheek and one in her chin. Henry was unable to see for himself and he felt mistrustful of the ambassador's description. He therefore sought for a more competent expert and remembered Wyatt, who must be supposed to share his tastes, since he also had loved Anne Boleyn. Henry had secret hopes that Christina might remind him of Anne, and he also hoped that Wyatt would suspect these hopes and would tell him whether Christina resembled the sorceress.

But when Henry's name was mentioned to her Christina pouted. She was of a lively disposition and very determined and wished to be allowed to make her own choice. In any case, she said, she had no liking for Blue Beards. This King Henry was altogether too fond of beheading. "If I had a head to spare," said she, "I might accept him." But she hastened to add that in all respects she was the humble servant of her Uncle Charles.

She was well aware that Charles had no wish to hand her over, and in the spring it began to be rumoured that Charles and Francis were drawing together and that Pope Paul III was urging their reconciliation, perhaps with a view to launching them against England. Both of them were shocked by Henry's anticlericalism.

Henry, Scourge of the Saints.

Henry's commissioners were burning miraculous statues, bursting open shrines and throwing the bones

[249]

of saints to the four winds, while Cromwell and Cranmer were whipping on the pack. Celebrated Virgins were smashed to pieces and they also destroyed the Blood of Christ which the priests preserved at Hales in a phial cut from a single beryl, the sacred candle lighted by Our Blessèd Lady Herself at Walsingham and the great crucifix at Boxley that had moved Its eyes and bowed Its head. The Prior of the Observantists at Greenwich, hung by chains above the flaming pyre, was harangued until he died, by Protestant bishops. They used as fuel to burn him alive a miraculous Madonna from a shrine in Wales. Such 'sports' as these served to while away the spring.

In August Henry was still hoping to marry Christina; Holbein had sent him her portrait, which he greatly admired. Her face was a long oval, her eyes slanting, and she had the grace that sometimes comes of the mingling of many races. Her fingers were slender, she was very young and seemed thoughtful, melancholy, perhaps voluptuous. The face appeared reserved, enamoured of delicate harmonies or of silence. Henry kept the portrait near him, Christina looked down upon him from the wall and her shade began to obliterate those earlier shades, for, as always, his imagination sought shadowy company. But this new apparition brought him soothing hopes; she would descend one day from her frame to his arms. He sent a Catholic as his messenger to Christina, his new representative, Risley or Wriothesley, but at home he continued to scandalize the saints.

The leader of the Catholic party was Cardinal Reginald Pole, the young theologian whom Henry had trained. Under the protection of Paul III, Reginald was now rousing Europe against him, urging Charles, Francis and James V of Scotland to invade England. Pole's mother and his two brothers had remained in the Kingdom and in August Henry sent the youngest brother, Geoffrey, to the Tower. For two months nothing more was heard of him; Cromwell was harrying his soul and the torturers his body. In the end he confessed to the existence of a plot and that his mother and his brother were in communication with Reginald, with a view to placing Exeter, Henry's cousin, upon the throne. In November Exeter and his wife, with Geoffrey's elder brother, were in their turn sent to the Tower, while their mother was confined to the precincts of a castle. These events supplied autumn excitement and Henry temporarily forgot about Christina.

It was now a year since Jane Seymour's death; Henry lived alone, a tolerably pleasant existence. He had no lack of agreeable mistresses. In October he discovered another amusement: he disinterred and burned the bones of Thomas à Becket, England's most venerated saint. Henry was unable to forgive the fact that Becket had once defied Henry II. He instituted legal proceedings against him and had him condemned as a papist and a traitor. For a period of three hundred and sixty-five years Europe had loaded Becket's tomb with offerings; the shrine in which he lay was encrusted with gems and Henry annexed the spoils, which filled seven coffers.

There was wailing from all the Catholics of Europe; from all those whose gifts had thus been seized. A King might have a perfect right to burn the living, but only a son of Satan could dare to rifle the sepulchres of the Saints.

For Love of the Sacred Host.

Henry wished to reassure the Catholics and in November he staged an imposing performance with a view to emphasizing his orthodoxy. He had been informed that an individual named Lambert had the temerity to deny the Real Presence in the Sacred Host, and he thereupon announced that he would debate publicly with this heretic and reduce him to silence. On the sixth of November the nobles gathered in the great chamber at Whitehall. Twelve solemn dignitaries, headed by Cranmer, formed the tribunal. Henry made his appearance, dressed all in white, obese and magnificent. Having seated himself upon the throne, he had Lambert brought before him and questioned him personally. Lambert, paralysed with terror, stammered and trembled while Henry reminded him that at the Last Supper Christ Himself had said, when blessing the bread, "This is my Body." Henry then left the discussion to the bishops and Cranmer spoke, followed by nine other prelates. The short November day began to fade, torches were lighted and still the bishops declaimed. Finally they exhausted their arguments.

"And now, Lambert," enquired Henry. "Are you convinced?"

Lambert remained silent.

"Choose for yourself. Do you desire to live or to die?"

Henry inflated his chest within the vast white doublet shaded by his red beard. He bent towards the trembling man; his eyes, sunk between rolls of fat, were narrowed.

The man, suspecting a cruel subterfuge, dared not reply.

"I place myself entirely in your Grace's hands," he finally murmured. "It is to God's hands and not to mine that you must entrust your soul." "I entrust my soul to God and my body to your Grace's clemency." "You deliver yourself to me? Well, then, you shall die; I am not in the habit of protecting heretics."

The tribunal consulted and put the question to the vote; then Cromwell rose and read aloud the sentence. Four days later Lambert was burned alive at Smithfield.

But within a fortnight Henry struck at the Catholic leaders. The Marquis of Exeter, his first cousin the eldest of the Pole brothers, and one of their friends were condemned to death and beheaded. A pardon was extended to the youngest Pole, Geoffrey, who, torn asunder by the torturers, had betrayed his own party. Exeter had formerly insulted Cromwell.

A little later Henry made a public announcement that, save for Papal Obedience, he remained a Catholic. He summoned together the principal bishops and imposed upon them a dogma of six articles which he himself had drawn up. In them he declared that Christ was in the bread and the wine; that the laity did not require to communicate in the two kinds; that any married priest must repudiate his wife and must observe the vow of chastity; that the faithful could have Masses said for their private intentions and that the sacrament of penance was maintained. Any person speaking against the Eucharist would be burned, while those violating the other five articles would be imprisoned.

Cranmer, dismayed, offered desperate opposition. The

interdict on the marriage of priests touched him closely, for his nights were still beguiled by the blond girl from Nuremberg. She was the sunshine of his existence, or rather the comforting domestic fire of his hearth to which he turned for repose from the flames of the stake and the odour of grilling flesh. Whenever Cranmer felt nauseated by his own vileness and cringing, he would find consolation in this faithful creature. He tried hard to persuade Henry that a holy bishop cannot be expected to live without the solace of a woman, but Henry, who held the key to the mystery and who was himself for the moment sleeping alone, allowed himself the pleasure of listening and arguing, of letting Cranmer hope against hope and then reducing him to abject silence. The worthy Cranmer's wife and children were forced to take the road to Germany and he remained desolate beside his deserted hearth, thankful enough to have retained his diocese. Two of his fellow-bishops who had proved over-recalcitrant had found themselves summarily deposed.

A Protestant Princess.

Cromwell cared little for either the Eucharist, the sacrament of penance or vows of celibacy. His God was definitely of the earth. But all the nobles were ranged against him; Howard and Brandon as well as Pole's friends, and all the nobles were Catholic; Cromwell wished to find Henry a Protestant bride. A Supreme Head of the Church, if he happens to be a King, cannot be expected to remain single. Saul and Solomon were undoubtedly married and heirs must be provided for the throne. The little Prince Edward might conceivably die and reasons of State made it highly desirable that two or three other small princes should be produced and held in reserve.

Henry was in excellent health, feeling himself sanctified and regenerated by his new laws against heresy. He inhaled the perfume of roses and of the new grass and his solitary nights seemed endless. From the wall Christina of Denmark still looked down at him, but a man who, in January, has made love to a shade, in May is apt to demand a living woman. Therefore, since Charles still withheld Christina and Christina was still content to be withheld, Cromwell proffered his candidate.

She was not by any means of the highest lineage; her brother ruled the sad flat lands of the lower Rhine adjoining Holland and was very poor. He had Cleves, Juliers, and lived at Düsseldorf, by the river, and was laying a claim to Guelders. His hopes and his ambitions vied with his poverty. The Castle of Cleves, which was said to date from Roman times, was known as Schwanenberg, the Mount of the Swans. This romantic name evoked the lovely legends of the Rhine and of the Scheldt, but the castle itself was a hovel. Duke William suffered from *folie de grandeurs* and thought himself a match for Charles. He reckoned on help from the small German princelings, the Electors and the Sovereign Dukes, and had married one of his sisters in Saxony. Thus this bull-frog of the Rhineland marshes sought to inflate himself to ox-like dimensions. A sister still available was thirty-four years of age and had formerly been betrothed to a prince of Lorraine, but the prince had fortunately changed his mind. Cromwell explained to Henry that the Duke of Cleves would win for him the support of the North Germans, and that from the Scheldt to the Zuider Zee the Low Countries would thus be lost to Charles; that Henry would then possess beyond the North Sea a people who, like himself, had cast off the Pope and who would also prove invaluable to trade. Francis, moreover, was friendly to the Duke of Cleves and might be drawn into the alliance.

Henry had been annoyed by Christina's refusal and also by Charles's arrogance, and he enquired regarding the appearance of the Duke of Cleves's sister. Cromwell promptly sent an envoy to Düsseldorf with peremptory orders to admire the Princess. Her name was a familiar one—Anne; but, after all, must memory always prove an obstacle? It was now three years since a sword had severed that slender neck and the anniversary was close at hand. Henry found himself hoping that another Anne, living, tangible, and smiling, whom he could clasp and caress, might stave off nightmares and banish the unwelcome ghost, so Cromwell sent an embassy to Anne of Cleves's brother and mother to ask for that princess's hand. They gave their consent, and so did Anne, who had none of Christina's fancies and was not in the least afraid of Blue Beard. It is true that she was eighteen years older than Christina and, moreover, was bored to death.

Henry, aroused by the thought of his new bride, became sentimental, forgot his Catholic edicts and swelled with Protestant emotions. It was a Protestant ambassador who was dispatched by Cromwell to Cleves to negotiate the details of the betrothal. The Catholics on the Council, led by Bishop Gardiner, expressed the deepest indignation. This Bishop Gardiner, a prince's bastard and a supple courtier at the time of Catherine's divorce,

had developed a fierce Catholicism. He was closely
linked with Howard and also with Brandon, in the hope
that Cromwell, Cranmer and their heretic supporters
might yet be overthrown and sent to the gallows or the
stake. Gardiner had put great pressure on Henry to
forbid the marriage of priests and thus it had been largely
owing to him that Cranmer's Grete had had to return to
Nuremberg. Gardiner himself kept two mistresses in his
house, but was careful not to marry either of them.
Moreover, in deference to decency and the laws of the
Church, he compelled them to wear male attire.

Henry soon silenced Gardiner; he even advised him
to absent himself from the Council and remain in his
diocese. Cromwell and Cranmer would very much have
preferred to see him disembowelled for treason or burned
as a heretic. But pious souls must frequently be content
with milder pleasures.

The Delights of Ripening Beauty.

Henry thought a lot about Anne of Cleves and
enquired whether she was tall. He was thankful when
assured that she was of large proportions, as he wished
for an imposing bride. He feared that a small, slender
woman might remind him unduly of the first Anne, and
he wished to avoid any caprices or follies of the flesh that
might lead him to regrettable actions. Also, he felt that,
being himself both tall and bulky, it was seemly that he
should present to his people a substantial spouse who
would be a fitting counterpart. Cromwell reminded him
that girls were seldom puny in the Rhinelands or those

of the Meuse, that Cleves was only about fifteen miles from Nimeguen, and that these were lands of fat pastures, of shining well-nourished cattle and of fertile placid beauty. Henry dreamed of ample breasts and of soft rotundities. At forty-eight a man is apt to prefer Pomona to Flora, and Henry, having up to that time known only English or Spanish bedfellows, had not yet experienced the pleasure of caressing delicately fattened limbs. It appeared to him that the time had come to experience these as yet unsampled charms. Persons of majestic stature were the fulfilling harmonies of life; they were not its trivial ballads but its powerful symphonies.

Henry spent the summer in such meditations and the ripening fruits seemed the sweeter to his palate; to him they appeared never to have been so heavy. In August Charles, scenting the danger of his alliance with Cleves, offered him the elegant Christina. But Henry refused her; he had been too long trifled with and was now bored with this immature though unvirginal morsel. He had Christina's portrait removed from his wall and, demanding a portrait of the comely Anne, he forthwith dispatched Holbein to the Court of Cleves. Cromwell trembled; he was well aware that Anne was no Venus and he feared that Henry might revert to Christina.

A Holbein Portrait.

Holbein saw Anne and painted her portrait and soon the picture arrived at the English Court. Henry gazed long at it and was enchanted. The subject was undeniably not the expected Pomona, but in his eyes she was something infinitely to be preferred. A chaste princess robed in heavy, parti-coloured, almost barbaric garments; a gentle countenance beneath an unfamiliar head-dress whose lines were simple and becoming. She had the kindness of the wide misty plains where the rivers flow lazily and the barges creep through the meadows, mingling their sails with those of the windmills. She was so meditative, so simply and warmly human, that it never occurred to Henry to study her features. He was too much of a musician to cling to a purity of outline and was ignorant of the Italian or Greek criteria of beauty. Nor was he accustomed to analyse his sensations; he was as ingenuous as a savage and untroubled by conflict. Anne was the gentle, generous peace of the home. When he looked at her picture his dreams became an anthem, solemn but benign, restrained but opulent: "I shall behold her seated opposite me at my fireside and the reflections of its flames will enhance her beauty." It pleased him that her garments should be heavy and so conceal her body; he visualized the gently swelling forms beneath her girdle, beneath the hands so modestly folded. He would say that the Court ladies were foolish indeed to display so brazenly their shoulders and their breasts. Two hands were all that a man should be shown, two folded hands, large but shapely, indolent perhaps, but suave. All the mystery of a woman might dwell in her hands: her strength, her kindness, her docility and her response to tender advances. Henry would think with rapture of the approaching day when he would touch those hands with his lips and feel them thrill beneath his moustache.

Meanwhile Charles was becoming angry and

threatening. He wished to prevent the marriage and spoke of an alliance with France, letting it be understood that he would then invade England. But Henry thought only of the new Anne, who at length left Cleves at the end of the autumn. She was accompanied by two hundred men on horseback and crossed the plains in the rain and mud of November. On the eleventh of December it was known that she had reached Calais, that she had thus set foot on the soil of her new kingdom. Henry had sent one of his ministers, Fitzwilliam, to meet her, but a storm arose and prevented Anne from crossing the Channel.

The most beautiful portrait in the world does not suffice to feed a lover for six months, and even Henry, despite his taste for tender harmonies, had his moments of lucidity. Sometimes, when a crude ray of light would fall on the portrait, its mystery and its gentle soulfulness would seem to fade. Henry would turn away, anxious to preserve his dreams, but the picture would remain in his mind, stripped of its poetical trappings. The eyes, the mouth would make him uneasy, and was not the nose, to say the least of it, original? The hands were undeniably overlarge . . . Henry would diligently thrust aside such thoughts, despising himself for what he felt to be these carnal distractions, but he was bound to admit that it was well that body and soul should harmonize. He was too simple to appreciate physical discords. He commanded his envoy Fitzwilliam to describe the Princess and Fitzwilliam replied that she appeared to be accomplished; he failed to supply any further details.

Cromwell by now was shaking in his shoes; he had drawn his own conclusions from Holbein's portrait.

Moreover, he knew that when a princess is handsome she soon acquires a husband or her parents succeed in marketing her; they do not leave her to blossom and fade on her virgin stem till she is thirty-four years of age. But must a woman necessarily be beautiful to please a man? Henry's taste was very uncertain; so were the senses of these Northern peoples, while Cromwell's own had developed in the pillages and rapes of the Italian wars. All things considered, he could hardly endure to wait until Anne should be safely established in Henry's bed. Had he believed in God he would have had recourse to prayer; as it was, he doubtless left such petitions to his friend Cranmer.

A Surprise.

On the twenty-seventh of December Henry learned at last that the mysterious princess had landed in England. In a lull between two gales Fitzwilliam had put to sea and the Channel, devoid of all respect, had punished Anne of Cleves. She suffered severely and so did her five German ladies. It rained and it blew and the deck was drenched with spray and they mourned for Cleves and its sleepy plains and the poor Mount of the Swans where they had been so bored. They longed for Düsseldorf and the great, quiet Rhine, and were unable even to land at Dover. The sea spewed them ashore a little further along the coast.

Brandon was awaiting them; he was ageing and concealed his wrinkles beneath a vast beard. He had brought with him his second wife, who glanced at the new Queen

and smiled. They set out in the rain along the sodden
roads, and soon the handsome coiffes of the foreign
ladies, soaked through and through, hung awry.

In order to see Anne sooner Henry had moved to
Greenwich, whither Brandon and Fitzwilliam sent him
messengers several times daily. But the descriptions they
gave him were vague, as though no normal terms were
adequate to portray so radiant a star. They travelled very
slowly, to avoid tiring their princess, and took two days
on the road between Dover and Canterbury. In this
latter town there were great rejoicings. Cranmer,
flanked by five bishops, met Anne at the gates of the city.
On that day the rain and the wind redoubled in violence.
The cathedral seemed empty since the removal of
Saint Thomas à Becket's shrine; the bitter December
blast whistled through the broken windows and the rain
fell in torrents upon the flagstones. The following day
Anne advanced a few miles further and came to a halt at
Sittingbourne. Henry, biting his thumbs with impatience,
sent continually for Cromwell; it appeared to him as
though all his emissaries, Fitzwilliam, Brandon and
Cranmer, were conspiring to prevent his seeing this new
Queen of Sheba.

At last, on the thirty-first of December, a messenger
came to announce that the princess had left Canterbury,
that she would proceed to Rochester, and would reach
Greenwich the next day, there to be the delight of his
eyes. This was a fine prospect for the dawn of the New
Year, but Henry could wait no longer. He was determined to see his mysterious bride, and perhaps even to
slip into her bed; he felt bold, lustful and ready for any
adventure. He summoned Brown, his Master of the

Horse, walked down to the river bank and had himself rowed to Rochester. Laid beside him on the cushions of the barge was a splendid betrothal gift, a magnificent mantle of sable furs.

At Rochester he learned that she had just arrived and was resting in her apartments with her women. Henry would have liked to appear before her eyes as a prince fallen straight from heaven. On reflection, however, he thought it prudent to be announced; after all, he was not a boy of twenty. In spite of his fine clothes he might prove a disappointment, and how great would be his anguish if the lovely Anne, taken unawares, should reveal her dismay, should show surprise at his belly. The eternal ulcer compelled him to limp and an incognito was always a risk. He came to the conclusion that at forty-nine a king is unwise to dispense with formality. He therefore entered Anne's apartments, but went no further than her antechamber. Thence he dispatched Brown to warn the Princess that the King had just arrived and craved her permission to lay his devotion at her feet.

Henry, listening from behind an arras, heard shrill voices speaking in an unknown and unmusical tongue. When Brown reappeared he looked very gloomy and his face had lengthened by inches. Henry sensed an impending catastrophe in the air, but had no time to question his emissary. Moreover, Brown seemed to be smitten dumb and the Princess's ladies were making their appearance, curtsying to the ground and drawing back the arras. Henry entered the room.

She stood awaiting him at the far end of the chamber; she took a few steps forward and curtsied. It did not occur to him to return her greeting; he passed his hand across his brow. He felt that he was dreaming, in the grip of a hideous nightmare.

She was staring at him now with her dull little eyes, eyes devoid of all mystery that blinked and shifted and then again sought his face as she made a miserable attempt to smile. She had a large, flabby nose, disastrously tip-tilted, an untidy mouth and wide pendulous cheeks that merged vaguely into the laces of her coiffe. Her neck was stiff and ungainly and her skin, pitted with smallpox, was coarse, greasy and pasty. The only light in the room appeared to be concentrated upon the shiny upturned tip of her nose, and at every movement she made this feature caught Henry's eye like a beacon. She walked in great strides with a swaying of her heavy red-and-blue gown and a clanking of barbarous adornments. A few strands of yellow hair, escaping from her coiffe, fringed her sallow brow.

Henry gasped, and felt the sweat running down his body. She made him another stiff curtsy, her five ladies following suit, and then she addressed him in her own tongue. She had prepared a speech which was translated by an interpreter, but Henry gazed at her and heard never a word. He thought of arresting Holbein and disem-bowelling him for treason, but how could he blame the painter? Holbein had depicted the woman as she was, had drawn her exact form and features. But as he had bent over the monster his brush had transformed her, impregnating her with his mysterious magic. For six months Henry, who had thought to love a living woman, had loved only a painter's soul.

He stammered a few words, drew back, made a vague gesture of greeting and stumbled blindly from the room.

He was rubbing his eyes, he felt himself to be stifling and perceived that he still clutched the sables in his hand; laying them down he left the house. He walked in dead silence, overwhelmed, his great back bowed and Brown followed him, not daring to utter a word. They made their way to the river, entered the barge and were rowed downstream, home to Greenwich. There Cromwell, sweating with terror, made his appearance. "She is frightful," bellowed Henry; "I have been deceived." By Cromwell's agents, he meant, and by Cromwell himself. "Never, had I known the truth, should she have come to this country; and now that she is here, how can I send her back again? I should be the laughing-stock of the whole of Europe. Her brother would demand vengeance and would make common cause against me with Charles, Francis and the Bishop of Rome on the grounds of my excommunication. They would all attack England . . . I must marry or perish." He was too desperate even to belabour Cromwell, but went off to his bed seething with fury.

Since his widowerhood he had been in the habit of always sharing his bed with a page or an equerry. The neighbourhood of their young bodies sleeping or waking was a protection against nightmares, and if he was pursued by a too importunate phantom with a vivid face and a long, slender neck, he had only to extend a hand and grasp living, vigorous flesh in order to dispel the obsession. These lads would undress him, massage him, comb and perfume his hair and wash the ulcer on his leg. But on the night of Anne of Cleves's arrival not one of them sufficed to soothe him, not even little Tom Culpeper, a poor relation of Howard's who was so winning, whom he loved above all the rest of them, and who seemed to feel no repulsion at his wound and dressed it with feminine gentleness.

All night long he raged: "The woman will come here, I shall have to put the ring on her finger and smile; I shall probably be compelled to kiss her. I shall be forced to endure her presence in my bedchamber; she will spread her great body in my bed. I shall hear her breathing for the rest of my life, for I am older and less robust than she is. She will be bending over me when my time comes to die, will give me my last potion and receive my dying breath."

Had he not been afraid that little Tom would hear him he would have broken down and cried like a child.

A Recalcitrant Bridegroom.

On the following day they came to inform him that the Princess had at last arrived. She had been installed in a marvellous tent erected at the end of a lawn. There she was being dressed in a gown of cloth of gold; and Henry was forced to put on his most splendid garments before going to join her in the tent. She smiled and held out her hand to him and in the broad daylight he thought her more astounding than ever. They mounted the horses that awaited them and set out between two files of observant courtiers while crowds of onlookers thronged the lawn. As he advanced beside this radiant monster Henry felt a flood of consternation inundate the long human hedge of beholders.

With the greatest possible speed he led her to her

apartments, where she disappeared behind closed doors. Passing to his closet he sent for Cromwell. "Well, sir, you have seen her? What do you think of her?" "She is tall and majestic and has the carriage of a Queen . . ." Henry cut him short: "I refuse to marry her; I utterly refuse. You must find a pretext for rupture." The marriage had been fixed for the following day, a Sunday. "Then we will postpone it until Tuesday and give ourselves three more days for reflection." Cromwell informed the priests and the Princess and arranged a postponement of the festivities. "There must be some way out. I repudiated Catherine, that exemplary woman, after twenty years of cohabitation. I must be able to deliver myself from this dragon whom I have barely seen and whom I should never in my life dream of touching. She was once betrothed to a prince of Lorraine." "But your Grace must remember that she was only two or three years old!" "What does that matter? The betrothal could not be annulled. Let the Lorrainer marry her! If I did so I should be a bigamist and beget bastards, and I have two bastards already which are more than enough for England." "But that betrothal was legally annulled." "Never mind; you must tell her women that I am tortured by scruples, that she is already married and that I cannot take her without sin." Anne's women were unable to grasp Cromwell's meaning, they jabbered helplessly in their low German. With the assistance of an interpreter they managed to explain that the alleged former betrothal had never materialized and that their beloved mistress was free. Cromwell, who desired the marriage, bore the reply to Henry, telling him that he had no alternative but to agree.

A further two nights were permitted to elapse, nights of impotent anguish for Henry. He was to be wedded on Tuesday. On Monday he sent Cromwell to enquire of the Clevan Princess whether she was quite sure that she was free to marry and whether she was prepared to make a statement to that effect in writing. By these means he hoped to terrify her: if she signed such a statement he might one day allege that she had lied, bring her to trial and send her to her death. She may well have felt that he was setting a grim snare, but she was weary of Cleves, of her thirty-four years of solitude, of the niggardly family hearth. She had already beheld the splendours of England. Even if she were one day to be slaughtered she intended to occupy the throne and to enjoy its privileges: she wrote out the statement and signed it.

Henry was still determined to resist, but Cromwell reminded him that his two enemies, Charles and Francis, were now reconciled and that at that very moment Charles was in Paris, doubtless preparing with Francis and the Bishop of Rome their prospective apportionment of England. Henry's courage failed him and he resigned himself to his fate.

The Fourth Marriage.

There was no alternative to draining the bitter cup to the dregs. On the sixth of January, the day of the Epiphany, after one last night of freedom Henry was compelled to don his white bridal finery. When little Tom Culpeper had dressed his leg Henry went to fetch

Anne and led her to the chapel. She had unbound her yellow hair. Walking at her side he could not see her, but he felt between his fingers the coarseness of her large hand. The organ throbbed, the choir sang, and they were made man and wife. The clearness of the treble voices moved Henry, even more than usual, and almost reduced him to tears.

The day proved a weariness, nay worse, a torment, for from time to time he discerned on the faces of even the most servile of his friends a faint smile of irony or of contempt. At the ball in the evening Anne shocked all susceptibilities and the ladies whispered that she lacked the most elementary deportment and could not long be tolerated. But the night proved even more cruel than the day. The fatal hour came when the intimate friends must lead the espoused couple to the nuptial bedchamber, when the bishops must bless their bed. There were many loud wishes for their amorous enjoyment and for numerous resulting progeny. Anne, who could not understand a single word of English, greeted these sallies with placid laughter.

They were both undressed and put to bed, the doors were closed upon them and they were left alone together. Henry had drunk heavily in search of courage; he controlled his nerves, seeking to persuade himself that facial beauty was not everything; that Anne was well developed, appeared to be plump and doubtless possessed hidden treasures. Love took as much account of the touch as of the eyes and by subduing the light and keeping the curtains closed he might yet recover his dreams. Henry had been a widower for more than two years and might well hope to discover resources in a strapping German virgin approaching maturity. The sheets were fine and perfumed and a pleasant warmth was diffused by Anne's recumbent form. He advanced, extended his hands and laid them on the stranger.

The gentlemen in waiting who watched on the threshold heard an outburst of profanity and then cries. Silence ensued and the gentlemen concluded that their master was taking his rest. Before dawn he made his appearance among them demanding to be washed and dressed. It was obvious that he had slept very badly and he was visibly foaming with fury. Cromwell, rudely aroused from slumber, came running to him and Henry fairly roared: "It is worse than I feared; her body is worse than her face, and, moreover, she is not a virgin! I am perfectly convinced that she is not a virgin, although I was unable to ascertain it." Cromwell's shrewd eyes registered astonishment: "No, sir, no, I tell you I could not do it. I touched her breasts and her belly, which more than sufficed me; for nothing on earth would I have gone further. But I give you my word, with that belly and those breasts, no woman could possibly be a virgin."

Virgin or not, they would have to keep her and every night he must sleep at her side. Night after night she encumbered his bed and they lay there as brother and sister. Nor had she any fear of his rages: if he looked at her shining nose her eyes would swerve to his ulcer. There was little affection lost between these two chaste bedfellows, but she felt quite certain that for fear of a war he would keep her, at least for a time. She was learning English and beginning to speak it, and she babbled with apparent innocence. One day her women asked her whether she were still a virgin. "Certainly not," she replied. "Every night the King, before getting into bed, takes my hand and kisses me, saying: 'Good night, my dear.' After that he settles down among his pillows and the two of us go to sleep. In the morning, when he wakes, he again takes my hand, kisses me once more and says: 'Good morning, dear heart.' Then he calls his gentlemen to dress him. So you see very well that I am no longer a virgin."

XIV

THE HOWARD ROSE-TREE BLOOMS AGAIN

(1540)

Cromwell Losing Ground.

THOSE two obligatory kisses irritated Henry and daily rekindled his fury. Every night as he fell asleep he said to himself: "I owe this bitter cup to Cromwell." Every morning, when he opened his eyes, it was Cromwell's odious countenance that obsessed him. But he was still afraid; Charles and Francis continued to conspire and he dared not face them unaided. Cromwell was capable and held all the threads, one could not kill so useful a man.

But Cromwell's enemies were not inactive. In order to reassure Henry, Howard visited Francis and urged him to abandon Charles. Moreover, the Catholic bishops were creeping back into favour. One of Cromwell's men, the Protestant Barnes, having insulted Gardiner in a sermon, was compelled by Henry to make public amends. But Cromwell held on and retaliated by sending a Catholic bishop to the Tower. Henry made him, Cromwell, Earl of Essex and gave him the property of thirty convents, but none the less, he was losing ground, owing to an essential miscalculation. This man, who had achieved greatness by divining and pandering to Henry's

lowest instincts, was now venturing to oppose them. He
had ceased to be his evil genius, his whispering familiar:
he had lost his initial clear-sightedness. If a man aims at
the control of another's being, he can maintain that
control only by constant inventiveness. Lovers can sometimes achieve this process, but the grip is soon lost, for
desire wanes. Cromwell's grip had also weakened, his
desire having been, not for love but for power. Undis-
puted chief minister, scourge of the courtiers, destroyer
of monks, beheader or creator of queens, he thought
himself secure, thought it safe to detach himself from
Henry, to become once more Cromwell undisguised.

The change took place almost imperceptibly: Cromwell
formed a Protestant party of his own while Henry
remained balanced between it and the Catholics. Day
by day Cromwell relaxed his hold on his master and
drifted further from him.

The fact was at first only vaguely suspected: in long-
standing marriages a routine persists which will serve to
conceal the fundamental fissures. Henry, out of aversion
for the Pope, would sometimes believe himself to be
Protestant. He allowed Cromwell to act, under a temporary delusion that he, the King, was being served, that
Cromwell was working for and preparing his happiness.
But the arrival of the Clevan swept away that illusion and
Henry was forced to realize that his velvet-gloved pimp
was no more, that Cromwell was destroying his pleasures,
was, indeed, substituting intolerable impositions.

Cromwell was fully aware of his danger, but he closed
his eyes, played for time, hoped against hope. Henry,
ageing, obese, semi-torpid, might yet accept the Clevan.
He had already slept for five months at her side. Satiated

libertines have been known to find savour in singular ugliness; the ugliness of Anne was undeniably exceptional and the rare may border on the exquisite. Henry was now drinking heavily in the evenings and drunkenness has its delusions. Might not the Clevan in the darkness of their bedchamber succeed in capturing his fancy? She certainly seemed less innocent than had been supposed and adults could not sleep together with impunity. Once the rubicon was crossed Henry might be agreeably surprised and reproach himself for having so long neglected a treasure.

But such suppositions were purely fantastic; Cromwell the realist was ignoring reality while others saw more clearly and were contriving his fall.

Catherine Howard.

Howard and Bishop Gardiner were working. Both were old and both were lecherous and they fully understood Henry's dissatisfaction, realizing the increasing boredom of his nights. Henry, with the passing of time, was growing desperate beside his Flanders mare; it made him sick to think of her lying near him, heavy, flabby and faded. He would dream of having her removed, strangled or possibly poisoned in order to avoid scandal. But in the mornings, when she offered her cheek to be kissed, he was sorry for her; she was too disastrously plain even to arouse his hatred, and he would be unable to take any pleasure in her death. What he required was a different victim: Cromwell, the traitor who knew his innermost mind, who had served him so long and who now had used his knowledge to place him in this insufferable situation.

He still hesitated, however. Cromwell had been the agent of all his murders, and on whom could he depend to murder Cromwell? Then he would resign himself for a time to his fate. Why, after all, should he send this woman away? She slept quietly enough on her side of the bed, and during the day-time he seldom saw her. Whom would he put in her place when she was gone? His equerries perhaps or little Tom Culpeper? And how would he replace Cromwell? Where should he seek others for his service?

Then the others presented themselves: they were Howard and Gardiner. They had their plan ready and had prepared the means with which they had hopes of snaring Henry. It was a simple snare, for neither the bishop nor the soldier was possessed of any imagination. They followed well-worn paths and said to themselves that when a man of fifty is thoroughly bored, a pretty girl is the best remedy that can be offered. Howard, thanks to his laundry-maid, and Gardiner, thanks to his two female pages, knew the restorative potency of a fresh young body. They sought a new wife for Henry.

Howard considered his family: Henry had only loved women of that tribe, its blood was irresistible to him as it had been to his relations. Margaret Douglas, his niece, had married Howard's brother and Richmond had chosen his only daughter. Howard now regretted the Richmond marriage; he should have foreseen that Henry would become a widower and have reserved his daughter for the emergency. He now recognized his error, but what could he do? He could not offer the King Richmond's widow, his own daughter-in-law.

Failing a daughter, however, Howard had nieces and could choose among the offspring of his sisters: there were Wyatts and Bryans. But these children all had fathers and brothers, and there would be a risk of their some day rebelling against their uncle and benefactor. Howard remembered the insolence of Anne Boleyn and decided that an orphan would be preferable. The clan abounded in resources and offered him all he required. Howard the grandfather in the course of two marriages had produced fifteen children, who in their turn had multiplied. Some of the younger sons had been unsuccessful in life; one of Howard's brothers had sunk to poverty while breeding ten children for the family to rear. Howard had been compelled to undertake their upbringing and they had grown up in the country under the vague supervision of his grandfather's second wife.

The eldest of these ten children was a girl who had been named Catherine in honour of the dead Queen. She was now eighteen, dark-haired and attractive. The dark hair was curly, her eyes were bright, she had a small aquiline nose and a wide mouth that was very red. She bore a faint resemblance to her cousin Anne, but was a simpler edition, devoid of all magic. At fifty years old and after so many trials Henry had lost any taste for magic. Howard and Gardiner judged of his weather-beaten heart by their own.

Catherine was no longer living in the country. At eighteen it is time that an orphan maid should look about her, earn a living and try to capture a husband, and husbands are seldom to be found in country castles.

Howard had therefore brought her to Court and she was given a post as maid of honour, waiting on the Clevan or, alternatively, on Mary, who was daily becoming more shrivelled. Both of them served to emphasize her youthful charms as she adjusted a veil or a crown or bore their trains. Having experienced poverty, she kept her eyes open, thinking of the future and discreetly angling for admirers. Her ambitions were modest or at any rate reasonable, for she was fully aware that powerful nobles, if they are young and handsome, do not marry penniless girls, that their mothers are there to prevent it. The nobles who were rich and elderly did not attract her, for she dreamed of more lively company. A strapping pleasant lad in a decent position, with hopes of advancement, appeared to her a reasonable objective. She surveyed Henry's equerries, his personal attendants, the former companions of his bed. Tom Culpeper was her first cousin; she cast an eye upon him and he responded. They saw one another several times daily, since Tom attended Henry while Catherine was waiting upon the princesses. They dallied together in the antechambers and in the evenings they danced together to amuse Henry and themselves. Tom understood that he was acceptable, for Catherine, the motherless girl, was by no means a prude, but they did not as yet realize that they were in love. They jealously concealed their respective feelings. Tom was already adept in Court intrigue and Catherine had her feminine subtleties.

The Two Old Men.

It was Howard who pointed her out to Henry and Henry observed her, at first discreetly, as he might have done a pleasing and graceful young animal, as he often would watch Tom Culpeper. Her laughter was melodious and he listened to it, enjoying it as though it were music. He scarcely took the trouble to study her face, knowing that he was too old to attract her, but he would linger in the apartments of his Clevan or of the surly Mary for the pleasure of seeing this Catherine moving about the room. She for her part had a heart more decided than his and very simple ideas in matters of sex. She divined his emotion, would brush against him as by accident, laugh inwardly at his consequent embarrassment and touch him again. He was a King and a terrible one; in her childhood she had been told the story of her cousin Anne and in her bed had lain dreaming of that romance. At twelve she had seen her grandmother and her aunts weeping over that cousin's death on the scaffold. It struck her as intriguing that she should now be able to disconcert a man who had a woman's blood on his hands. She had always pictured him as handsome and mighty; he was ugly and paunchy with pendulous jowls, he turned his feet out when he walked and leaned on a stick. She thought him ridiculous but suppressed her smiles . . . it was not safe to laugh at Blue Beard. But she would bait him just sufficiently to give herself a thrill of fear, a thrill in which she found enjoyment. She would wonder if he still remembered her cousin Anne, whose portraits she would study, seeking to resemble her, dreaming that she might one day avenge her. It would amuse her to see Henry's glance alight upon the new Anne, to see his eyes narrow and close with distaste. Then Tom would come in and she would pretend not to see him and resume her manœuvres with Henry. To her Blue Beard was now no more than a grotesque admirer, an old puppet whom she used to spur on the man of her fancy.

But she singed her wings, for there came a day when her uncle Howard drew her aside, told her that Henry loved her and that in three months she would be Queen. She thought of Tom, but dared not speak his name. Howard fixed his heavy gaze upon her and she realized that she was trapped and could hope for no escape.

She was taken to see Gardiner and that libertine bishop, well versed in the art of entangling maidens, spoke to her gravely of her Catholic duty, telling her that it lay with her to redeem England, to bring it back to the Faith and to crush the heretics. He reminded her of her poverty, of Tom's lack of money, and made her feel that she would be utterly helpless should she ever attempt to defy her uncle Howard. She was versed in the exploits of that noted commander, slaughterer of the Scots and of his own wife. "He would take Tom between his finger and thumb and break him. And in any case, are you so sure of loving the lad? He is no more than a servant, a subservient bedfellow, a pander to debauchery. He himself, at a word, at the first suggestion, would lead you to Henry. He might weep, but he would obey. God has called you to give happiness to a glorious king; you should go on your knees like Esther and Ruth and render thanks to the Lord for His favour. Who are you to set yourself against

Heaven's decree? Are you prepared to be a rebellious daughter of the Church? Are you prepared to reject a crown? Every girl in England will go pale with envy. You will take precedence over the poor Queen who for your sake will be dismissed and may even lose her life, and before that arrogant Mary who has so often snubbed you. You will be given all the jewels of the treasury, Catherine's necklaces and the crowns worn by your cousin Anne. All the dressmakers and the embroiderers in London will be set to work in order to make you beautiful; you will wear the rainbow in your garments, your hands will be filled with gold and you will be able to shower it on your little brothers and sisters; on Tom himself, should you so desire it. But will you then have any memory of Tom? These lads of twenty are fickle creatures and not to be compared with a maturer husband. An older man is faithful while a young one quickly tires and is off before you know it in search of new adventures. For a woman there is happiness in fearing no rival, in knowing herself to be secure of her future. And as for the vaunted pleasures of the flesh, since we must consider all aspects, they are not always what young girls expect. Thirty years of experience are not to be despised and a mature husband fully understands his duties. His wife can be certain of careful, painstaking attentions which are entirely devoid of selfishness. Too violent pleasures are frequently evanescent."

Catherine listened to him and reflected. Gardiner and Howard returned to the charge with insistence. Howard was brutal, Gardiner tender and moving. Together the two old men persecuted the girl until she dreamed of them at night. She could hear them whispering until they merged together into one dark and threatening obsession. Then a bulky shape would make its appearance, and they in their turn would seem to be absorbed into it. Her terror was such that she sweated with anguish; then she yielded, said she would obey and that she was ready.

Secret Pleasures.

A number of secret meetings were arranged. Gardiner gave dinners at his Episcopal Palace on the further side of the Thames, at Lambeth, at which Catherine would be seated next to Henry. It was May once more and once again the scent of flowers was wafted in through the windows. Henry gazed at Catherine with rapture; she was slender, she seemed pure and she told him that she loved him. He would have liked to be alone with her, to become a child again and weep in her lap. He found enchantment in a breath, in a silence, recovered his early innocence and forgot the rancours of his life. His senses were becoming keener and more subtle.

A different type of man would have enjoyed Catherine in private while retaining the Clevan for public ceremonies, but Henry would have felt that he was debasing himself and endangering the salvation of his soul. A pious monarch marries the woman he loves. On the ninth of May he summoned a meeting of the Privy Council and it was thought that he intended to rid himself of his minister and of the obtrusive Clevan. Already Howard and Gardiner were sharing out Cromwell's honours and property, were gloating over their prey, but Henry changed his mind and dismissed the Council. He needed the energetic Cromwell to squeeze an enormous tax out of the Commons. The tax was voted at the end of the month and Cromwell appeared to be more powerful than ever. Three Catholic priests were condemned for treason and there were rumours in London that Gardiner had fallen and that he was going to be sent to the Tower.

Fall of Cromwell.

On the morning of the tenth of June Cromwell appeared in the House of Lords as Head of the Government. After midday there was a meeting of the Council. Howard, Fitzwilliam and Gardiner arrived early at the Palace; they were talking together in undertones and visibly fidgeting with impatience. Finally Cromwell also appeared: "You came very early?" Howard had already sprung to his feet, crying, "Do not sit down; this is no place for a traitor." He summoned six guards who were waiting outside the doors and they attempted to seize Cromwell, but they were not dealing on this occasion with one of those effete and amenable aristocrats. He defended himself, butting at them and using his fists; he howled as they overcame him and bore him to the ground. The nobles joined the guards and trampled upon his prostrate body crying, "Traitor, traitor!" Howard wrenched off his Collar of the Garter while Fitzwilliam tore the Garter itself from his leg. When they had kicked him, stamped on him and belaboured him until he was reduced by exhaustion to silence they had him removed from the hall by the six guards, who bore him to the river, threw him into a barge and took him straight to the Tower.

Hiding in an adjacent room, Henry had been listening and holding his breath. Having heard the cries, the blows, the sounds of a body being dragged down the stairs, he sent his agents to Cromwell's house to seize his possessions and make a detailed inventory of them. He had fully expected to lay hands upon a vast treasure, but his men found little of value.

Free at last, he dismissed Anne and relieved his bed of her presence. He explained to her that the summer heat appeared to fatigue her, that she would be better in the country, and that he had prepared Richmond Palace for her reception. He spoke to her very slowly so that she understood his words, for she had made considerable progress in the English tongue. But the fact of her doing so had given Henry no pleasure; he found her sour and cross and regretted the time when she had been silent. When she learned of her dismissal the Clevan trembled: what could be the meaning of this country holiday? Catherine of Aragon had breathed her last in rural retirement . . . but what was the use of resisting? She departed.

Howard and Gardiner wanted Cromwell's head while Henry thought it as well to burn the now useless tool. Moreover, he wished to annex his property and even for a king inheritance was preferable to confiscation. Nor could Henry forgive Cromwell those six months of married tedium. Nothing could be easier than to send him to his death, since Cromwell himself had perfected the methods and had shorn judicial procedure of all superfluous ceremony. By recent decrees he had suppressed the interrogation of the accused, the need for their appearance or for the depositions of witnesses. By these means he had effected great economies for the treasury, since witnesses were notoriously an expensive item. And what was the use of permitting the accused to speak when they might prove insolent to those who meant to kill them, or might possibly reveal some embarrassing detail? Cromwell had even abolished the court and the jury, deciding that in dealing with cases of treason, the two Houses of Parliament, the Lords and the Commons, should vote in the matter and give their decision. This felicitous system was promptly applied to its originator whom Henry accused before both Houses of being a heretic and of having abused his authority. The Lords and the Commons, whom he had trained for ten years, rose like one man and declared him a traitor. Their vote was unanimous and he was delivered over to the King's good pleasure.

Cromwell Seeks to Defend Himself.

Even then Cromwell refused to give way to despair, being too strong-minded to renounce his own defence so long as the breath remained in his body. Any means were good enough, even the most abject. He wept and implored, feeling it no shame to grovel if by momentary abasement success could be achieved. Perhaps for the brave man his greatest courage may lie in consenting to be thought a coward. Cromwell knew Henry and his colossal egoism, but also the sensibility of his nerves, and he knew that he was lost if he resigned himself to silence and allowed Henry peaceably to plan his murder. By uttering despairing shrieks, by acting a fear he did not feel, there was a chance that he might trouble the King and arouse that alarm that had invaded him twenty years earlier at the time of Buckingham's execution. It was a very faint chance, but the only one that remained. Cromwell had no choice but to try it.

But how was he to contrive that his voice should be heard, enclosed as he was between four walls with a patch of sky for his horizon? He might well have felt himself to be haunted by the ghosts of all those whom he himself had sent to this dark prison, there to suffer and to die. Several of his victims still lingered in its cells: the aged Lady Salisbury, whose son and grandsons he had murdered; three Catholic priests and one of Queen Catherine's confessors, condemned by him as a traitor and now awaiting hanging and quartering. But Cromwell remained unperturbed; he had no imagination and fancies did not trouble him.

The Protestants deserted him; they had gone to earth, fearing to provoke unwelcome attention which might lead to an accusation of unbelief in the Real Presence. Their nostrils scented the potential stake and in any case they cared nothing for Cromwell. He had been to them an ally but never a friend and they knew him to be capable of selling everything: his own soul first, then that of his allies and finally their sentient bodies also. Cranmer, however, thought it incumbent upon him to make some effort on behalf of his former comrade and with shaking pen and a cowering spirit he sat down and wrote to the King. In this bishop there existed the elements of the pliant reed and of the slug: he dared not declare that Cromwell was no traitor, but he wrote that such treachery would surprise him: "His only security lay in your Grace . . . he loved you as he loved his God . . . he had never any thought but your wishes and your pleasure . . . he was wise, diligent, faithful and experienced . . . or so, at least, I believed . . . such was my humble opinion . . . I loved him as a friend, but above all because I thought him devoted to your Grace . . . But now he is a traitor and I regret that I ever loved or trusted him and am happy that his treachery was discovered in good time." This valiant voice was the only one raised in Cromwell's defence and the gentle Cranmer did not insist and ended, like the rest of them, by voting for his death.

Cromwell, however, was kept alive for some time; Henry needed him for the purpose of verifying some accounts and especially required his aid in the repudiation of Anne of Cleves. All things being weighed, Henry thought it would be wiser to put her aside than to kill her. The axe would have aroused surprise, poison would have caused scandal. Moreover, either of these methods would have involved loss of time, and Henry, infatuated with Catherine, had no intention of being kept waiting.

The Divorce of Anne of Cleves.

On the eleventh of July he sent two of his friends to Anne. He had selected Brandon for his elderly authoritativeness and for his beard, and also one of his Catholic secretaries, Risley, who was beginning to make his way, having a certain shrewdness not unlike that of Cromwell. When she caught sight of them the Clevan was convinced that they had come to seize her, to drag her before the Council and shut her up in the Tower. Robust though she might be, she fell down in a dead faint. They called for her women, who slapped the palms of her hands, loosened her stays and unlaced her bodice while Brandon and Risley reassured her. The King, they explained, regarded her with tender affection and had no idea of cutting short so worthy an existence. His only desire was to divorce her and he ventured to hope that she would agree to his doing so. The disgrace and death of Catherine should serve to discourage her from opposition, a King being possessed of many means of persuasion. Anne understood.

She had not the slightest wish to raise difficulties, being no less bored in the conjugal bed than was her too tranquil husband. She also was possessed of senses and of the remnants of her youth and was weary of her virginal matrimony. Nevertheless, she made certain conditions. She had no intention of returning to Cleves; she was sick to death of the Mount of the Swans and of its too familiar domesticity. She wished to remain in England, to have a residence and an income and to live according to her inclinations. She could imagine the welcome she would receive at Cleves, her brother's reproaches and the wails of her mother, and she refused to resume her spinster's life as an old maid with embroidery and housekeeping as her only relaxations. She had now been a wife—at least in name—and she intended to retain the advantages of that state. Brandon and Risley promised that Henry would be very generous and she thanked them with her most ingratiating smile. That night she laid herself down peacefully in her solitary bed: at thirty-five life was sweet and still had plenty to offer her.

The Lords, the Commons and the clergy quickly pronounced the divorce, using the pretext of Anne's former betrothal to the little Prince of Lorraine. They pointed out that the present marriage had never been consummated, since Henry had only agreed to it under constraint. Nobody enquired who had imposed the constraint in question. Cromwell sent the King a long memorandum explaining the situation; as a postscript he added: "Most gracious Prince, mercy! Mercy! Mercy!" Henry made use of the memorandum but ignored the postscript.

Anne received even more than she had asked for. She was given Richmond Palace and another residence in order that she might have change of air. She was given a large income and was adopted by Henry as his sister, taking precedence next to his daughters. He sent one of his bishops to Cleves to explain matters to her brother and offer him a generous gift of money. The brother refused the money and lost his temper. But Anne was more practical and pocketed the disdained tip. She was also supplied with furniture and innumerable adornments and she was so happy that she wore a different gown every day. The good soul was indeed a trifle tactless. A brief period of retreat would have been more seemly, a few days of melancholy, of grey, mauve or quiet-coloured gowns in such shades as "the end of a lover's dream" or "lost illusions." But Henry was not even aware of her behaviour; he did not even care to be regretted.

Death of Cromwell.

By the end of July everything was settled and Henry could rid himself of Cromwell. He spared him the disembowelling and gave orders that he should be beheaded. It being out of the question that a plebeian should perish on Tower Hill he was taken to the common execution ground at Smithfield, and Cromwell, so soon as he saw that the game was up, ceased his supplications and died quietly, like a soldier.

Two days later the London populace were given another entertainment, as Henry decided to illustrate the impartiality of the law by killing three Catholics and three Protestants simultaneously. The six were laid on hurdles and dragged through the streets. On arrival at Tyburn the three Protestants were burned. As for the three Catholics, they were made to suffer in every detail the interminable mutilations reserved for traitors.

The Fifth Marriage.

Henry loved to mingle marriages and executions, and on the very day that saw Cromwell led to the scaffold he wedded little Catherine Howard. The ceremony took place in a secluded castle at some distance from London, at Oatlands. It was very private, for he did not feel that Catherine was adapted to ceremonial. He loved her so dearly that he did not even wish to display her, and seated beside her in the shade of the trees, enjoying the beauty of a July morning, he allowed his mind to dwell upon the agony of Cromwell being dragged through the howling of the mob. He felt a definite relief at the thought that those sharp eyes would never again meet his and that that ponderous head would never more meditate and scheme. Cromwell was associated with all his past crimes and Henry felt that in slaying him he himself was purified. He was throwing that dark soul in propitiation to the shades of his victims, casting that prey to the Furies. "They will fling themselves blindly upon his carcase, will tear him asunder and devour him and, being satiated with the servant, will cease to remember the master." Offerings appease the dead.

Two days elapsed. They dragged the six victims on their hurdles, but Oatlands knew nothing of the odour of the burnings or of the shrieks of the mutilated martyrs. The executioners' assistants threw the ashes of the three Protestants to the winds and placed the limbs of the quartered Catholics above the ramparts of the City of London, while Henry, feeling peaceful and very innocent, contemplated the sky, the meadows and Catherine's young bosom.

XV

THE ROSE WITHOUT A THORN

(1540—1542)

Love at Fifty.

THE Furies were doubtless appeased, for Henry enjoyed a happiness as deep and as inexhaustible as were the long August days. But August itself has its moments of melancholy; the meadows are shorn and the fields are harvested and the grey earth shows through the stubble. The birds have stopped singing and there is in the air something suggestive of desolation. The leaves take on too sombre a green and their sap has ceased to flow and one longs for the first showers of autumn while knowing that their coming will bring destruction. But Henry, with Catherine always beside him, had no thoughts but of her, for in her flowed a sap so young and so vital that the very air seemed renewed as it touched her and would appear to him to form an aureole around her. He would sit in his gardens and draw her to him, gently pressing her down beside him. The shadows of the leaves would dance upon her cheeks and patches of sunshine would play on them, so tremulous, so luminous that they seemed not to come from heaven, but to be born of her flesh like ephemeral flowers. They would glide over her neck to the rhythm of her breathing, widening and diminishing with the rise and fall of her breasts, shimmering, scattering and dancing fantastically. With her eyes closed, Catherine would lie laughing.

Henry would raise his heavy head and would prick his pointed ears. He was more affected by sound than by colour or form and he also would close his eyes the better to absorb through his hearing. The sight is a sense of relative purity, it is almost chaste, but hearing resembles the sense of touch and there is even in it a deep element of secrecy that the touch of the hands fails to achieve, that is hardly evoked by the most intimate recesses of the body. Sound is ephemeral and offers the profound pleasure of that which is passing, that will never be recaptured exactly, that can never be repeated. The shape of a body may seem eternal, the softness of the skin, its very perfume change so gradually that they appear to endure for ever. But what can be more evanescent than spontaneous laughter or a cry, an inflexion? What, for that matter, can be so exquisitely sad? Such things are the more vividly alive in that they die as soon as they are born.

When Catherine, throwing her head back, began to laugh, it was as though a little bubble rose and fell at the base of her throat, giving her skin the delicate hues of mother-of-pearl. It was hard to determine whether her laughter gave greater delight to the ears or the eyes.

Summer was coming to an end and autumn was at hand; then came winter. Henry might have watched their passing without troubling to raise his eyes, for Catherine appeared to have a kinship with the earth itself, she seemed to absorb the seasons. With September she grew languid, revived in the October woods to exhale the vital perfumes that precede decomposition. She grew rosy in the humid fogs of November and fresh and cool as the snow itself, crystalline and fragile as the hoar frost in December. With the first days of March her breasts swelled in unison with the burgeoning of the trees.

Henry forgot Kingdom, taxes, and conspiracies; the days were monotonous but immeasurably rewarding. England also relaxed, enjoying peacefully an unaccustomed happiness. No more stakes were kindled and the sound was no more heard of carpenters' mallets hammering the boards of the scaffolds. There arose no more exhortations of the condemned, the bells ceased to toll and the April sunshine, striking the walls of the City of London found no more bleeding quarters but only bleached bones bereft of all horror and pure as rocks in which bees could make their honey.

Henry had not had Catherine crowned; he was tenderly jealous of her, fearing lest the eyes of the crowd should soil her. She was to him less the Queen than his wife, she belonged not to England but to himself. He even shrank from having to show her to the ambassadors, to his friends and to the courtiers. Nevertheless, he allowed her to be approached; he knew that she was loved and delighted in seeing her generous and extravagant. She had brought her brothers and sisters to the Court and rained gifts upon the Howards; she even gave to those who could have no love for her and to poor Anne of Cleves, whom she pitied for her dismissal. She sent Anne jewels and passed on to her gifts received from Henry. Henry made no demur, merely replacing them with others more beautiful. She also sent gowns and mantles to the aged Countess of Salisbury who was suffering from the cold in the Tower and whom her gaolers kept in tattered rags; and again Henry made no attempt to interfere, although the old lady lay under sentence of death. She obtained a pardon for her cousin Thomas Wyatt who, in a new spirit of poetical independence, had ventured publicly to bewail Cromwell's execution. Wyatt was associated with memories of Anne Boleyn and it was thought that Henry would like the opportunity of being rid of him; but Henry's disturbing visions had ceased and Wyatt remained alive. Catherine then admitted among her ladies another person whose past had involved Henry in anxiety: that Lady Rochford who had married George Boleyn and who had accused her husband of incest with his sister. Catherine had no belief in wickedness; she was alike incapable of mistrust and of contempt. Henry was amazed at her incomparable innocence and called her his rose without a thorn.

The days were delightful, but he longed for the return of nightfall, for at night he had her all to himself. She would let her garments drop from her until she was naked, having no modesty where he was concerned. She knew that she enchanted him and abandoned herself to his gaze, while he wondered to realize that now nothing on earth moved him save the sight of her rounded and perfect body.

She lived only to please him; she sang to him and danced. Others had also sung, especially Anne Boleyn; but the singing of Anne had torn at his vitals and had roused him only to intolerable suffering, to a feeling of uncomprehended impotence. For Anne he had burned with desire, but with a desire that was insatiable, that no pleasure could allay, a thirst that could never hope to be quenched. Anne had hated him as she hated all men, as she hated her own existence. She had hurled herself toward death out of self-weariness and also in the hope of bequeathing him eternal suffering. This one was all caresses, but caresses devoid of monotony or of Jane Seymour's foolish and insipid submissiveness. More than her singing or her dancing, more even than her laughter, Henry adored her silences, her languors, her drowsiness. There was nothing morbid in these moods of quiescence. She was lively and compound of health, but the joy of living would sometimes exhaust her. Henry would watch her as she lay asleep. To him she was health, balance and youth incarnate. He would forget his troubles, would forget to blush for the malformations of his body, for his many lecheries. By the very fact of her presence she made him feel regenerate; she gave him confidence. In summer he would withdraw the bed-clothes from over her: he wished to see her lying naked, her knees slightly drawn up like an infant in its cradle, her beloved weight nestling in the soft mattress of the bed. A breeze from the open window would touch her limbs and make her sigh and she would turn her head, murmuring a few unintelligible words and shaking out the waves of her masses of dark hair. Anne's hair had whipped her flesh like a mantle of living reptiles and had seemed alive with an accursed vitality. Catherine's was soft and warm and inviting to the touch; in it also dwelt a sensation of animal vitality, but it was of a gentle nature, like a sleeping, purring animal.

Henry would not bring the candles nearer but would

lie bending over her resting upon his elbow, his small
ears pricked like those of a lascivious faun too timid to
venture to waken the hamadryad.

Never before had he loved as he loved now; he would
indeed ask himself whether he had ever known love. His
caprices and his passions seemed to him to have been no
more than imperfect trials, a long prelude to reality.
The various sentiments that had possessed him, his
voluptuous but rather timid desire for the first Elizabeth,
his respectful tenderness for the first Catherine, his
young man's passion for Bessie Blount and for Mary
Boleyn, the consuming flame with which he had burned
for the sight of Anne, all were born again at contact with
Catherine, were mingled and harmonized into one new,
deep and multiple emotion. At times he would be
assailed by a shade of sadness, as the remembrance came
to him that he was fifty years old. Man learns to love very
late in life, and when the heart has knowledge the body
is failing. For himself he cared not that his fires were
dying down; his own fulfilments were profound, but he
feared that he might not satisfy her. Not that it ever
struck him that she might escape him or give him pain,
but he deeply desired to make her happy.

It has been said that the greatest happiness lies in
anticipation, but there is another, which is that which
cries to time to stand still, or which is even so utterly
fulfilled that it has no thought of arresting time and is
prepared to accept instant dissolution. In Henry's love
for Catherine there was no desire for change nor any
particular hope for the future. The essential impulse of
passion, the craving for a child, the urge for perpetuation
in the body of another, that of mingling with another

being, Henry no longer experienced. From Catherine he neither expected nor wished for a child. She herself was much more his child than either Mary, Elizabeth or even Edward, who had long since become strangers to him, creatures similar to the rest of mankind, devoid of interest. Catherine was considerably younger than Mary; she had been born when Henry was thirty-two years of age, she reached him across a bridge of two generations. There was something faintly unnatural in their union, just sufficient to give it an indissoluble tenderness.

Their peaceful existence endured for fifteen months and Henry continued to forget his enemies. Nevertheless, in the spring, to celebrate the anniversary of their union he sent his aged cousin, Lady Salisbury, to the scaffold, but she had been under sentence for several years; indeed, to execute her was almost a deliverance. She fought for her life, however, on the scaffold, fell in her efforts to escape from the executioners, who were in the end compelled to hold her down and literally hack off her head.

In the autumn Henry took Catherine with him on a progress up North, a part of the country where he had not ventured to show himself since the Pilgrimage of Grace. He had hopes of a meeting with his nephew, James V of Scotland; James did not make his appearance, however, but the forests were none the less beautiful for his absence. There was hunting and dancing and at the end of a month they set out once more for London. But they did not go to Whitehall; they stopped at Hampton Court Palace. The plague had come to London and the dead were being buried in cartloads.

The Plotting of Cranmer and the Seymours.

Cranmer remained at Henry's side, but ever since he had witnessed the falling of Cromwell's head, he had lain low, seeking safety in allowing himself to be forgotten. He had advised the adherents of his party to cease being obtrusive with regard to the Bible and the Eucharist, to hold their tongues and to wait; the future being always the reward of the patient. Ill-doers and heretics would not triumph for long and Cranmer was laying odds upon some error of Howard's or of Gardiner's, watching for the little Queen to commit some imprudence. He had on his side many folk who were powerful or who hoped some day to become so; Jane Seymour's two brothers, Edward, the elder, rather slow-minded but very steady, and Thomas, the younger, slightly eccentric but charming, full of vitality and imagination. With these were arrayed Cromwell's surviving friends and various hangers-on of their party. Cromwell's son and heir had married one of Jane's sisters and was therefore allied to the Seymours. These Seymours intended one day to rule England; as uncles of the little Prince Edward they planned to become his guardians and his regents. Henry was daily growing heavier and more bloated; ardent and too greatly desired wives are not beneficial to husbands approaching the critical age. Prince Edward was still in petticoats and fifteen years must elapse before he would attain to manhood. Nobody believed that Henry could live another fifteen years; there were good days ahead for the Seymours . . .

But it was meanwhile essential that Henry should

accept them. Both the Seymours were in excellent health, but none the less the stroke of an axe would suffice and Howard was eyeing them with an unwholesome interest. Catherine, if Howard schooled her, might easily set Henry against the Seymours, reminding him that they were heretics and had designs upon his inheritance. There might indeed arise yet more perilous complications; Catherine, so healthy, so radiant, might easily have a son, for Henry, at her side, was recapturing a third or fourth springtime. Once such a son was born, any childish ailment would suffice, an attack of measles or of diarrhœa, to send little Edward to another world and make of the newly born the heir to the kingdom. Howard would then be uncle to the new prince and consequently prospective regent. The Seymours, their brother-in-law Cromwell, and their holy friend Cranmer would then find themselves completely outclassed. Once Henry was dead, Howard and Gardiner would easily institute proceedings against them for heresy and treason and the bishop would be burned while the laity would be hanged, drawn and quartered.

When Henry and Catherine returned to Hampton Court, they found Prince Edward ill of a fever.

During fifteen months, those same fifteen months in which Henry enjoyed perfect happiness, Cranmer and the two Seymours were busily reflecting. They had no intention of losing their lives and they sought industriously for a means of defence. Any intrigue against Howard or Gardiner would be sheer waste of time. In the event of dismissal they would not fail to return, with Catherine there to be their advocate. And even if they remained in exile, Catherine would be with

Henry and might at any time conceive a son. It was Catherine herself at whom they must aim, they must contrive to destroy that womb.

Cranmer Strikes.

On the second of November the Mass for All Souls was said in the chapel at Hampton Court, and Henry was careful to attend it. He loved all ceremonies and upon that feast it was customary to sing very melodious music. Moreover, he had many dead to pray for and assist, and since he had approved a continued belief in purgatory, it was his duty to give his prayers to the souls detained therein. The King his father was doubtless burning for more than one political misdeed; Jane Seymour's demise had been so unexpected that it was licit to doubt of her perfect contrition, and there was also that other who appeared at last to be appeased and whose name it was safer to leave unmentioned but who might be none the worse were she thrown an occasional prayer. Catherine, at his side, followed the Mass inattentively. She murmured her orisons, reflecting that the chants were unnecessarily tedious and that it must be pleasant outside on the terrace.

Cranmer glided up to Henry's armchair; he was pale as though hesitating between two apprehensions. He whispered a few words in Henry's ear and handing him a paper closely folded begged him to read it only in the utmost seclusion. The man with his furtive feet which were barely visible beneath his priestly habit seemed to instil mystery into every situation.

[300]

Henry hid the paper in his hose and Catherine pretended to have seen nothing; she seldom took any interest in affairs of State. Henry suspected that Cranmer was denouncing some more or less fictitious plot, seeking to undo Gardiner or Howard. Nevertheless, he was troubled, as he invariably was when anyone denounced his friends. A thrust with a dagger is quickly given and a king lives surrounded by traitors. Like Catherine, he began to find the Mass unnecessarily long and he ceased to meditate on purgatory. Mass over, there followed a few subsidiary prayers and he finally left the chapel, made his way to his bedchamber, closed the door and opened Cranmer's paper.

In it Cranmer accused Catherine of having formerly had lovers. An old servant of Cromwell's had come to him and had related painful, unlovely incidents. This servant had learned of them from his own sister who had been a maid in the household of the Howard grandmother and had known Catherine herself as a child. It all sounded most lamentably authentic, for Cranmer, before dealing his King so terrible a blow, had been careful to verify his evidence. His heart bled at being compelled to denounce Catherine, but he could not endure that his King should be immersed in such an ocean of iniquity and turpitude. He had sought advice from men deeply devoted to their master, to wit, among others, the two Seymours, and all had advised him that it was his duty to speak. But, doubtless in his fear lest his voice might fail him, he had preferred to write his accusations.

Henry crumpled the paper in his hand and then sent for Cranmer. He was indignant that this old priest should dare to touch, to soil her who was to him as his own flesh. He had no belief in Cranmer's assurances of affection as coming from a man whom he had a thousand times humiliated and frustrated and whom he had compelled to repudiate his wife and children. He guessed that Cranmer, at one time wounded in his dearest attachments, found pleasure to-day in being able to avenge himself while serving his own interests and overthrowing his enemies. Henry seemed to hear him saying: "You deprived me of my wife and her absence grieves me, but at least I am not jealous; I know that I can trust her, while she whom you have chosen has wallowed in the gutter."

When Cranmer appeared Henry asked himself whether he should not strangle him; it would be quite easy and Cranmer, gripped by the neck, would be unable to cry out, would not utter a sound. The accuser dead, Henry would know nothing, he could continue to trust Catherine; he had only to burn the paper. After all, it contained nothing incontestably new; he had always had his suspicions of her purity. A girl of her vitality could scarcely have attained to eighteen years without her lips having known those of young men. Why was this bishop meddling in the matter? But then he reflected: Cranmer's death would serve no purpose; it would not slay facts, since the Seymours knew of them, and others also, Cromwell's former servant and all those who had known Catherine in her childhood, all the household of her Howard grandmother, Howard too and Gardiner, who had thrust Catherine into his arms. They all knew, they had all laughed at him and had made him fall into their infamous snare. Such shame could

only be washed clean with blood; he himself could not
now bear to live on in ignorance.

A servant announced the archbishop and he came in
trembling. It had always been his fate to have a timorous
soul and to be compelled to master his fears and hurl
himself into terrible enterprises. Henry ordered him to
tell what he believed to be the truth and sitting down he
began, in his studied priestly accents, to relate the details
of his carefully concocted story.

How Little Girls Amuse Themselves.

When she had been thirteen or fourteen in her grandmother's house, Catherine had looked too attentively at
her music master. Music has been known to turn youthful brains. The name of this master was Manox and he
taught Catherine the virginals. Their fingers would
sometimes meet on the keyboard and when she would
bend forward to study the music, Manox would bend
forward also. His lips would linger on the nape of
Catherine's neck, would somehow pass from her neck
to her mouth and thus they would forget their studies.

Nor did they remain content with kisses. The spinet-
player was possessed of nimble fingers and knew how to
find his way beneath a gown; Catherine had allowed him
to venture, to contemplate; he knew of a secret mole and
could tell where it was situated. Cranmer, as he related
this detail, modestly lowered his eyes, but did not fail
to observe that Henry blushed.

Cranmer, having thus produced his effect, proceeded.
The adventure with Manox, he said, had been of short

duration. Old Lady Howard had one day come in unexpectedly, had dismissed the musician and lectured Catherine, who was hurriedly adjusting her skirts.

There had followed a youth, bolder, and more favoured than Manox; it was indeed uncertain whether the Queen did not still love him. He was a cousin of the Howards, Derham by name, yet another of their poor relations. He had been learning social usages in the Howard establishment, serving as page and as esquire. He had fallen in love with Catherine and had crept at night into her chamber. At the beginning the meetings had been innocent; other Howard children, sisters or cousins of Catherine, had slept in the room beside her. A servant, Jane Bulmer, had also shared their chamber and Derham had had to content himself with words. Later, however, he had brought the children sweetmeats and had bribed the servant. Then he had been able to creep into Catherine's bed in the darkness; he had kept on his clothes, but they had clasped each other through their garments.

Henry mopped his brow, remembering the nights that he himself had spent thus with Anne Boleyn. These Howards were doubtless all alike; he visualized the two childish bodies lustful and frustrated.

Cranmer sighed and then resumed his narrative: "Nor did they always retain their garments." The testimony of the servants was circumstantial and all are aware how such adventures develop. Derham and Catherine had continued to meet for several years; she had been fifteen, sixteen and then seventeen. At first Derham had removed his collar under the pretext that it choked him; then, on a summer's evening, his doublet, remaining in his hose of fine wool that closely moulded his legs. But wool is a material harsh to the skin, and presently he had also removed his hose. Catherine had helped him with her delicate hands. He could not very well lie naked on the outside of the bed without shocking the servant and surprising the little girls, so he had slipped in beside Catherine, under the bedclothes.

"But how was this thing discovered?" asked Henry dully.

The music master had given them away. He had not dared to challenge Derham, who was well skilled with sword and dagger, but nevertheless he had been consumed by jealousy. He was unable to forget Catherine's little secret mole or to endure the thought that another should be reaping the harvest that he himself had sown. He wrote to the old Duchess and placed the letter on her prayer-stool, thus lending sanctity to cowardice. The grandmother had consequently tiptoed up the stairs and had surprised the lovers abed one night with the servant guarding the candle. She had rained indiscriminate blows upon all of them impartially and Derham had fled, his hose over his arm. An uncle of Catherine's to whom the grandmother had gone for advice had counselled silence. Since Catherine had been careful or fortunate enough to keep her reputation, her future must be considered. The young man flung out of the house, joined the army and travelled; he went over to Ireland and became a pirate.

"But where is he now, this Derham?" enquired Henry. "Is he here?" "Yes." "Does he see her?" "The Queen has taken him into her service as groom; he is now her Groom of the Bedchamber. She also employs the servant who watched with such fidelity; she is that Jane Bulmer whom your Grace has doubtless seen." "Very well," said Henry, "Derham must be arrested; we shall find the means of making him speak."

An Energetically Conducted Enquiry.

He dismissed Cranmer, but did not seek out Catherine, to whom he sent orders to remain in her chamber. He heard that she had summoned her musicians to divert her and accompany her dancing. He countermanded her directions; this was no time for dancing.

He called together his usual advisers: Cranmer, of course, and Fitzwilliam, the man who had gone to fetch the Clevan; Catholics also: Gardiner and Risley. Howard was in London and at first Henry dared not send for him lest he should bring the plague; but later he made up his mind and brought him to Hampton Court, where he dined with him alone in a private pavilion and then took him to join the others. On the fifth of November the sitting lasted through most of the night.

The suspects were arrested and were divided among the counsellors. Fitzwilliam tackled the brother and sister who had originally denounced the affair to Cranmer, and they repeated all that they had said before. Cranmer, with Risley to help him, took the music master to his palace at Lambeth and he made a full confession, admitting that he had loved his pupil and also the nature of the lessons he had given her. From Lambeth Palace Risley proceeded to the Tower, where he found Derham safely in custody. Risley had undertaken to unseal the pirate's lips; he had efficacious means at his disposal.

Catherine remained confined to her chamber. Her Uncle Howard asked to see her and Henry gave his permission. Possibly he hoped that Howard would suggest some means of defence, some falsehoods that might, if necessary, be used to stop the mouths of the accusers. But Howard was not the man for such subtleties and by-ways and he lacked Cromwell's instinct, his power of reading Henry's heart. His only desire was to exonerate himself, to prove his zeal by overwhelming Catherine. He questioned her brutally and she refused to answer. He returned in a fury to the Council. Cranmer took his place and visited Catherine; he was adept in the confessing of women. He adopted the tones of a friend, of an elder brother. "Tell everything, my child; you know that the King loves you. He is far from desiring to harm you in any way; he reserves for you treasures of leniency. After all, these stories refer to ancient occurrences, before you had ever known him. At that time you owed him nothing, therefore speak to me frankly and I will repeat only so much as we think wise. There is deep satisfaction in a full confession of sin and you will experience a blessed relief. You will feel as pure as the newly baptized babe. You must realize that the King is already fully informed, therefore you must try to touch his heart by your confession and complete submission. He has certainly no thoughts of a trial; he could not live without you. He may possibly command you to withdraw for a short while. You may even, at any moment, see him appear before you so that you may fall at his feet. He can refuse you nothing and all will be forgotten."

During an entire afternoon he tempted her. She was all alone and she was terribly afraid. The grey November day drew to a close and servants brought in the candles. She was utterly worn out and she wanted to weep and suddenly she weakened and spoke. She admitted that the music master had seen her body, that she had caressed Derham's bare legs under her bedclothes. Cranmer wrote to her dictation with many reassurances: these were not very serious, these peccadilloes of childhood. When he had finished he asked her to write her name at the foot of the statement and Catherine obeyed.

Cranmer again sought Henry, entering his room on soundless, slippered feet, and silently showed him the paper. Henry perused it and saw Catherine's signature, the sprawling signature of a child. He visualized her wide frightened eyes, her shaking hand, and he understood that in signing that confession she had ruined herself, that here was something that he could not hope to destroy, that he no longer had the right to forgive her and would see her no more. He had not even the strength to hate Cranmer who had set this snare. He bowed his head sadly as Risley arrived from the Tower. Risley had seen Derham; trapped between four walls, handled by the torturers, the handsome pirate had spoken. He had confessed the nocturnal adventures of his youth, his amusements in Catherine's narrow bed.

The Tears of a Too-Loving Husband.

Henry was now unceasingly in Council. The chiefs of

the enquiry arrived at intervals with new minutes and interminable interrogatories. They gloried in devising new torments for the witnesses, in drawing from them yet further admissions. They would sit together around the table, leaning one toward another, comparing their documents. Cranmer's eyes gleamed when he saw Derham's confession, while Howard cried out that his niece was an infamous prostitute and that no fate could be too bad for her. Then he would sympathize with the King's misfortune. Henry, when he read Derham's deposition, lost all control. Before the eyes of these men whom he despised he allowed his tears to flow and burst into heart-broken sobbing. They wept in competition but they glanced sideways as they wept, looking at him, mocking the huge, grotesque body as it sobbed, gasped and hiccoughed. What was his grievance? A neglected little girl who was bored in the country had sought amusement in allowing herself to be petted by her music master, and later by a good-looking young cousin. She had not even met the King in those days, had owed him no fidelity and had made him no promises, could not even have suspected that he would ever look twice at her. Was this seemly behaviour for a man who ruled two kingdoms, for a Pope who had announced himself as the inspired of Heaven? Cranmer thought of the tears he himself had been compelled to hide, to restrain or to swallow when he had dismissed his Nuremberger, she and those children who had been his life's happiness. Others sat remembering the victims of this weeping king, the beheadings, the burnings, the quarterings at Tyburn.

But Henry had been premature with his tears; he had

still to learn of more painful disillusions. He had not yet drunk the cup to its dregs.

The Handsome Tom.

A woman of the bedchamber, one Madge Norton, stated that the Queen was probably now unfaithful to the King; that in any case she certainly loved another man. Commanded to be explicit she said that one day, at Hatfield House, she had surprised one of the Queen's glances. That her eyes had rested upon a handsome young man, and that her gaze had been visibly tender. The ministers demanded the name of the young man and the witness replied: "Thomas Culpeper."

Hurrying to Henry they triumphantly announced their discovery. They were yapping and squirming like a pack of hounds who, being hot on the scent, are anticipating the kill. Tom Culpeper had long annoyed them with his spoiled, childish airs; Tom, who mocked them to the King and who obtained favours and monasteries. Tom was young, handsome, well-dressed and a ne'er-do-weel, the most dangerous type of minion. They themselves were ugly and decrepit and were probably being deceived by their mistresses. One and all they sided with Henry; the old Scaramouches were determined to be revenged on Harlequin.

It is not known whether on this occasion Henry again wept. Possibly his suffering was too intense. He adored Catherine, and Tom he also loved. In their company he had been used to forget politics, ministers, Cranmer's dreary face and Howard's murderous countenance.

With them he had been able to brush aside fears and anxieties; he had been confident and had felt himself to be kind and now those two beings had united to insult and betray him, to inflict upon him a mortal injury, and, yet more criminally to awaken in him forgotten yearnings, to inflame him anew with the torments of desire.

Tom was at that time in attendance at the Palace, only a few yards away from his master, waiting and ready to serve him. Henry, separated from Catherine, had resumed his former intimacies; he had allowed Tom to witness his anguish and Tom had been anxiously attentive, had seemed perturbed. And so doubtless he had been, not out of affection but out of fear. Henry did not send for him; Tom would have wept and implored. He had him quietly removed by a few of his guards. He was put in a barge and taken downstream, like so many others before him of more consequence, to the Tower of London.

Witnesses are Frequently Superfluous.

Henry waited. He felt himself weighed down and almost paralysed by his sorrow. It was not a piercing, vital anguish but a dull, dreary despair. That fine flame of youth which Catherine had rekindled in him was now for ever spent and he no longer knew whether he cared to go on living. The heavy November skies numbed his perceptions and he looked at those about him as though they were ghosts. A sudden outbreak of shrill voices would rouse him, after which he would sink back into an interminable silence. At times he clung to the hope that he was living in a dream; he would say to himself:

"Presently I shall wake. I shall find her, innocent and faithful, lying asleep beside me. I shall once more take her in my arms and warm myself at the fires of her youth; I shall slake my thirst from the inexhaustible fountain of her vitality."

But when he opened his eyes he would see only the empty place beside him and, lying at his feet, the page who had replaced Tom Culpeper.

She had not left his house and he learned that she wept and wailed, that she was refusing either to eat or to drink. She was only a child who had sinned out of ignorance.

At times he would long to go to her, whether to forgive her or to strike he did not know. Would it not be sufficient to behold her weeping at his feet for a few moments, a few hours? That response, that emotion which he had never been sure of obtaining from her, would now be aroused by her devastating terror. He would watch the orgasm possess her being and divine, beneath her labouring breast, the panic of her heart. Then he would raise her up, would take her on his knees and drink her tears, but then he would remember that all his ministers knew, that the servants were whispering, even the very pages. He reflected that he would be laughed at, and to that he preferred death.

Two weeks had gone by and he could not keep her any longer in the Palace. He did not, however, send her to the Tower, but to a convent in the country, a few miles from London, at Syon. He hoped to leave her for a time in this empty house, to give her the opportunity of repenting in seclusion, never to take her back but to visit her from time to time, finding refreshment in her society. Perhaps he would allow her to grow old in captivity, wasting that youth which she had failed to dedicate to him; possibly he had thoughts of killing her by means of some painless poison, without her being warned of her impending death. For five or six days he disappeared from Court and went, accompanied by a handful of servants, to hide himself in the depths of the winter-bound forests.

The Heaviest Punishment is Reserved for Those Least Beloved.

He returned and commanded his ministers to rid him of Derham and of Tom Culpeper, the two men who had so deeply wounded him. On the first of December they appeared before a tribunal of the Council. Derham maintained that he had sported with Catherine only at a time when she had still been free. He was, however, condemned for treason. Tom related his story: "I loved her deeply from the first moment of her coming to Court. We were practically betrothed when the King took her from me. I submitted but I was unable to console myself; every day I saw her and we played and laughed together. My passion for her increased, but for a long time I controlled it. Finally, one evening at a ball, I slipped a note into her hand asking for an assignation to which she agreed. After that we met secretly sometimes, but I was not her lover." Throughout Tom's narrative, Howard had not ceased to snigger and to nod his old head and when Tom had finished the elder Seymour, who was president of the tribunal, observed: "You have told us sufficient to forfeit your life," and he was condemned, like Derham, for treason.

The two men had been tried in the heart of London in the full publicity of the Guildhall. They had been deliberately exhibited to the populace as though the ministers, scenting Henry's indecision, were courting scandal with a view to forcing his hand. The prisoners were led back to the Tower and remained there for another ten days: Henry could not make up his mind to kill Tom.

Nevertheless, he knew him to be guilty, for other servants had witnessed against him. Several times, in September and October during Henry and Catherine's progress in the North, Culpeper had secretly crept to her chamber. He had also met her on a narrow staircase and later in a secluded room. Once he had lain all night in her arms. Henry visualized them clasped heart to heart, those two bodies that he knew so well, that he could evoke with such devastating precision. The servants could hear him howling in his bedchamber. One day he suddenly demanded a sword; he would go to Syon Convent, seize the adulteress and plunge the sword into her heart.

Then his hatred would evaporate and he would find it unbearable to think that Tom should be drawn and quartered, that he must suffer a lingering and hideous death. On the tenth of December Derham was led to Tyburn to the agonizing torments reserved for traitors, while Tom, whose crime had been infinitely greater, merely laid his head upon the block.

Forty Days of Anguish.

Catherine was still at Syon and Howard was urging Henry to agree to her being burned alive. But Henry ended by losing his temper and dismissing Howard from his presence. Sometimes he would desire to have Catherine tortured: "I will have her subjected to such various torments that they will efface the memory of her pleasures." He would be convulsed with desire: either by means of joy or of pain he would tear a response from her body. Catherine begged him to spare her the cries and the curiosity of the populace and to allow her to die in privacy.

But he dared not consent; he was profoundly conventional and in his eyes a king who ordered that a criminal be stabbed was nothing less than an assassin, while a king who deputed the business to a tribunal and executioners was justified even were the victim innocent. And Henry always aimed at self-justification. He required it in order to deceive the populace, perhaps also to deceive himself and to buttress himself against future nights of remorse and against the accusations of certain phantoms.

After the execution of Derham and Culpeper followed forty days of complete silence. Catherine ventured to breathe and her spirits rose. Henry was subjecting her to childish punishments, such as forbidding her to wear any adornments. For company he had given her George Boleyn's guilty widow, that Lady Rochford who had helped her to meet Tom and who had kept watch during their meetings. Threatened with death, Lady Rochford had agreed to spy upon Catherine and to repeat all her utterances, and Henry feverishly awaited her reports. In the middle of January he decided that Catherine must die. The two Houses having been summoned he presented them with a bill of attainder against the Queen, asking them to declare her a traitor and to vote her death. Then, almost immediately, he ordered them to desist and adjourned the debate.

Two weeks later he informed the Houses that they must resume their labours, but without his taking the initiative. The Lords obeyed him and sent a deputation to Syon for the purpose of asking Catherine to confess. She denied that she had ever been Culpeper's mistress; she was not an adulterous Queen. Whereupon the Lords threw themselves at Henry's feet and begged for his permission to examine the Queen, or, in other words, to condemn her, while Catherine sent word to Henry that she would not defend herself to strangers but would accept her fate only at his hands.

On the tenth of February the Constable of the Tower arrived at the convent of Syon. On this occasion it was no longer Kingston who had so conscientiously spied upon Anne Boleyn but John Gage, a man of the newer generation, a fine gentleman with an elegant beard. When Catherine beheld him she wept and made an attempt at resistance, while Lady Rochford shrieked like a lunatic. They grew calmer, however, and followed Gage to the river and were placed in a small wherry. As they were approaching London they saw two great barges rowing upstream towards them. One of these was commanded by Brandon and the other by Fitzwilliam and both were crowded with guards. The helmets and cuirasses of the soldiers gleamed dully under the January sky while the two barges drew alongside the wherry and silently escorted it on its way.

To Die, but to Die Gracefully.

On the following day Catherine was informed that both Houses had voted her death. She wept. Lady Rochford was also condemned and they were to die on the morrow. When Henry was told of Catherine's tears he postponed the day of execution. He would not let her die unreconciled and thus risk the loss of her soul. So long as he knew her to be alive there remained some warmth round his heart; desperately he prolonged her existence.

Next day he was told that she was resigned to her death and he realized that it was the end, but he delayed it yet another day. He refused to allow her to die in private, compelling her to face the last public ordeal; and she was afraid of dying badly. Not that she lacked courage or had any tears left to shed: she had now achieved resignation. But even the most self-confident of actresses, the most experienced of coquettes is liable to error if she has not studied her gestures or repeated her part before a mirror. Catherine asked the Constable to describe the scaffold, the width of its planks and the number of steps leading up to it. She was particularly anxious with regard to the block. She had never seen a block and she desired to kneel down before it with dignity, to be graceful in her farewell to life. They brought the block for her to see, and she practised, seeking the best position for her knees and for her head, laying her lips against the grain of the wood and asking her women to criticize the attitude of her neck. When she felt sure of her movements she had the block removed and made an effort to obtain some sleep. She wished to appear rested when she faced the crowd. Also she rehearsed the sentences of her intended speech.

It consisted of a few emotional phrases that she had chiefly selected for their romantic content in order to leave behind a passionate impression that would linger in the minds of all those young men who would stand below the scaffold to watch her die. She considered also the young men of the future.

As in the case of her cousin, the scaffold had been erected in the courtyard and, like Anne, she distributed largesse. She climbed the wooden steps and advanced to the balustrade. In the foremost ranks of the crowd she saw the ministers: those who had offered her to the King and those who had been her undoing. They were all there with the exception of her Uncle Howard, who had been exempted by Henry from attendance. Her lovely eyes surveyed the crowd in search of younger and more comely faces; how handsome were these lads, young nobles, squires and even simple apprentices! She would have liked to caress them, like Derham, like poor Tom!

It was to them that she addressed her last speech. She said: "Brethren, I am setting out on a very far journey and before I go, I swear to you that I did not betray the King." That much she must say to win their approval, for young men despise unfaithful wives, even if they profit by their infidelity. But she did not labour the point; she had no wish to remain in their minds as the respectable bourgeois wife of a paunchy old husband. She had not sinned in body, but her mind had remained free. "I have always loved Tom. I loved him before the King ever noticed me." She mentioned neither Derham nor the music master; what was the use of appearing promiscuous? She loved Tom with an eternal devotion. At that moment she probably believed it and had forgotten the two others. "When the King spoke to me for the first time I should have told him that I already loved another. Tom wished it and had I done so I should not now be upon this scaffold and he would still be alive. I had rather have had him as husband than have possessed the entire world." This might be open to doubt, so she hurried on to admit her errors. "I was blinded by sin." What sin? She did not specify. "And more particularly by my desire for worldly eminence. In this I was sinful and I must now pay the price." She implied that her fault had lain, not in betraying Henry but in having deserted Tom, and she added: "If I suffer to-day, it is at the thought that Tom died because of me."

It was impossible to imagine more poetical sentiments. Then she turned towards the executioner, saying: "Do your duty quickly." In accordance with custom he knelt at her feet and received her forgiveness. She was very small and the man in red towered above her when he rose and drew back while she walked to the block. The fatal moment had arrived. She knelt and with a graceful movement of her body adjusted the folds of her gown, glancing towards her women for assurance that all was seemly. She raised her head again, she had one thing left to say by which she intended to unite for ever the two principal elements of her life, to be remembered both as Queen and lover. "I die a Queen, but I had rather have died the simple wife of Tom Culpeper. May God have mercy on my soul. Pray for me."

They began to pray and she was still smiling when the axe fell. She had sported so gracefully with death that she scarcely felt herself die. They removed the slender body and the severed head and brought Lady Rochford to the scaffold. She mounted the steps, melancholy and morose. "I am innocent of the crime of which I am accused, but I die justly because I lied long ago when I myself accused my husband George and the Queen Anne of incest."

XVI

TWILIGHT

(1542—1547)

The Dangers of Melancholy.

AT twenty nothing is more enjoyable than a fit of melancholy. Musicians discover by its means their most moving melodies, while it provides poets with their tenderest sonnets. It is a phantasy of the spirit and a relaxation for the body in which the organism, exhausted by sensual excesses, recuperates its energies. There is no better preparation for enterprises or for the less chaste categories of adventure.

But Henry was over fifty years old and that is an age dangerous to those who suffer from ulcers, to those who are gluttonous and to the obese. Catherine's death hurt him far more deeply than any young man's despair, but he was on his guard against giving way to his grief, fearing to sink so low that he would never rise again. He knew that for him there would be no pleasure in his pain and that he would be unable to find in it either poetry or music. He never touched his lute and his suffering wore him out, leaving him without even the strength for dreams. He was too much numbed to feel remorse or to see visions and he grew to regret the times when he had been used to see Anne's bleeding head. It seemed as though those fifteen months of his happiness had consumed all that remained to him of life, leaving him despoiled even of the power to remember.

A Variety of Distractions.

He set to work to organize the present, giving banquets and balls and amusing himself with watching comely women dance and partake of delicate dishes. He guarded himself from any sentimental adventures, having no longer sufficient self-confidence to believe that he could be beloved. As for purely physical escapades, he left those to the young and contented himself with reigning.

Never in his life had he been so powerful; there was now no minister left to obstruct him. Catherine's death had discredited the Catholics, Gardiner and the Howards, but had not crushed them. The two parties were finding their level, both of them being led by seasoned advisers, men who were experienced and devoid of imagination, while Henry remained aloof from both as sovereign arbiter. He would play off one party against the other, affront or gratify them, make them tremble with a word. Being absolute master and meeting only mediocrities, he was able to believe in his own genius.

He had compelled both Houses to vote a law which had transfigured him into a species of god before whom every woman must tremble with awe. On the actual day of Catherine's condemnation the Lords and the Commons had passed three amazing decrees: Should be held guilty of high treason any maid who, not being virtuous and being asked in marriage by the King, should fail to confess that she was not a virgin. Should also be held guilty of high treason any person who, being aware of such a damaging fact in connection with the intended bride of the King, should not immediately communicate that knowledge in the proper quarters. Should also be held guilty of high treason any queen who should attempt to be unfaithful to her husband. The guilty party should be hanged, drawn and quartered at Tyburn unless his Grace, in his infinite mercy, should commute the sentence to decapitation.

His matrimonial future thus guaranteed, Henry turned once more to religious questions. The claims of the Lutherans annoyed him and he could not tolerate the idea that any fool might open the Bible and seek in it his personal interpretations. He was of opinion that when dictating the Bible God had not always necessarily made Himself clear to the multitude and, in common with the Catholics, he held that the Scriptures, being very ancient and having been written by an Oriental people, required commentary by scholars and enlightened experts. There not being always perfect agreement between the Old and New Testaments, it was necessary to establish a hierarchy between the various aspects of the truth. Certain psalms, certain passages in the Old Testament contained sentiments that were undeniably violent and that might conceivably encourage the poor to set themselves up against the nobility and their rulers. Henry restricted the sale of the English translation of the Bible and confined the reading of the Word to persons of leisure who were educated and of moderate views.

He also occupied himself with foreign policy. On the Continent Francis and Charles continued their monotonous quarrels. Henry approached Charles; not that he had any intention of assisting him, but he had thoughts of intervention in Scotland, of engineering some chastisement for James V, that disrespectful nephew from whom he had failed to filch Mary of Guise, and Francis was allied to James V.

In the autumn Henry sent an army into Scotland commanded once more by the evergreen Howard. As always, Howard pillaged, burned, sacked and then retreated. James V mobilized his forces with the intention of invading England. Being intensely Catholic, although yet more licentious, he had received letters of authorization from the Pope. His object was to depose his uncle Henry and to re-establish the Roman Faith. The Scottish had no confidence in the success of this enterprise and they implored James, in view of the fact that he had as yet no legitimate son, not to expose his person to danger. James protested but was compelled to give way and retreat and the Scots were pursued and beaten by the English. They were as foolhardy as they were brave, full of imagination and liable to the most groundless panics. Once more the bare legs and kilts were beheld in complete rout and James was so infuriated that he took to his bed and died within three weeks. It being by then December, Henry began the New Year very comfortably and felt no undue emotion on the anniversary of Catherine's death. Such trivial memories appeared to him to be unworthy of his attention, God having vouchsafed him proof of His love.

He remained concentrated upon his political

distractions, interweaving his schemes at home with foreign complications.

Surrey.

Since the war in Scotland Howard had acquired undue importance. Nothing had ever been known to disconcert him. He had survived Catherine's trial as he had that of Anne and was now preparing a new matrimonial project. His present candidate was not a young girl, believing as he did that Henry was cured of love. The heir to the crown being only five years of age, he could not as yet be contracted in marriage. But Howard had a son, the Earl of Surrey, for whom he determined to obtain the hand of the unhappy Mary, Henry's daughter, who was ageing in semi-disgrace. Could anyone be sure that the little Edward would survive? And in that event Henry's death would place Mary on the throne, with young Surrey to occupy the place at her side.

Surrey's physical appearance was really astonishing. He had a narrow head, a crooked mouth, a pointed chin and crazy eyes which rolled in huge, hollow orbits. But he was brave to excess and the most exquisite of poets. Mary, at twenty-seven years of age, appeared too mature to fall in love with so bizarre a suitor; a man some years her junior, adventurous and addicted to plotting, but he was also dissolute and ostentatiously impious, and the mystical Mary might have dreams of converting him.

Surrey knew how to unite shrewdness with prowess. Henry was fond of him, had given him forces to command and had bestowed upon him the orders of chivalry. But a few months after the Scottish successes he determined to put a curb on the Howards. He informed the brilliant Surrey that he regarded him as a child and imprisoned him for nocturnal brawling and for having eaten meat in Lent. The alleged nocturnal brawling had aroused his suspicions of a possible attempt at revolt.

The Sixth Marriage.

The Protestants believed themselves to have the upper hand and they rallied round Cranmer and the two Seymours. Cranmer was grovelling more abjectly than ever and Edward Seymour was eagerly hoping that Henry might die of surfeit, having previously appointed him regent and guardian to little Prince Edward. Thomas was growing steadier and was even contemplating marriage.

He had fallen in love with a Protestant, thirty years of age, not very good-looking but sensible and intelligent and who had already had two husbands. She appeared to have devoted herself to old men and had buried the first when she was only sixteen. The second had lasted considerably longer, but he also had recently expired after twelve or thirteen years of matrimony. The lady had every appearance of discretion, but she must have had her secret emotions, for she agreed to a betrothal with Thomas Seymour, a Protestant out of policy but a confirmed pagan by disposition.

This very consolable widow came of an excellent family and her name was Catherine Parr. Her nose was long and hooked, her neck decidedly on the short side and she had the respectable portliness of a piously learned woman who for fifteen years has slept with a partner, but without enjoyment. Her eyes were round, black and staring, surmounted by arched and rather bushy eyebrows. She wore few jewels but wide spotlessly laundered collars and irreproachable white coiffes. Her mouth was well shaped and surprisingly suggestive of temperament.

This Catherine had been known to Henry for a long time, but he had scarcely troubled to look at her. He generally avoided married women and Catherine was certainly not of those whose flashing, fatal personality lends to adultery a dignity worthy of kings. An adulterous relationship with Catherine Parr would almost have assumed respectability. Despite her leanings to science and theology, she was domesticity personified and if the brilliant Thomas Seymour was genuinely attracted to her it must have been in the spirit of a Don Juan who, weary of Bacchantes, had acquired a perverted taste for the seduction of virtue.

In the spring of 1543 Henry, who was once more veering towards the Protestant camp, towards Cranmer and the two Seymours, was brought into contact with this worthy widow. It was May, a month that always seemed to cause him unrest, and feeling himself assailed by desires he was fearful of succumbing to some new folly. Catherine struck him as a potentially appetizing bedfellow, an excellent bourgeoise, a protection against passionate entanglements. Unless the body is to lead a man astray it must be accorded some measure of satisfaction. He was unaware that Catherine was betrothed; or, what is more probable, he feigned ignorance. One day he drew her apart gently into a corner and informed her that she was the object of his choice. She grew pale and uttered a cry, exclaiming: "I, your wife?" An imprudent ejaculation that was self-revealing! Henry insisted and doubtless promised that in no circumstances would he sever that agreeably plump neck. He then communicated his intentions to the younger Seymour and Catherine resigned herself to becoming Queen. Henry married her at Hampton Court, where Cranmer had staged his attack on Catherine Howard. The King thus resumed his conjugal life in the very place that had witnessed its interruption. Thus wisely, in a spirit of continuity, he linked the past to the present.

His nights may possibly have been rather prosaic, but Catherine Parr, by means of long training, had grown adept in the art of pleasing the elderly. If her thoughts occasionally strayed towards the handsome Seymour she would remind herself that Henry was not immortal; and she cared for his children, for Elizabeth and especially Edward. She proved an admirable stepmother, telling herself that after Henry's death the affection of the little king might be a valuable asset. She might even hope to succeed in ousting the elder Seymour from the regency and installing the younger brother in his stead. Thomas had no thoughts of marrying elsewhere; he waited patiently for Catherine Parr.

A Recrudescence of Warlike Youth.

Henry was extremely happy with Catherine and they passed a peaceful summer and winter. He was successful everywhere, reinforcing his power in Ireland, interfering in Scotland and royally emptying English pockets. He was preparing for war, returning to the projects of his youth, and he dreamed of conquering some portion of French territory. At the moment of his marriage with Catherine Parr he had entered into an alliance with Charles and had sent him troops to aid him against the French.

These English forces joined those of the Germans at Hainault, in the green and rainy country of the Sambre, and with them they undertook the siege of Landrecies, finding war on the Continent decidedly entertaining. Then Charles arrived on the scene; he had been chastising some of his vassals, particularly the Duke of Cleves, brother of the disappointing Queen Anne. The unhappy Cleves had been roughly reminded that his resources were meagre, that a frog is not a bull and that it is wiser to respect the powerful. Charles had deprived him of Guelders and had made him understand that he was lucky to retain Cleves and his Mount of the Swans. The ex-Queen Anne congratulated herself that she had elected to remain on the banks of the Thames. In spite of her unprepossessing features she had now no difficulty in finding agreeable bedfellows. Few were the gentlemen who resisted the honour of slipping between the sheets of a former sovereign, of the King's adopted sister; of secretly becoming Henry's brothers-in-law and of providing him with morganatic nephews. For Anne proved fruitful. But pleasure had doubtless taught her tact, for she was careful not to embarrass Henry and she kept her new family concealed. He would sometimes go and pay her a visit, embracing her fraternally and never failing to maintain her allowance. However, he permitted his ally Charles to sit heavily upon Cleves and its little duke.

The English were not given time to grow bored at Landrecies, for a French army soon made its appearance. Francis had come in person with the intention of attacking Charles, but it was a Francis grown old and ravaged by disease, a Francis bereft of chivalry and daring. Charles was, however, compelled to give up Landrecies and Francis pursued and was about to capture him when suddenly, for no visible reason, he abandoned the pursuit. The English, believing that success was in their grasp, pursued in their turn, but met with unexpected resistance and were beaten. Winter supervened and put an end to the fighting.

In the spring of 1544 Henry decided to go to France in person. In April Charles, in spite of some reverses in Italy, announced that he would enter France from the North-East and that he would march on Paris. He sent an invitation to Henry to join him. Henry had always dreamed of seeing the Seine and claimed to be the only legitimate King of France; the project of invasion therefore appealed to him and he desired to be of the party. In the meantime he sent the elder Seymour to Scotland with a view to taking Edinburgh. Seymour failed in the attempt but consoled himself with pillage.

Charles was preparing a powerful army, having rallied the Protestants and united Germany by promising her a free hand in conquered France. He urged Henry to hurry to Calais and to attack. But Henry had never been hasty or audacious; he was a heavy vehicle that sank into every rut. Charles continued to wait for him until June and then set out alone, crossing the Barrois and hurling his army across the Marne. Saint-Didier held him up for a while, but fell at the end of June, and Henry decided that it was time to embark.

The Last Expedition to France.

It was the fourteenth of July. The sea was calm and Henry had brought with him everything necessary for his own comfort. He was accompanied by thirty thousand soldiers, to which Charles added another fifteen thousand. But Henry was in no hurry; he had not seen Calais since that November long ago when Anne Boleyn had appeared to return his love. He did not, however, allow himself to be weakened by too poignant memories, but gave his thoughts to his plan of campaign. He reflected, wondering whether he had not been foolhardy in agreeing to Charles's project. Now that he was in France its dangers struck him as more apparent. If he advanced on Paris some French force might cut him off from the coast, prevent him from retreating should he be defeated, prevent his taking refuge behind the ramparts of Calais as a preliminary to a prudent return to England. Charles was doubtless a powerful sovereign and a fine leader, but his audacity had frequently landed him in danger. Three years earlier he had lost his entire fleet in attempting to take Algiers, and the enemy had almost succeeded in making him a prisoner. In spite of his pacific appearance he delighted in risks; was he not a descendant of Charles the Bold? A sensible man like Henry could not be expected to follow his advice. He therefore decided to remain on the coast and to allow Charles to attack Paris alone while he himself besieged Boulogne. Sieges are leisurely operations well adapted to persons of bulk, and Henry was also thinking of the future. When peace was declared each belligerent would doubtless retain his captures and the English, should they by then have occupied Boulogne, would be able to remain there. Boulogne would be a useful pendant to Calais. So, far from going to support Charles, Henry employed the fifteen thousand Germans who had been sent him in laying siege to Boulogne on his own behalf.

Thus July and August went by, and Charles advanced as far as Château-Thierry. If Henry had consented to move, Paris would have been theirs, but Henry was quietly absorbed in his siege. Then Charles, exhausted and, moreover, harassed by revolts in Central Europe, left Henry in the lurch and made a separate peace with France. Henry had taken Boulogne and was contemplating seizing Montreuil, but he said to himself that the French, with Charles off their hands, might easily march towards the coast and interfere with him. He therefore relinquished all thoughts of Montreuil, returned to Calais, and by the beginning of October was back in London.

The following spring Henry remained at home. He had had his fill of exploits, but the French had no intention of allowing him to rest in peace. They determined to attack him in his own country, to invade England. Francis went to Rouen and collected a vast fleet, while Henry sought to reassure himself by repeating that the French had never been good sailors. The British fleet was anchored at Portsmouth and Henry paid it a visit to encourage it to defend him. He even went on board the flagship, but while he was afloat they came to tell him that the French fleet had been sighted and that an engagement was doubtless imminent. As his life was too valuable to England for him to think of exposing it to danger, he immediately ordered his barge and returned to land. As soon as he stood upon the quay and felt the solid earth beneath his large feet he decided that he could safely pause, that the French would probably be defeated, that the spectacle would be amusing and that he would be at hand to receive the acclamations of the victors. But the Frenchmen, manœuvring unskilfully but boldly, promptly sank one of the largest British ships, the *Mary-Rose*, and Henry watched her go down with all hands aboard. Five hundred English seamen were drowned and Henry returned home thoroughly disgusted with war.

A Sermon on Charity.

He resumed his meditations upon the next world. Catherine Parr was quiet and contented, or at any rate she appeared to be so, and if she sometimes glanced at Thomas Seymour she did so with incomparable discretion. Thomas waited for her the more patiently in that he did not fail to amuse himself in the meantime. Henry was putting on weight and his blood was growing more sluggish; he suffered from tingling sensations and his ulcer was suppurating. Catherine would place a footstool beneath his aching leg and every morning she dressed the wound. If she was less amusing than poor Tom had been, her hands were undeniably quite as gentle.

Henry, between accesses of indigestion, felt himself to be piously evangelical. Towards Christmas, before his united Lords and Commons, he made a paternal-fraternal speech tinged with the tenderest love and charity. In it he adjured all his subjects, his children, to refrain from quarrelling with regard to religious doctrines. They might read the Bible should they desire to do so, but always in a spirit of loving-kindness: "Do not make use of the Scriptures as a weapon against your priests or your preachers. Do not insult them or subject them to mockery." He himself had always been fearful of mockery and he pointed out to his audience that one thing particularly shocked him; his dear children appeared to him to be lacking in charity, whereas he, no doubt from personal experience, had learned all the delights to be drawn from that virtue. Doubtless his teachers had been the stake, the gibbet and the block. "Never has charity been less practised among you; never have public morals been so reprehensible." Despite the example set them by an exemplary king, it was notorious that the English were scornful of chastity. "God Himself has never been more meanly served. Live in peace the one with the other, as brothers. Love, fear and serve God; such is my request. It is what I ask of you as your sovereign, as your Supreme Head." The Lords and Commons wept with emotion and Henry's own paternal heart was moved. He descended pompously from his throne, leaning upon his staff.

The Game of See-saw.

His favourite pastime, the very foundation of his policy, had always been to preserve the balance between the Catholics and the Protestants. If he conferred a favour on Cranmer he promptly conferred another on Gardiner. In marrying Catherine Parr he had encouraged the Protestants, but a few weeks later he burned three heretics who had dared to deny the Real Presence in the Host. Therefore Gardiner and the Howards, father and son, did not lose courage; they were determined to overthrow Catherine Parr, to compass her death as Cranmer had compassed that of Catherine Howard. To each his turn of diminishing the Queen by a head.

Catherine being very cautious, they tried to ensnare Cranmer by denouncing him as a Lutheran; Henry nodded but kept his Cranmer. He was well aware of all his secret thoughts and of his views on the Eucharist, but he liked to manipulate such flexible material, a nature that tacked and tacked again in anticipation of the merest breath. Cranmer was too cold and too slimy to excite anger or to arouse Henry's instinct of cruelty and Cranmer had rendered him a thousand services. It was he who had pronounced the three divorces, he had been involved in all the important events. Henry's other tools had all been killed or were in the process of dying, and only Cranmer remained to discuss old happenings, to listen to recollections, to supply a date or a precise detail. If Henry had decided to burn Cranmer, he would have been sending to the flames a great part of himself. And then Cranmer's vileness, his unlimited ductility, amused Henry, and he would avenge himself gently and patiently upon the man who had denounced Catherine Howard, who had robbed him of his last love. He compelled him to remain separated from his wife and his children, to live and to grow old in solitude. He forced him to persecute his Protestant friends, to impose universal respect for the Catholic catechism, to deny by his every act his own private convictions and his God. It was well worth while keeping him alive, but Gardiner and Howard, unable to understand, ground their teeth.

There were also the ramifications of foreign policy. Henry had lost interest in Continental affairs and was preparing to make peace with France, but he continued to interfere in Scotland, where there was now a little three-years-old queen, Mary Stuart, who was a bone of contention between the various parties. Henry had vainly attempted to gain possession of her in order to marry her to his Edward and thus add Scotland to his realm. But his agents proved unsuccessful, though he did contrive after several years of effort to have Cardinal Beton, the leader of his adversaries, stabbed. This was a happy augury for the spring: the month of May had always brought him success. The murderers hung the Cardinal's body from the battlements of St. Andrew's Castle.

An Indiscreet Preacher.

These murderers being Protestants, Henry lost no time in moderating the delight of Cranmer, of his dearest Catherine and of the Seymours. There was at that time in London a most energetic evangelist, an apostle in petticoats who was preaching the new dispensation. This ardent female had neglected to study Saint Paul, or possibly she thought herself justified in despising the instructions of a saint so unfavourable to her sex. She therefore deserted her husband and children, being convinced that God required her for the snatching of souls from the darkness of idolatry. Being of gentle birth and well connected, she contrived to influence some very great ladies, including Brandon's second wife and Henry's dearest Catherine. She had been arrested on several occasions but had been released, and after thanking God for her rescue from misfortune she had stoutly resumed her ministry.

As a good Protestant, she could not endure the idea that God should be present in the Sacrament. Henry therefore caused her to be seized and taken to the Tower. Her husband also was put in prison, for no visible reason, seeing that she had deserted him and had even changed her name. The husband was left to moulder in gaol unmolested, but Henry dispatched to the eloquent lady one of his chosen inquisitors, that excellent Catholic Risley, who had become chancellor. Risley did not have recourse to the torturers, but operated personally with the assistance of one of his friends, a minister almost as eminent as himself. They entered the evangelist's cell, locked the door, flung her upon the ground and inflicted upon her the most exquisite torments; incidentally, she was young and attractive. She asked for nothing better than martyrdom, and was only too willing to confess, so that Henry was able to condemn her immediately and she was given over to the flames one fine day in July, at Smithfield.

The Imprudence of Catherine Parr.

This incident delighted Gardiner, who said to himself that since it marked a return to the execution of women

·it might well be possible to reach the Queen, and
Catherine at that moment was affording him an opportunity. Together with several other women of the Court,
all of them friends of her who had just been burnt, she
was reading, commenting and discussing the Bible.
Conversation thus assumed a new vivacity, avoiding Court
gossip, private scandals and personalities. But unfortunately Catherine took her fancies seriously and she
decided that she had been inspired by God as a means
of establishing the new doctrine. Thus had Esther been
placed at the side of Ahasuerus. She therefore ventured
upon some allusions before Henry and permitted herself
a slight supercilious smile when he spoke to her of the
Eucharist. He grasped the situation and was deeply
offended, but encouraged her to talk, to entangle herself.
She responded and went so far as to risk an argument.
Henry pretended to reply, to recognize her learning, to
be disconcerted. But one day he remarked to his
Catholic ministers that he was uneasy regarding the
Queen's spiritual state.

They thought their hour had dawned and replied that
she was a heretic, and Henry declared that no affection
would deter him and that he would punish heresy, even
in his own bed. Possibly he had cast an eye upon some
more comely maid of honour . . . In any case Gardiner
undertook to draw up an act of accusation. He was very
prompt in bringing it to Henry, who signed it. There
remained only to prepare an apartment in the Tower and
to summon the guards.

But Henry hesitated. He wished to know what
Catherine would say and sent one of his people to warn
her. Catherine had no aspirations to martyrdom. She

still expected to get some happiness out of life and cared more for Thomas Seymour than for any questions of religion. She fainted, only recovering consciousness to scream and cry and to make an inconceivable amount of noise. Henry was interested; he had not expected such wails and such distraction from the sensible Catherine. He lost no time in hurrying to witness them and Catherine literally rolled on the ground at his feet. He soothed her and promised to forgive her; God Himself does not desire the death of the repentant sinner.

As soon as he had left her Catherine pulled herself together and set to work to muster a defence, to evolve excuses. Having decided upon the course to adopt, she made her way, leaning upon her sister's arm, to the King's apartments and into his presence. She had no intention of leaving him to reflect, being well aware that he might change his mind. She knew him to be both secretive and shrewd. He greeted her, assuring her yet again of his affection, but she quickly realized that he still bore a grudge. He spoke to her of theology, obviously with a view to testing her.

"But I know nothing," she replied. "It is for you to instruct me. A woman's proper place is at her husband's feet."

He demurred.

"Not in your case; you are learned, you are a scholar and must teach us."

But Catherine lowered her eyes.

"I am nothing. I only talked of religion to distract you. I knew very well that I should say something foolish. But your leg was causing you pain and I hoped to entertain you . . .''

"Well, Kate; let us forget it. We are friends as before."

He was much too shrewd to believe in her submission, but he had succeeded in reducing her to a seemly servile status, and knowing that he had sealed her lips for ever, he no longer bore her any malice. His health was daily becoming less satisfactory, Catherine knew all his little intimate ailments, and she was also privy to all his equally intimate fancies. He was not going to gratify Gardiner by a change of nurse or the loss of a friend.

He took Catherine for a stroll in the garden and was leaning heavily on her arm when Risley made his appearance with half a dozen guards. He approached with an air of great solemnity. Henry, who had entirely forgotten his mission, nearly suffocated with fury and raged at him for a fool and a scoundrel. He would very likely have struck him as he had used to strike Cromwell, but he was no longer sufficiently active. Risley, dumbfounded, swallowed his insults and as soon as he could made his escape.

Death.

Henry remained fairly lively through the summer with Catherine nursing him patiently and perhaps almost too solicitously; she was thirty-four years of age and could not continue to wait for ever. In the autumn he seemed to collapse; he was only fifty-five, but he was dying of obesity and of over-eating, and the blood was surging up to his brain. He was unable to move about and a species of heavy vehicle was constructed to take him from room to room. Then his arm became paralysed and he was no longer able to write his name, but nobody was authorized to sign on his behalf, for he still intended to remain absolute master. He had a stamp made which was entrusted to the joint care of three secretaries, who were only permitted to affix it in his presence and in that of each other.

His mind was becoming clouded. Catherine had been waiting for this moment, knowing that so soon as he should be dead the Howards would attempt to turn out the Seymours and seize the person of the little king and the regency. She therefore lent her aid to Cranmer and the Seymours in their efforts to destroy the Howards. They told Henry that young Surrey had intentions of marrying Mary and would doubtless murder Edward, and they accused Gardiner of being involved in the plot. On the twelfth of December the ministers in full Council summoned Gardiner and Surrey to reply to questions. Gardiner had realized the impending storm and had succeeded in conciliating Henry, but Surrey found himself thrust into the Tower, accused of having adopted the royal arms. Howard was also imprisoned, but being shrewder than his son proceeded to defend himself.

Towards the twentieth Catherine and the Seymours feared that their game was foiled. Henry had had another stroke and was in danger of dying before he had killed the Howards. But he was carefully nursed and once more he rallied. On Christmas day he was decidedly better and on the following morning they submitted to him the former decree in which he had provided for the regency. They persuaded him to exclude from the government Howard, Gardiner and another Catholic minister. They also prepared for him a new will which was brought to him for signature a few days later. In it Henry bequeathed the throne to Edward and after him to Mary followed by Elizabeth, but refused to recognize any claim on the part of his niece Mary Stuart, the little Queen of Scotland.

Throughout January his improvement was maintained, while Cranmer, Catherine and the Seymours pressed forward the Howards' trial. Surrey was in the Tower, polishing his final poems, while Howard implored the King for mercy, enumerating his past services and offering all his possessions. The father and son were not being tried together. Surrey, in spite of his royal blood, appeared on the nineteenth of January before an ordinary tribunal, who declared that he had aspired to the throne and condemned him.

But it was in Parliament that Cranmer, the Seymours and all the crew who were nursing Henry and keeping him closely confined in his chamber demanded Howard's head. On the twenty-fourth of January the Lords and Commons condemned Howard unheard and on the twenty-fifth Surrey mounted the scaffold and laid his long, peculiar head on the block.

Custom demanded that Howard's death should be delayed until after the dissolution of Parliament, but on the twenty-sixth Henry had yet another stroke. Catherine and the Seymours felt that he was going to slip through their fingers and quickly dispatched the order for Howard's execution, together with the assurance that Henry had signed the warrant.

On his immense bed, in the room with the heavy hangings, in the grey January dawn, Henry lay dying.

Catherine was at his side; he was still conscious and his eyes dwelt on the shadows. In the evening the doctors announced that the end was at hand and that it was time to inform him of this, so that he might turn his thoughts to God. A gentleman approached the bed and fulfilled this duty; his words did not appear to cause Henry any surprise. His former terrors had entirely vanished; life for some time past had been so monotonous that he expected nothing more of it and was resigned to leaving it. "I have made many mistakes," said he, "but the Lord Jesus is merciful and would forgive my sins even were they greater than they are." It was very visible that he felt his soul to be at peace. The gentleman enquired whether he wished to see a priest. "Yes," he replied, "I should like to see Cranmer. But not now, later; now I wish to sleep." He then fell asleep and Cranmer arrived.

With his suavity of manner and his humble gestures Cranmer was a man adapted to receive final confessions. But Henry said nothing; he had waited until it was too late and his small eyes could only roll in his purple countenance. "Do you die in the Faith of Christ?" enquired Cranmer, taking his hand. But Henry made no reply, he no longer beheld the earth.

At the Tower they were busy erecting the scaffold while Howard listened to the blows of the hammers. He was thinking of his dead son, of the coming dawn and of the executioner, while beside Henry's bed Cranmer and Catherine were praying. The Seymours were waiting in an adjoining room, wondering whether the inert old body would hold out until morning and give them time to kill their enemy.

Midnight struck and Henry was still alive, but finally his laboured breathing grew fainter. His immense body was seen to collapse and without a struggle he expired. Cranmer, Catherine and the Seymours barred the way to his chamber and secretly set about preparing their regency; but they dared not kill Howard and ordered his release.

They sent for the little King. Edward Seymour took the Kingdom, Cranmer the Church and Catherine her handsome Thomas. She hastened the funeral and married within a fortnight, being determined to make up for lost time.

They laid Henry to rest in the Chapel at Windsor beside the remains of their sister, the pale Queen Jane.